Dukakis

An American Odyssey

Dukakis

An American Odyssey

Charles Kenney

AND

Robert L. Turner

Houghton Mifflin Company

BOSTON

1988

To Anne and Charles Frederick
To Otile, Julia, and Maggie

Copyright © 1988 by Charles Kenney and Robert L. Turner

ALL RIGHTS RESERVED.

For information about permission to reproduce
selections from this book, write to Permissions,
Houghton Mifflin Company, 2 Park Street,
Boston, Massachusetts 02108.

Library of Congress Cataloging-in-Publication Data
Kenney, Charles.
Dukakis: an American odyssey / Charles Kenney and
Robert L. Turner.
p.   cm.
Includes index.
ISBN 0-395-47089-7
1. Dukakis, Michael.   2. Massachusetts—Governors—Biography.
3. Presidential candidates—United States—Biography.   I. Turner,
Robert L., date.   II. Title.
F71.22.D85K46 1988
974.4'043'0924—dc19   87-36761
[B]   CIP
Printed in the United States of America

A 10 9 8 7 6 5 4 3 2 1

Acknowledgments

WITHOUT THE SUPPORT of our friends and colleagues at the *Boston Globe*, we would have been unable to write this book. We received time and encouragement from Jack Driscoll, Marty Nolan, Tom Mulvoy, Ben Taylor, Sandy Hawes, Kirk Scharfenberg, and Ande Zellman, who also read the manuscript and offered valuable advice. Charles Liftman and Sean Mullin were wizards with the computer system. *Globe* photographers Stan Grossfeld, Janet Knott, and Mark Wilson were there when we needed them, as was the staff of the *Globe* library, particularly Lisa Driscoll.

Jonathan Ramljak, our enthusiastic researcher, was diligent and productive. Our work was also helped by people at Swarthmore and Bates colleges, Brookline High School, and the *Brookline Chronicle Citizen*. We are grateful as well to Mark Mulcahy of the *New Bedford Standard Times* and Barbara Anderson of the John F. Kennedy Library.

Scores of Dukakis's relatives, friends, colleagues, adversaries, and acquaintances offered useful information and insights, and many of them spent hours racking their brains, answering questions. Within this book are hundreds of quotations from scores of people, but none is from an anonymous source. Those who comment, analyze, speculate, praise, or criticize are identified by name. We would like to thank in particular Graham Allison, Mikki Ansin, Sandy Bakalar, Paul Brountas, Beryl Cohen, John DeVillars, Euterpe Dukakis, Joan Hertzmark, Haskell Kassler, Dick Manley, Fran Meaney, Dan Payne, John Sasso, Frank Sieverts, and Nick Zervas.

We have covered Dukakis for the *Globe* for twenty years, from his time in the legislature to his campaign for president, in office and out, from Brookline to Greece. We also conducted several interviews with him for this book, and we appreciate his time and patience.

Julie and Molly Greaney cared for Julia and Maggie Turner with love and good sense and, from Julie especially, a generous gift of her time.

Agnes Hagerty, whose good cheer, patience, and reliablility are boundless, took perfect care of Charles Frederick Kenney.

John Kenney not only worked my shifts with the kid, but also read the manuscript and offered advice and encouragement. And my brothers Timothy, Patrick, Thomas, and Michael, as well as my father, provided essential moral support.

Bob Levey, Ellen Goodman, Jim Carroll, Dayton Duncan, Ben Bradlee, Jr., and Tom Winship were true friends in many ways.

Luise Erdmann's exacting manuscript editing was crucial, as was her good cheer under pressure.

And, finally, we owe a great debt to Michael C. Janeway, our editor at Houghton Mifflin, whose guidance was much appreciated, and who had the vision, when others did not, to see the possibilities here.

Contents

———

"A man doesn't spring like Athena out of the head of Zeus."

"Michael cried . . . [He] was just shattered. He was sitting on the wall, the tears were coming down his face . . ."

"He's got to be reckoned with."

"This is not a plot on the part of a cigar-smoking, old-line, conservative Irish-Catholic Democrat to try and pull you down. You've done this yourself."

"You've been a pretty good governor, but I'm not voting for you."

"It was horrible . . . horrendous . . . It was like a public death."

Illustrations

Following page 116

Ed King, Dukakis's nemesis (*Boston Globe*, Bill Curtis)

Paul Brountas, Dukakis's closest friend (*Boston Globe*)

Bob Farmer, fund-raiser extraordinaire (*Boston Globe*, Keith Jenkins)

John Sasso, in the governor's office (© 1985, Peter Jones)

In Iowa, milking no cows, petting no pigs (*Boston Globe*, Suzanne Kreiter)

The Dukakis presidential message (Dan Wasserman)

The Dukakis family (Pamela Price)

Introduction

CHARACTER HAS DOMINATED presidential politics since Watergate. It elected Jimmy Carter and Ronald Reagan, and it has terminated several other candidacies. Starting early in the 1988 campaign, questions of character had far more impact than questions of policy.

This book grows out of our conviction that character is central, not only to a candidate's prospects of winning, but also to his potential for serving effectively as president. In judging a man's character, his life—his own actions as well as the people and experiences that shaped him—is far more telling than anything said in the heat of a campaign.

We believe that whatever it is called—character, strength, vision, moral gyroscope, ethical compass—the essential stuff of which a person is made is revealed not by analyzing his rhetoric about the future, but by examining the events of his past.

From the first, Michael Dukakis said character would elect the president in 1988. In announcing his decision to run, Dukakis said that "the next president of the United States will face challenges that no campaign position paper can possibly anticipate. But what *can* be measured in advance is the character of the person who will confront those challenges."

Values, motivation, flaws, ability—a candidate or officeholder does not acquire these the day he or she embarks on a campaign or takes the oath of office. They are part of a life story.

A chronicle of Michael Dukakis's campaign for the presidency will not be found here. This book is a biography, the story of a man whose life has been far more dramatic than many people, including some of his closest friends, realize. In this story there is loss and vindication; there is personal strife and great achievement.

Dukakis has been viewed by some people as the most transparent of national leaders, by others as the most enigmatic. But for those interested in evaluating the man, his life is by far the best gauge.

Our intention here is to portray Michael Dukakis not as he or anyone else might wish him to be, but as he is.

1. Beginnings

*"A man doesn't spring like
Athena out of the head of Zeus."*

O N THE FIRST DAY of his first trip as a prospective presidential candidate—February 4, 1987—Michael Dukakis strode into a storefront pizza parlor in the small
southern Iowa city of Osceola and plunged into a conversation
with Gus Thorakos, co-owner of Gus and Tom's Pizza. It was not
an ordinary chat between a politician and a voter. The two men
were conversing in Greek, a language spoken by a handful of
Iowans and one presidential candidate. To the amusement of
onlookers, the two men peppered each other with questions,
asking where their families were from and when they had arrived in this country.

A few minutes later, Thorakos was telling reporters he would
be Dukakis's "head man" in Osceola if he ran in 1988. The next
day, Dukakis told Democratic party leaders in Iowa that Thorakos was an example to their party of economic opportunity offered and seized, of the great American immigrant history. "Any
community that has a pizza house run by Gus Thorakos is headed for success," Dukakis said to the well-dressed gathering at a
$500-per-person party fund-raiser in Des Moines.

He did not electrify the crowd at the party in Des Moines, but
he has never been the sort of politician who walked into a
room and commanded rapt attention. His height, five feet eight

inches, has something to do with that, as does his less than inspi-
rational oratory. As he spoke that night, his arms and hands,
characteristically, were in perpetual motion, punctuating his upbeat, self-assured delivery. He looks exceptionally fit for a man
of fifty-three and seems, particularly when he smiles his broad,
infectious smile, to be younger by a half-dozen years at least.
While he does not exude charisma, Michael Dukakis has dark
good looks: a thatch of black hair, flecked only here and there
with gray, setting off a strongly featured face with dark eyes and
bushy eyebrows, accentuated by a prominent nose. Here, clearly, is a man of pride, a man who takes himself seriously.

Six weeks after the party, Dukakis declared himself to be a
candidate for the presidency, and the "pizza connection" quickly
became a symbol of what the campaign was all about. It was an
emblem of what Dukakis thinks is important about his ethnic
heritage, the values and personality traits that he emphasizes:
honor, diligence, independence, and success. It was a symbol,
most of all, of Dukakis's life story as a first-generation son of
immigrant parents.

When Michael Dukakis was a young man and a fledgling politician on the rise, his Greek roots were for the most part well
covered by the rich soil of upper-middle-class America. The
growth of his ethnic identification is similar to that of many first-
generation children, with the difference that his has been played
out in public. It began to emerge in 1982, during the campaign
to exorcise his most painful defeat. In retrospect, it's not surprising that in his hour of greatest need he would call on the reserve
of strength that is his heritage. He is the son of a man and
woman whose story testifies to a remarkable combination of intelligence and drive.

When Dukakis began his presidential campaign in 1987, his
mother, Euterpe, and his father, Panos, were very much on his
mind, for the central theme of his campaign—its heart and
soul—was his family's immigrant saga. He emphasized it at even
the briefest campaign stops and spun it out with growing detail
for groups of Greek Americans. In large part, it is, as he claims,
the story of America, the classic tale of poor immigrants who
came here in search of a better life and found it. It is a story as

old as the *Mayflower* and as new as the latest Thai refugee to swear the oath of citizenship.

It is a story of hardship as well as success, discrimination as well as opportunity. It is also a family story, about an odyssey that began even before the spring of 1912, when Panos S. Dukakis, age sixteen, passed through Ellis Island, or April of the following year, when Euterpe Boukis, age nine, arrived. Her parents, Michael and Chrysoula Boukis, were rugged mountain people who had been born and brought up in the northwestern region of Epirus. According to Euterpe Dukakis, her father's mother died at the age of ninety-five, "and I remember her telling me that *her* mother died at a hundred and five—and then after an accident, though I suppose it was her time." Euterpe was born into humble circumstances, a bookkeeper's daughter, on September 4, 1903, in Larissa, one of the largest cities in central Greece. She was the fifth of six children—two boys followed by four girls. Even before the last child arrived, the family had planned its move to America. First Nicholas would go, then Adam, and they would make enough money to send for the rest. But the family was hoping the last child would be a boy. "In those days, you see, girls were really a burden," Euterpe Dukakis told us. "The family had to provide a dowry." So when the sixth child arrived, "my mother said, 'Oh, Nicholas, another girl,' but he said, 'Don't worry, Mother, I'll [work] another two years and bring her over, too.' "

When Nicholas arrived in America in 1907 or 1908, he followed thousands of other immigrants to the mills. For him it was first the shoe mills in Manchester, New Hampshire, and eventually the mills in Haverhill, Massachusetts, "The Slipper City of the World." Despite low wages, strong, determined young immigrants willing to endure oppressive conditions were able to earn some money. Nicholas and Adam, who joined his brother in about 1910, were evidently determined. By 1913, they not only sent for the rest of the family but were able to provide housing. "They had bought a little property just before we came," says Mrs. Dukakis. "Three lodging houses in the center of the factory district, and they had a flat for us."

Nicholas, who was to become Michael Dukakis's godfather,

met the family in New York and took them on an overnight steamer, complete with musical entertainment, to Fall River, then by train to Haverhill. Adam greeted them with a sumptuous feast; "lamb chops, french-fried potatoes, and a salad—I'll never forget it," Euterpe Dukakis says. It was their first meal in America as a family. Indeed, as the food and the flat testified, the boys were successful, but only by mill town standards. The family was still careful with every penny. Apart from their own space, the three lodging houses, which had been bought from an older Greek, were run as a small business on the side. Soon, Adam began working part-time in a men's clothing store in Haverhill, and after he learned the business the two brothers bought the store, renaming it Adam's Men's Store. All this time, however, the brothers and other family members were working long hours in the mills.

Socially, the family experienced the clash of cultures so common to immigrants. Their neighborhood, home, and church life were all heavily Greek, yet they were eager to learn American ways. None of the Boukis family spoke English on their arrival. "How could we?" asks Mrs. Dukakis. "We just took it in through the pores." Yet the brothers pushed them to learn more quickly. Within a few weeks of their arrival, she says, "Adam in particular was impatient [that] we weren't learning the language faster. But after six months we spoke as if our tongues were loosened."

The key was the public schools, as it was for so many immigrants, and it was there, particularly at the Winter Street School in Haverhill, that Euterpe began to stand out, even as a young girl. "I had very long, long dark brown hair, and for some reason that seemed to attract attention," she says with a hint of a smile. Also, she adds, "I suppose I wasn't stupid, so it helped." Indeed, the young Greek student developed relationships outside school with several of her teachers. "I was introduced to their home life—they were very fine people."

Standing out in this group was the principal, Stanley Gray, a native of Castine, Maine, who became a mentor and friend to Euterpe until his death in 1938. Gray took the young girl to museums, libraries, concerts—"things I would never have known," she says. "He introduced me to book reading as a pleasure, not just for study," and she sped eagerly through the classics. With Gray's encouragement, she became, she believes, the first girl among the three thousand or so Greek immigrants in Haverhill to go to college. She did not waste the opportunity, graduating Phi Beta Kappa from Bates College in Maine in 1925. Bates, she says, was a positive experience in many ways, particularly in its diversity. There was a healthy mix of male and female students, she says, as well as more black students than many schools enrolled at the time. Her yearbook praised "Tippie" Boukis as a scholar and enthusiastic cheerleader, referring to her as "the hidden soul of harmony." Tuition was $125 a year, with room and board an additional $375. Euterpe's college study was clearly exceptional and was supported by the family financially as well as emotionally, she says, but she worked, both at school and in a shoe factory during the summer, to earn all of her tuition and some of her room and board.

Though Stanley Gray and Bates College were opening the world to young Euterpe, she also felt the sting of discrimination. Applying for a job as a public school teacher in a small town south of Boston, she thought her academic record and a strong interview would win her the position, but in the end she was rejected. She was stunned. In a scene she remembers vividly more than sixty years later, she went to the office of the Abbott Teachers Agency, in the Little Building in Boston, and asked, " 'Was it because I have a foreign name?' and they said, 'Yes.' "

She was also rejected for a teaching job in Salem, New Hampshire, though years later a school administrator there told her that an active Ku Klux Klan chapter in town had effectively prevented their hiring any foreigners or Catholics. "It wasn't the first time I had felt discrimination," she says. "It was really quite rampant, especially for Italians and Greeks and Jews."

Euterpe did find a job in the high school in Ashland, New Hampshire. It was a small school—senior and junior high grades were all in one building—and she taught a variety of subjects, including English, history, French, and Latin. She became a United States citizen during her two years there, then moved to Amesbury, Massachusetts, and taught in its junior high school for two years before getting married.

Euterpe Boukis had met Panos Dukakis when she herself was in junior high school in Haverhill; he was more than seven years her senior, and there was no romance until much later.

"He always said that from the first time he saw me he knew he was going to marry me," Mrs. Dukakis says with a laugh. Then, after a pause, "I think he was telling the truth . . . I'm sure he was." She says that her husband wanted to get his education and establish himself before giving any thought to a family, or even romance. "When he was ready, he came after me," she recalls. "I was willing."

The Greek roots of the Dukakis family are quite different from those of the Boukises. Panos S. Dukakis was born on January 15, 1896, in Edremit, in Asia Minor, a city that is now part of Turkey. His parents were both from Lesbos, a Greek island in the Aegean Sea. Like many island-dwellers around the world, the people of Lesbos have a reputation as adventurers. In its general outlines, however, the story of Panos Dukakis's immigration is strikingly similar to the Boukises'. The oldest brother, Arthur, came first, established himself in the mills and as a tailor, and then sent for others in the family. George was next. According to his son, Arthur G. Dukakis, now regional director of the U.S. Census Bureau in Boston, George soon established himself in the restaurant business. First he worked in Lowell, in a place called Plaza Lunch, then he and his brother Arthur opened their own restaurant with the same name, Plaza Lunch, in Lawrence, another mill city not far away.

Panos arrived in 1912, followed soon after by the boys' parents, Stelianos and Olympia Dukakis. Panos had picked up a smattering of English during a brief stopover with relatives on Lesbos. From the first, he was determined to get an education. Working in the mills and behind a lunch counter—including cleaning the meat cases in Saunders' Market in Lowell, his nephew Arthur recalls—Panos experienced a cultural collision much as the Boukis family had. There was a period when his desire to assimilate was apparently so great that, in the mills, he was called Peter Duke. Arthur remembers hearing that Panos once wanted to change the family name to Duke but was talked out of it by George. Euterpe Dukakis remembers hearing that it was the eldest brother, Arthur, who considered shortening the name. In any event, the effort was brief. Panos and his brothers

stuck to their full Greek name and never moved to change it again, even when it threatened to cut off educational possibilities for Panos.

While working in the mills, Panos hoarded every hour he could find to pursue his education at night, attending Lowell High School and American International Academy (now American International College) in Springfield, where there were many foreign-born students. He then did a year of premedical work at Boston University and another at Bates in 1919–20, a year before Euterpe Boukis's arrival in 1921. Like the Boukises, Panos Dukakis's family rallied behind his ambition to get a good education and then to become a doctor. Financial and moral support came most strongly from his brother George, who became the head of the family when both their father and oldest brother, Stelianos and Arthur, died during the influenza epidemic of 1918–19.

When Panos applied for admission to Harvard Medical School, an assistant dean discouraged him, saying there was little hope for a young man with his background at that door. Panos traveled north to Dartmouth College, in Hanover, New Hampshire, where he was quickly accepted at its medical school. He had even agreed to take a room—one that had once been occupied by Daniel Webster, he was told—when a telegram arrived from Harvard. He was in.

In 1924, Panos Dukakis became the first Greek immigrant ever to graduate from Harvard Medical School, and he did it just twelve years after his arrival at Ellis Island with almost no money and less English.

Dr. Dukakis then settled in. He soon opened an office, which he maintained for more than half a century, at 454 Huntington Avenue in Boston, across from the Museum of Fine Arts and only a few blocks from Harvard Medical School. He quickly developed a large practice; none of his patients were more loyal than his proud family. "When Pan became a doctor, we all had to go to him," Arthur Dukakis recalls. "His prognosis was God. He knew all the answers."

He then began courting Euterpe Boukis, and although she was "willing," as she says, and there was no long delay in their engagement, one prerequisite was honored. "Before I said yes,"

Mrs. Dukakis recalls, "I took him to see Mr. Gray in the hospital. He was . . . quite ill [following an operation], but as we were leaving he whispered to me, 'I have an okay in my pocket.' " Panos and Euterpe were married on September 4, 1929, just a month before the stock market crash. They lived in an apartment down the hall from Panos's office for four years, and it was there that their first son, Stelian, was born. For the next seven years the family lived on Boylston Street in Brookline, where Michael was born. It was "a lovely apartment, eighty-five dollars a month with heat and a garage," Mrs. Dukakis remembers. In June 1940, the family moved to 210 Rangeley Road, South Brookline, where Mrs. Dukakis still lives. Dr. Dukakis had a general practice, specializing in obstetrics, and delivered some three thousand babies, a population that became a consistent source of support for his son as he campaigned around the country. He worked regular office hours six and usually seven days a week until he went into semiretirement in 1978, at the age of eighty-two. A year later, Panos Dukakis suffered heart failure following a stroke and died. His practice had included many poor families who were never sent a bill, his son often remarked. Nevertheless, he established two trust funds, which, by the time they were made public in 1987, contained some $1 million each.

This tale of immigrants realizing the American dream of success and independence became a central theme of the Dukakis presidential campaign, though Dukakis usually passed over the fact that both his parents were preceded by siblings who paved the way. Mentioned briefly to small groups or recounted with anecdotal filigree to gatherings of Greek Americans, it was the one part of Dukakis's campaign rhetoric that was included in almost every spiel. He would tell the story with obvious pride and affection, often with emotion, the latter a quality that has frequently been found lacking in him. Dukakis said during the campaign that no matter what he accomplished, he could never achieve as much as his parents had.

The heart of this message was opportunity—that Dukakis knows about it from his parents' lives, and his own, and therefore that he has something very specific in mind when he talks of "opportunity for all." Inherent in his message is the emphasis

that an immigrant past is a common denominator among all Americans. (Once, when an American Indian challenged this view of history, Dukakis replied that the Indian's own ancestors had immigrated over the Bering Strait.)

Still another aspect of his message is specifically Greek. Like many immigrant families, Panos and Euterpe Dukakis experienced the strong and conflicting tugs of two cultures. In many ways, they tried to maintain both. For years, Panos Dukakis was the school physician at Hellenic College in Brookline. The Dukakises named their two sons in the traditional Greek way; the first, Stelian, for his father's father, and the second, Michael, for his mother's father. Their home was bilingual to a substantial degree, with both sons fluent in modern Greek from an early age, principally because their grandmother Olympia Dukakis, who always spoke Greek, lived with them until Stelian was ten and Michael, seven. According to Michael, he and his brother were so involved in sports later on that they refused to go to Greek school, but for one year their parents hired a tutor and made them stay at home for an hour on Saturdays to learn to read and write Greek.

In other ways, however, the Dukakises were not clannish. The young doctor and his wife moved to neighborhoods with few Greeks, settling in one of the most suburban neighborhoods of Brookline, an area with old trees and quiet streets and comfortable, though not extravagant, single-family houses on well-maintained lots. The area is usually referred to as South Brookline, but it is in the zip code of Chestnut Hill, one of the wealthiest addresses in the United States. As the boys grew up, Greek holidays were celebrated but there was little formal Greek training or education—for example, Michael attended Swarthmore, a Quaker college. Apart from relatives, the family made no special effort to associate with Greek Americans. Michael didn't go out of his way to date Greek women, and, in fact, he married a Jewish woman. During his first term as governor, from 1975 through 1978, he came under heavy criticism from many active Greek Americans in Massachusetts for appointing too few Greeks to high positions in state government and for failing to attend enough traditional Greek events.

Nonetheless, it is clear that Dukakis has maintained some de-

gree of ethnic identification throughout his life. It is no accident, for instance, that two of his closest friends are Greek
Americans, and highly successful ones at that: Paul P. Brountas,
a senior partner at Hale & Dorr, one of Boston's most presti-
gious law firms, and Dr. Nicholas T. Zervas, chief of neurosur-
gery at Massachusetts General Hospital.

Some people close to Dukakis, including his wife, Kitty, remember ethnic identity as an essential part of his campaigns
from the start. "We had Greek bands at every single event we
ever had," she says. But the emphasis did not come until later.
In fact, as a state representative from Brookline, which has a
large Jewish population, Dukakis used to joke that "people in
Brookline often think I'm Jewish, and I never tell them otherwise."

But it is clear that Dukakis's family history and his concerted
effort to make the Greek connection did not come into play
publicly until he was a presidential candidate, when it became
the centerpiece of his campaign.

Peter Agris, the longtime editor of the *Hellenic Chronicle,*
which is published in Boston but has a nationwide circulation,
says Dukakis has benefited from the support of Greek Americans through the years, but this is generally "not because of the
political philosophy, it's just because of ethnic pride." In particular, he says, many thought Dukakis was too liberal—too
much for government intervention—in the first term, because
"the majority of Greeks believe in doing it yourself." Another
leading Greek American, Elias Vlanton, says the Greek response
to Dukakis's presidential candidacy derives from personal qualities. Vlanton, information director for the fifty-thousand-mem-
ber American Hellenic Educational Progressive Association
(AHEPA), says that Dukakis "invokes his Greek heritage and the
values that Greeks hold dear—love of family, the need and importance of public service. He projects integrity."

During his first term as governor, Dukakis went on a seventeen-
day vacation to Greece that Paul Brountas feels "was sort of an
awakening" for him. With Brountas and his wife, Lynn, and
Kitty and her parents, Jane and Harry Ellis Dickson, Dukakis
left on September 13, 1976, for a trip of discovery. He had

never before seen his parents' homeland, and Brountas says, "I don't think [his ancestry] meant a lot until he went to Greece."

Brountas may well be right, but the impact wasn't immediate. On a scorchingly hot day, he clambered up the Acropolis in wingtip shoes. At one point, Dukakis was troubled that a number of people he saw in Athens seemed tired and spiritless, lacking the ambition that he associated so closely with the Greeks he knew at home. It was suggested to him that the populations might be self-selecting: that many ambitious Greeks might have emigrated while the less ambitious remained, but this did not satisfy him.

Most telling was Dukakis's visit to his mother's childhood home in Larissa. The small, stucco house still stood, a testament to the cramped poverty and hardship that were nearly inescapable to most Greeks at the time. There, seeing the house and touring the area where his mother had been raised, listening to bits of remembered history from distant cousins and neighbors, Dukakis seemed curiously detached. At a reception afterward, he said, "I'm not an emotional guy, but I got kind of choked up walking around my mother's home, I really did." The words, however, were accompanied by little outward emotion. In truth, he had seemed more interested to learn that the neighborhood was threatened with demolition for a new highway. Having fought successfully against new highways in Boston, Dukakis talked animatedly to the people about organizing the community politically. As it happened, the highway went through, and the house no longer stands.

Though Dukakis seemed cool at important junctures on the trip, it was apparently not so much because of hardhearted indifference as culture shock: he simply didn't know how to absorb so much that was new all at once. His curiosity worked overtime as he rattled off questions endlessly from the first day to the last.

And if he was not overflowing with emotion during his visit among the Greeks, Dukakis was clearly impressed with theirs. From strangers on the street to the highest government ministers, Greeks greeted him with genuine enthusiasm, saying how much it meant to them that a Greek American had achieved political prominence. Part of this was clearly relief after the embarrassment of Spiro Agnew, though that name was almost never mentioned. But most of the enthusiasm seemed to come from genuine pride at a Greek American's success, and Dukakis was touched.

Though the trip was ostensibly a vacation, Dukakis spent much of the first three days meeting with top officials, including Premier Constantine Karamanlis. At a formal dinner, Undersecretary of State Constantine Stavrapoulos toasted the governor's achievement and predicted more: "I am sure you are not going to stop there," he said.

On a trip to Delphi, Dukakis was supplied with a chauffeur-driven Ford and whisked on his way by a relay of twelve policemen, ten in cars and two on motorcycles. Military men snapped to salute and village chickens flapped crazily off the road as the little motorcade sped through the countryside with siren blaring, ignoring red lights and speed limits. Dukakis, who rode the subway to work and shunned the trappings of office in Boston, emerged in Delphi with a predictably stiff remark. "Back home, I can stop this kind of thing," he said, seeming, however, more amused than outraged.

The trip made Dukakis think about his roots. In the Lesbos village of Pelopi, where his father had lived briefly as a boy, the townspeople, three hundred or more, turned out to see and honor the Greek American who had done so well. As the men clustered around him in the town square, he looked up the streets and saw women and children leaning from windows and doorways, fascinated as the village leaders presented Michael Dukakis with the original birth certificate of his father. He looked up at the children, at the Greek faces of the little boys and girls, raven-haired, olive-skinned—precisely as he was. He recalls that he thought, "There but for the grace of God go I." This is how his life might have been, in a remote and primitive Greek village, had his parents not been so determined.

He also gave a brief talk at the Athens airport on his arrival (his mother had helped with the vocabulary) and, with some emotion, at the formal dinner. Most important, though, was the reception. "The people were very excited," Brountas remembers. "Greek TV was following him everywhere, and he was surprised." In Brountas's view, Dukakis "became aware and proud of the heritage" as a result of the trip.

This feeling emerged when Dukakis ran for re-election two years later. There was no Greek theme, but he was more vocal about his roots than another Greek American running for high office, Paul E. Tsongas. In 1978, Tsongas was the Democratic congressman from Lowell, trying to unseat the Republican U.S. Senator Edward W. Brooke, successfully as it turned out. "I vividly remember being concerned whether there would be a backlash," Tsongas says, "with Greeks running for two of the three top offices in the state. I would avoid it like the plague, but he would invariably, when we were together, raise it." In retrospect, he now says that, although Dukakis lost that election, an anti-Greek backlash was not a factor, and the governor was right to make an ethnic appeal. In fact, there may have been a different kind of backlash voting from some elements of the Greek community itself, people who were offended that Dukakis had not celebrated his background enough—either through appointments of Greeks to high office or by participation in Greek events. "During the first administration," Brountas concedes, "there were certain big Greek events that he was expected to attend, and he didn't. It was different in the second administration."

In the rematch election of 1982, when Dukakis took back the governorship, the Greek theme was a bit more visible. With the encouragement of his media adviser, Daniel B. Payne, Dukakis made a television ad in which he told some of the immigrant story while standing in front of a house in Lowell that his father once lived in when he was working to save money for school. As bouzouki music plinked in the background, Dukakis, in a blue plaid sports shirt, said, "Dad came over from Greece in 1912. He settled in Lowell and lived right here. Even though he was only fifteen or sixteen, he worked very hard, but he always said this was the greatest country in the world . . . A few years later, I decided to run for office. I guess it was what my father always told me: much has been given to you; much is expected of you . . . I've always been a Democrat, because the Democratic party is the party of opportunity, the party that gave a couple of

Greek immigrants a chance to succeed in America. I'm proud to be a Democrat. You might say it's in my blood."

Dukakis never explained his parents' debt to the Democratic party, an odd assertion since their success began largely during the Republican administrations of Harding, Coolidge, and Hoover, and since Panos was a Republican until his son ran for office. Still, the commercial was very popular within the campaign and was aired widely. Dukakis's aides called it the Zorba ad.

Taking office as governor again on January 6, 1983, Dukakis ended his inaugural address by reciting what he said was a paraphrase of the Athenian oath of citizenship: "We will never bring disgrace to this, our commonwealth, by any act of dishonesty or cowardice. We will fight for the ideal of the commonwealth, both alone and with many. We will revere and obey its laws and do our best to incite a like respect and reverence in those who are prone to annul them or set them at naught. We will strive unceasingly to quicken the sense of civic duty. Thus, in all these ways, we will transmit this commonwealth not only not less, but greater, better, and more beautiful than it was transmitted to us."

"Like so much that is Greek," Dukakis said of the oath, "it is as meaningful today as it was twenty centuries ago."

Since his return to the governor's office, Dukakis has been more overtly ethnic, claiming Mediterranean kinship with House Speaker George Keverian, an Armenian American, and practically anyone else with European roots. Even Walter Mondale, whose presidential candidacy Dukakis supported enthusiastically in 1984, became the object of an attempted ethnic transplant. He suffered from the charge that he was an excessively frigid Norwegian, but Dukakis, with a grin, introduced him on several occasions as "Walter Mon-*doll*-i" and claimed he was Mediterranean at heart. Dukakis also took to making more frequent ethnic references. When pressed about a program or appointment that was taking a long time, for instance, Dukakis called up "the old Greek saying, The sweetest honey is made only slowly."

On March 6, 1987, shortly before announcing as a presidential candidate, Dukakis made a speech in Bedford, New Hampshire, that introduced a keynote of his candidacy. After talking at length about Democratic tradition, education, competitiveness, Star Wars, Nicaragua, tax enforcement, and integrity, Dukakis suddenly paused. "Seventy-five years ago," he said, "a young Greek man arrived in Manchester from a town in western Asia Minor. He spoke very little English and had about twenty-five dollars in his pocket . . . He had a burning desire to get an education, and he used to run from his job in a restaurant at 17 Broadway in Lawrence, where he worked until five o'clock so that he could be in his seat and on time at his English classes at the Lawrence Y. Eight years later, that young man was entering medical school.

"A year after he arrived, another Greek immigrant family came to Haverhill. They lived literally in the shadow of Haverhill's shoe factories. They worked in those factories, and they worked very, very hard. One of them was a little girl of nine who went off to the Winter Street School . . . The principal, a Down East Yankee named Stanley D. Gray, saw something in that little Greek girl. He encouraged her to study. He helped her to develop a lifelong love of reading . . . He urged her to go to Bates College in Maine . . . When her second son was born she gave him the middle name of Stanley—the best way she knew to remember the man who had opened the door of opportunity to her in a very special way."

The audience, like dozens of others later in the campaign, listened attentively as the story unfolded. But the New Hampshire gathering was in for a surprise. At this point, Dukakis stretched out his hand and said, "That young Greek man was my father, and that little Greek girl is here tonight. Mum, would you stand up?" Mrs. Dukakis sprang up from her seat at a table facing the podium, her energy belying her eighty-three years. The dignified, immaculately dressed woman surveyed the audience, her widely set eyes expressing delight in the burst of applause. Dukakis continued:

"When my mother and father arrived in this country, they could not possibly have dreamed that someday their son would be the governor of Massachusetts. But they never let me forget that this was, as my dad used to tell me all the time, 'the greatest country in the world,' and that there was nothing my brother and I couldn't do if we just put our minds and our hearts into it—and our shoulders to the wheel . . .

"When I speak to you as I have tonight, and when I talk about building a nation in a world at peace, with genuine opportunity for every one of our citizens—rich or poor, young or old, black or brown or white—in every part of our country, it is part of what I am and who *we* are.

"And it is why we Democrats believe so deeply that all of us, from every walk of life, have a responsibility to give something back to our community and to our country. Not just governors, but those citizens like yourselves who empower leaders with their votes and through their active participation in caucuses and primaries . . . not just public officials but the teachers and the engineers and the architects and the dreamers . . . not just the managers but also the workers."

To enthusiastic applause, Dukakis concluded with an exhortation to "let the future begin here," an appeal that was widely and correctly taken to be a prelude to his announcement, ten days later, that he would in fact run.

The Athenian oath appeared again that day, March 16, and yet again on April 29, when he made his formal declaration. Both speeches also used the marathon metaphor for the campaign. People were encouraged to think that Dukakis was particularly suited to the race because he is Greek American and because he ran the Boston Marathon thirty-seven years earlier.

Many Greek Americans see certain personality traits as particularly Greek. Zervas says most of his countrymen are "hard-working, tough, hard-headed, clannish—a very strong-willed people." Brountas emphasizes their independence: "Ninety-nine percent of the Greeks who came over opened businesses on their own." Tsongas identifies some "very clearly defined values: family, education, and hard work." Some of this is borne out by Census Bureau data. In a 1975 study of twenty-four second-generation ethnic groups, Greeks were second in income (behind Jews) and first in educational attainment. Although wealth has never been the goal of Dukakis or his parents, economic success was an important by-product of their achievement. And of course education was the essential staple in the family.

Tsongas sees the progress of Dukakis's ethnic identification as not unusual for a first-generation child. "You're so driven to compete and learn American values," he says. "You strive to succeed in a system of Yankee values, and then you realize there is another part of you that has worth. It can be very fulfilling."

At the same time that his presidential campaign has found Dukakis more publicly Greek, it has also found him more openly emotional. In the early years of his public life—through his campaign for redemption in 1986, really—Dukakis kept his emotions under strict control with very few exceptions. His manner "used to be quick, cold," in Brountas's view, partly out of a sense of what it means to provide leadership: "You have to think of the image you're presenting, of the stature you convey ... In many cases he didn't think it was right to show your emotions." Since the beginning of his third term, however, Dukakis has been close to exuberant on several occasions, most of them connected with his presidential campaign, and he has also been seen with tears in his eyes with some regularity: during the dedication of a memorial to President Kennedy, when his wife revealed a previous dependency on diet pills, at the funeral of a State House lobbyist killed by an alleged drunk driver, and when his father-in-law retired from the Boston Symphony Orchestra. And his sadness was apparent when his closest adviser resigned from his presidential campaign.

In none of these cases, however, did Dukakis seem to lose control. He was still self-reliant and self-contained, not allowing himself to move out of the grasp of his own rationality. In his speeches, he was telling people that voters judge presidential candidates on character more than they do candidates for any other office, and at the same time he was allowing his own public personality to grow. It was clear that he felt he could reveal more of his emotions, and more of his ethnic heritage, and still be very much in control of himself.

His mother believes that contemplation of the candidacy, and of being president, have widened Dukakis's horizons and have deepened his sense of his roots. "Is it a very small thing he is doing?" she asks. "No, that is a very, very big thing . . . Why does a man aspire to this? Maybe his parents had something to do with this. A man doesn't spring like Athena out of the head of Zeus."

2. Brookline

"Michael cried . . . [He] was just shattered.
He was sitting on the wall, the tears
were coming down his face . . ."

COMPARED WITH the bootstrap beginnings of his parents, Michael Dukakis started life on a cushion. Panos and Euterpe Dukakis provided their two sons with a comfortable and stable home, stimulating surroundings, and ready access to some of the best schools in the country. Yet the Dukakises had no intention of using their success to shield their children from the hardships they had experienced in Greece and the New England mills. In the Dukakis family, success would not be, as it was in many immigrant families, a vehicle for escaping the past, sending the next generation forward without looking back. For Panos and Euterpe, the goal in raising children was not comfort but character. While they provided their children with what was, in many ways, an upper-middle-class style of life, they continued to exemplify many of the traits that brought them success: strict self-discipline, frugality, and hard work, with an expectation of achievement. And they demanded the same from their two children, Michael and his older brother, Stelian. Michael was shaped by this environment in many ways that have not diminished through the years. To it he brought, from birth, other qualities: one is a highly developed sense of self, of independence, of aloneness, of will, of self-containment; another is a determination to strive, an ambition to achieve.

Stories of Dukakis's childhood independence are remarkable. According to his mother, "the first word he ever spoke was in Greek, *monos mou*, 'by myself.' He was an independent little fellow. He never wanted me to help him."

In an interview in 1974, Mrs. Dukakis said that Michael was an unusually persistent child from the first. "He never gave up. He was terribly persevering," she said. "Our home was bilingual," she added, "and as a little fellow we would find him standing by himself, mouthing a word over and over until he got it right."

When Michael was very young, about three, his mother recalls now, the two found themselves in a test of wills. "I chose a pair of socks for him to wear," she says, "and he said, 'No,' he wanted another pair. I said, 'The pair I have picked for you will go better with what you're wearing.' But he said, 'No.' So we went at it a little bit. Finally I said, 'Mother knows best,' but he still wouldn't put them on, so I said, 'Go into your room and come out when you understand.'" He went, as ordered, to his room, and there he stayed. Mrs. Dukakis remembers well checking the time. Fifteen, twenty, thirty minutes passed. Finally, a full hour later, the little boy grudgingly appeared, wearing the socks he'd been instructed to put on. And although she was firm on that occasion, Mrs. Dukakis says she and her husband saw Michael's self-confidence as a positive quality, even though it spilled over into stubbornness at times. "We didn't want to discourage it too much," she says. "We didn't want to weaken the spirit."

"We've always felt that he's had a very strong sense of himself," Mrs. Dukakis said in 1974. "It is part of his own strength of character and integrity."

These earliest stories come from the period when the Dukakis family lived on Boylston Street in Brookline. Stelian had been born on July 11, 1930, ten months after his parents married and when they were still living on Huntington Avenue in Boston. But when another child was expected, the family moved to Brookline. Michael Stanley was born on November 3, 1933, and has lived in Brookline all his life. He is named for his maternal grandfather and for Stanley Gray, his mother's mentor. In fact the Dukakises broke slightly with Greek tradition in naming their second-born, since all sons were normally given the name of the father as a middle name—as they did with Stelian Panos.

As education had been the key to success and to a rich intellectual life for both parents, its importance was made clear to the children from the start. Stelian began kindergarten early, at four years and two months. When Michael's time came, no kindergarten was offered in their neighborhood, but the Dukakises and several other families discovered that space was available at Brookline High School. In what became a celebrated example of community action in the town, they lobbied school administrators successfully to open the space for a kindergarten, though the parents paid for the teacher.

The next year, Michael went to the Runkle School, the highly regarded public elementary school where Stelian was already enrolled. Subsequently, the family moved to South Brookline, and the boys went to the Baker School, another superior elementary school. Going into the Baker, Stelian repeated a grade. He had not had any problem with his studies, but he was young for his class and his parents felt he would get along better. And since all his schoolmates would be new, there would be no stigma.

The boys found that life at home was markedly more disciplined and demanding than it was for many of their friends. Neither boy was ever given an allowance. Any spending money they wanted had to be earned, and both boys had paper routes and found other jobs to bring in a little cash. Household chores were not jobs for pay but an expected part of family life. To this day, Michael's domestic proclivities at least equal those of his wife, Kitty. One of the first presents he ever gave her during their courtship was a waffle iron, which he used more than she did. And throughout their life, including all his years as governor, Dukakis has done most of the food shopping and a fair amount of the cooking. In fact, the corn muffins he makes from scratch are a Sunday morning tradition.

As the boys were growing up, Dr. and Mrs. Dukakis set standards in their own lives. Both were industrious, abstemious, and frugal, and the sons followed along. Though they can be taught some things by instruction and admonition, Mrs. Dukakis said years ago, "children learn by example more."

For Panos, a strict, disciplined man, family and work were

virtually his whole life. Sunday afternoons, and the evening meal on weekdays, were family times; everyone was expected to be there and to share. It is a practice Michael Dukakis maintained with few exceptions until the last of his children left for college—including most of two terms as governor. The only thing that could pull Panos away from the family was a sick patient. "Work was very important to him," says Michael's cousin Arthur Dukakis. "Many a time he left the dinner table because that call came in for somebody who needed him."

Panos was taciturn, a man with few social needs apart from the satisfaction he drew from his practice and his family. "He was a guy of very simple tastes," Michael says now. "His one indulgence was going into the market district and coming home with crates of fruit." Like her husband, Euterpe has extraordinary self-discipline, but she has always been more outgoing, more voluble, and her side of the family is more openly political. She also found it easier to be flexible with her sons when they showed signs of independence. "I never dreamed for my children," she says. "I always wanted them to have their own dreams."

Euterpe's intellect also flashed more visibly than did her husband's. Arthur Dukakis says he always saw a distinction between his two cousins. "Stelian was more a Dukakis," he says. "Michael is more like his mother. I think that's where he gets his smarts."

The stubbornness and determination evidenced by Panos and Euterpe are among the more obvious personality traits handed down to Michael Dukakis, traits that some of his family and friends consider particularly Greek. Another inherited characteristic may have broader roots in the immigrant experience generally: his attitude toward money and things material. His reputation for parsimony is legend. Virtually everyone who knows him at all well seems to have two or three stories demonstrating his tightness, and each story is different. His frugality is also the characteristic for which he is most lampooned. As a candidate, Dukakis himself has frequently added to the store of fables on this subject, telling Iowa farmers, for instance, that he usually buys generic, no-name groceries, which are often even cheaper than coupon buys. But his mother bristles at any suggestion that he goes too far. "Michael is not cheap," she declares with measured emphasis. "He's thrifty, and he doesn't waste." Poverty, of course, was the mother of this penchant. "We grew up in poor families," Mrs. Dukakis says. "We never threw anything away that could be used. There was always plenty of food, a clean house. But nothing was wasted. To this day I just hate waste."

There is more than simply an abhorrence of waste, however; there is also a rejection of materialism. "It seems to be in the air that you buy everything in sight. If it's there, you buy it," says Mrs. Dukakis, shaking her head. "I don't have a dryer. I enjoy hanging my wash out in the summer and folding it. In the winter I have lines in my cellar. It dries in two or three hours, the towels overnight. I don't want another thing to wait for a service man for." She also describes a recent purchase, a standard, four-sided metal grater that she bought for $1.59 in a supermarket to replace the one she had used for fifty-eight years, since her marriage. "It was a great decision," she says, smiling at her own internal debate. But she couldn't bring herself to discard the old one right away. It seemed to have some use left in it still.

As the boys were growing up, food that was put on a plate was expected to be eaten. "We did not waste food," Mrs. Dukakis says. "God's blessings are not to be wasted." If there was any hesitation, the boys were reminded of the poor children in Greece or India who didn't have enough to eat. One day when she urged Stelian to eat his spinach, however, she recalls that he replied, "Mother, give it to the little Greek children."

Throughout his life, Michael Dukakis has practiced thrift and often celebrated it, flashing his monthly discount pass on the subway system and showing off his latest suit from Filene's Basement, a Boston store famous for its bargains. Sometimes there has been a hint of moral superiority in his attitude, an unstated suggestion that those who are less frugal are profligate. A quarter century of bombardment from his wife, whose taste can run to more expensive items, especially in clothes, has softened Dukakis only slightly. He still insists on buying only wash-and-wear shirts, which he launders himself. Dukakis does have a snowblower for his short driveway, but it is a relic; his neighbor and aide Ira Jackson calls it a candidate for the Smithsonian. Dukakis also shocked a few neighbors not long ago by acquiring a gas barbecue grill, but some of them suspect he figured out that gas was less expensive than all those bags of charcoal.

Thrift is one of the qualities that is found in most immigrant families, but it is not always passed on. To some, the whole point of success is to liberate themselves and their offspring from the hardships they endured along the way. But in the Dukakis house, both parents set a clear example. One bit of advice Dukakis remembers coming most insistently from his father was: "Economize, Michael, economize." Thrift was seen as an integral part of the character that was essential to a worthwhile life.

As was education. Both Stelian and Michael were good students, but for Michael, schoolwork seemed to come unusually easily. In fact Dr. Dukakis, whose own academic achievement was nothing short of extraordinary, began to worry at one point. "Mike seemed to work not too hard," he said in a 1974 interview. "It was six-thirty, and I would say, 'Have you done your homework?' And he said, 'No, not yet.' Then he would shut the door and come out in an hour. And I said, 'Have you prepared all your lessons in an hour? I used to spend four or five hours.' I was afraid all the time that it would not be satisfactory, but it came back all A's." Dr. Dukakis still pondered whether the schoolwork was demanding enough, but finally concluded that his second son was "awfully bright, awfully intelligent." Though life was spare in many ways for the boys, there were rewards. When A's appeared on their report cards, they were taken out for one of their favorite foods, fresh clams or oysters on the half shell.

As youngsters, Stelian and Michael had different personalities, but they were constant playmates and competitors. The brothers often seemed headed down the same bright path. Both stood out academically and athletically, and both developed an interest in politics. They were also musical. Both tried their hands at the small piano in the house; then Stelian took up the clarinet and Michael played the trumpet. In particular, the boys shared a passion for sports. Dukakis remembers seeing Lefty Grove pitch when he went to his first Red Sox game at the age of four or five, and he can still tick off the names of most of the Sox starters that year. The boys' favorite sports were basketball, long-distance running, and baseball. "We used to organize track meets in the driveway," Dukakis recalls. "The whole neighborhood would come over and we'd put bamboo rods on barrels and turn them into hurdles, and we'd have one long-distance run which was my favorite . . . We were always playing ball in the street, up against the garage door, up at school, and so on." Once, though he was younger than the others—"a little pipsqueak," he says—Dukakis ended up catching for the Baker School seventh-grade baseball team when Stelian was pitching. "He had kind of a cute curveball," Dukakis recalls. "We beat Pierce [School] twenty-seven to nothing; I'll never forget it . . ." Years later, in a softball game among state legislators in Boston, a Republican colleague broke his leg badly sliding into a Dukakis tag at home. To this day, Dukakis refuses to take any blame. "It was a bad slide," he says, with only a hint of a smile.

The family always took an interest in public affairs. Panos regularly had everyone listen to the CBS radio news at 6:00 P.M., and when the 1940 Republican National Convention was broadcast, six-year-old Michael helped his older brother keep a state-by-state tally sheet as Wendell Willkie won the nomination to oppose Franklin Roosevelt. Both boys also had lively curiosities and easily found ways to entertain themselves. "They never once said, 'What are we going to do now?' " their mother recalls.

Almost three and a half years older, Stelian was also two or three inches taller than Michael when both were full-grown. During their early years, competition was sometimes fierce, but Stelian was the leader. "They were very close friends, but the sibling rivalry was something awful," says Mrs. Dukakis. "It wore me down and it wore me out." Michael remembers their fighting "like cats and dogs," though he says it was no more than "most brothers do." In spite of the conflict, says Mrs. Dukakis, the boys "were inseparable."

While Michael was eager, ambitious, and self-assured from the first, Stelian had a softer personality. "He was a very shy child," his mother says. "He was a very gentle kind of young man." She says he was the kind of person who could be drawn out with encouragement. "He needed lifting," she says. Early in their childhood it was clear that "Stelian didn't have that aggressiveness that Michael had, but yet Michael followed his lead in everything."

Soon Michael began to excel, sometimes beyond Stelian's accomplishments. Michael, for instance, was an Eagle Scout and completed the work for merit badges almost faster than his scoutmaster could approve them. "I can remember, in his room, he had the merit badges all displayed," his cousin Arthur recalls. Stelian was also an accomplished Boy Scout, but did not achieve the rank of Eagle Scout; Michael believes he was a Star Scout, two ranks below Eagle. Michael's scoutmaster, Felix Knauth, now ninety-two, still remembers Panos bringing his eleven-year-old son to his first troop meeting. His memory of Michael is remarkably consistent with others from the period. Michael, he says, was "a very, very likable boy, very ambitious—clean as a whistle. And whatever he started, he won." In grade school, according to his mother, Stelian had been vice-president of his class; Michael was elected president on the only two occasions when class officers were chosen—in the third and eighth grades.

Even in those early days, he began to develop a reputation that spilled out beyond his own neighborhood. Katharine Dickson, a youngster at the Runkle School, heard that "there was this brilliant Greek kid on the other side of town," Kitty Dickson Dukakis now recalls. "I certainly knew about him." Kitty, three years Michael's junior, caught up with him at Brookline High when she was a freshman. She remembers seeing him in the hallways, but for Michael, recognition of his future wife did not come until a full decade later.

Brookline is a rectangular town that looks on the map as though it had been jammed, like a piece of a jigsaw puzzle, into the City of Boston, which surrounds it on three sides. It is a mixed community with urban neighborhoods adjacent to Boston University and Fenway Park, along with leafier, wealthier areas bordering Newton, an affluent bedroom community. The Brookline in which Michael Dukakis grew up was a mix of old Yankees and Irish, with a large Jewish population; lately it has seen an influx of Asians and other minorities. A constant through the years has been the town's unyielding commitment to providing the best public education possible. Indeed, Brookline's schools have gained a national reputation for excellence.

Brookline High School, in particular, has a tradition of accomplishment. When Dukakis began to run for the White House, a few stories began to circulate about persons who identified him early on as presidential material. One comes from Marilyn Tanner Oettinger, who along with Dukakis was voted "most brilliant" when they graduated. In an ancient history class during their freshman year, Oettinger says, the teacher, Newton Rodeheaver, was especially impressed with Dukakis's work one day. "Sometime," he said to the class, "Michael Dukakis is going to be president of the United States." Ira Jackson, who also graduated from Brookline High, advises against giving too much weight to such tales. "You could say that about a thousand Brookline High grads," he says. A classmate of Dukakis's, Bob Wool, says that success and ambition were "just part of the air" at school. "Working hard, studying, getting into a good college—that was part of your blood," he says. Another classmate, Mikki Ansin, now a photographer in Cambridge, agrees that "a lot of stars came out of that town. We all got the message—we were headed somewhere."

Even so, some schoolmates insist that Dukakis looked like a standout from the start. One is Barry Bunshoft, who now practices law in San Francisco. He says that for four years he started the day with Dukakis and their classmates in homeroom 238. He later renewed the friendship at Harvard Law School. When Dukakis was in high school, says Bunshoft, "you knew he was a winner from the first. He just had leadership in him."

As a freshman, Dukakis was elected vice-president of his class, an office he kept for three years. In his senior year, he decided to challenge his friend and basketball teammate Bob Wool for class president. It was the first of several times Dukakis would run against a friend. Wool, now a writer in New York, was the most popular boy in the class and had been president for the first three years. In addition, both Wool and Dukakis had dated the most popular girl in the class, Sandra "Sandy" Cohen. After a campaign that none of the three can remember as particularly personal or eventful, Wool won. The tally is lost to history, but Dukakis doesn't remember it as being close. "I got my head handed to me," he says. Wool's recollection: "I beat him pretty badly, I think."

But the setback was an exception. Dukakis was involved in a multitude of school activities. One was the marshals, the group headed by Edgar "Sugar" Robinson, now vice-president and treasurer of the Exxon Corporation in New York. The marshals were designated, according to the school yearbook, as "the enforcer of the laws set forth by the school council." Wearing blue armbands, the marshals supervised their schoolmates in hallways and the cafeteria. "We were gentle authorities," says Sandy Cohen, now Sandy Bakalar, a social worker who still lives in Brookline, but the job had some bite to it; marshals acted as prosecutors on the infrequent occasions when students were brought before the all-school court. The role of marshal seemed to fit Dukakis, who always had a clear sense of right and wrong along with a moralistic streak. Because of his activity with the marshals, Dukakis was a member of the Student Council, and in his senior year was elected its president. For Dukakis, it was in high school that politics became a central part of his life, both in school elections and in issues stirring the nation. As a candidate himself, Dukakis showed some early signs of the ambition that would become a hallmark. In grade school and high school, the ambition was always clear. "Whatever it was, he ran for it," his mother says.

For years, Dukakis has listed John F. Kennedy and Joseph R. McCarthy as the major influences on his young political consciousness—one as an inspiration, the other as a source of outrage. But it seems clear that McCarthy, the scourge of alleged Communist sympathizers, came first. During Dukakis's high school years, Kennedy was a cautious young Democratic congressman learning his way in Washington. And although he had been born in Brookline, it was not in his congressional district. The Wisconsin Republican, however, was already in full cry against "pinkos" and "fellow travelers" in government, the media, and the arts. A guiding spirit to Dukakis and many others at Brookline High was the basketball coach, John Grinnell, who was fierce on the subject of McCarthy. (Ira Jackson has remarked on the intensity of political awareness in Brookline; only there, he says, would the basketball coach be a major political influence.)

That Dukakis would be stimulated so early in his career by something he saw as fundamentally wrong, rather than by the pursuit of an abstract, ideal good, is no surprise to people who have followed his career. His key campaigns, the first entry into Brookline politics and the state legislature and the rematch campaign for governor in 1982, were essentially negative campaigns run against opponents he pictured as corrupt or bumbling backroom politicians. In late 1986 and 1987, as he made his decision to run for president, the Iran-contra scandal brought daily revelations of the secret actions of Lieutenant Colonel Oliver North and others who had violated the code of public service that he holds virtually sacred.

Scholastically, Dukakis was at the top of his high school class. Stelian had been a good student, too, a member of the Alpha Pi honor society, but Michael was the president of Alpha Pi. His class yearbook has a caricature of Dukakis with the inscription "Big Chief Brain-in-Face," labeling him the "most brilliant" boy in the class. He also played trumpet in the school band, a skill he continued in college, then let lapse for thirty years until his presidential campaign.

In sports, Dukakis was a starter on the varsity basketball and cross-country teams and captain of tennis. In athletics, as in later life, he was often underestimated. At five feet, eight inches, he was certainly not an imposing presence on the basketball court, and he was not flashy at running or tennis either. Rather, characteristically, his strengths as an athlete were steadiness, discipline, intelligence, determination. He played within his abilities, keeping the ball in play, rarely trying difficult shots or making unforced errors. There was nothing wild, or out of control.

One cross-country teammate, Beryl Cohen, now a lawyer in Boston, thinks that Dukakis was especially suited to long-distance running because he has the essential quality: pace. A cross-country race cannot be won with a jackrabbit start or a tremendous finishing kick, Cohen says. "It begins and ends with the same pace. The point is not to falter, or break down, or change your pace. More than other sports, it requires control and discipline, which of course he has. He's very organized and dogged about it."

The one aspect of school life in which Dukakis's self-assuredness gave way was his relationships with girls. Mikki Ansin puts it succinctly: "He was always smart and always square." Sandy Bakalar probably did more than anyone to help him overcome this awkwardness. "Michael was a little shy. I think as an adolescent he wasn't very comfortable with girls." But they dated, going to ball games, the symphony, jazz clubs. And Bakalar also taught Dukakis how to dance. "It was like the blind leading the blind," she says. One reason he was a bit backward in boy-girl relations, she believes, is that his parents, particularly his father, seemed skeptical of teenage dating. "Michael was brought up that way, that you don't waste time with frivolous things," she says. When she first went to dinner on Rangeley Road, she recalls, "I was really scared of Panos. I could not swallow the food." She did not feel singled out; the question was, "Did he really approve of Michael having girlfriends at all?"

Bakalar and Dukakis ended up having some real affection for one another, though the path was a bit rocky and the romance faded after the two went to college. Bob Wool, Bakalar's other regular date, asked her to the senior prom and she accepted. Then Dukakis called. "I really loved Michael," she says, "so I called Bobby and asked if I could break the date, but he wouldn't let me." Dukakis, of course, wouldn't encourage her to break a commitment unilaterally, so he attended alone while she and Wool went to the prom, where she insists to this day she did not have a good time. High school heartbreak is in some ways timeless, but Bakalar remembers her experience as "so different than it is today. It wasn't sexual. We were so innocent. Times have surely changed."

Though Dukakis was clearly a superior student at a superior school, one trait stood out above all—his extraordinary sense of self. "It was very unusual," remembers Wool. "He had some very strong sense of who he was, what he was doing, what he had to do and accomplish. He wasn't driven the same way we were. We were peer-driven. Acceptance and popularity were so important to us. We were guided very much by the standards around us. I think that's fairly normal at that age. But he listened to a different inner drummer."

His close friends in high school discount stories that he talked of one day running for governor even before he went to college. But in retrospect, Wool believes that ambition for public office was stirring even then. "I would suspect when he ran for senior class president that he [knew he] was going to come back to Brookline and start a political career, and being president of the class could be useful."

Wool, Bakalar, and other classmates say that Dukakis's sense of self is best illustrated by his disdain for the informal clubs that were an important part of life for most Brookline teenagers at the time. Organized outside school, they had different specialties—sports, culture, and the like—but they were basically social. They had names like the Trojans, the Spartans, and the Clover Club, a girls' club of which Bakalar was president. "Michael used to kid me about it," she says. "He thought it was divisive, elitist. 'What good did they do?' he asked. What good *did* they do?" she asks now. "They gave us a sense of belonging." But he did not need that. "Michael was an iconoclast in some respects," she says. His cousin Arthur noted the same trait in another context. Arthur was active in a Greek youth group, the Sons of Pericles, but Michael simply wasn't interested.

It wasn't that Dukakis was antisocial, not that at all. If he was not quite as popular as Wool, he was respected and genuinely liked throughout the school. More than anyone in her class, Bakalar feels, Dukakis "bridged all the gaps that kids place between each other—the athletic jock group, the intellectual student group, the social group, all of them." She says Dukakis also bridged the principal ethnic division in the school, the "polarization between the Jewish kids and the Whiskey Point [neighborhood] Irish kids. Michael especially was friendly with both groups."

Graduation in 1951 capped what was indeed a stellar high school career for Dukakis. Athletically, he added a final achievement on April 19 by running the 26-mile, 385-yard Boston Marathon, finishing fifty-seventh in a field of 191, in what he still reminds people, accurately, was a "very creditable time" of 3 hours, 31 minutes.

Then suddenly, with no warning, this glorious spring of achievement and happiness was smashed by family grief. Stelian, a junior at Bates College in Maine, had a severe attack of depression. He returned home and shortly thereafter tried to kill himself. Family members are extremely reluctant to discuss the incident, and usually refer to it as a "nervous breakdown." But Mrs. Dukakis confirms there was a suicide attempt. Asked what happened, she replies, "Do we have to talk about it?"

Of Stelian's breakdown, Michael says, "It came out of the blue, just bang-o." He believes it was late in the spring, after the marathon, probably in May, that they heard from Stelian. "He called up and said he was coming home. He was deeply depressed, couldn't function. It was a total breakdown almost." Stelian had broken up with a girlfriend shortly before, but Michael thought that hadn't seemed a severe blow to his brother. "There had been no history of problems or troubles," Michael says. "My folks couldn't understand it."

Incredibly, Michael says he does not remember whether Stelian tried to kill himself. He remembers the breakdown, but recalls few details. Asked specifically whether his brother tried to take his own life, Michael replies, "He came close." But then, whether it was kept from him or he has repressed it, he doesn't elaborate. "I don't quite remember what happened," he says. "I remember my dad was involved. I remember a doctor being called . . . This was at home, after he came home." Asked if Stelian took pills, Michael answers, "Might have, but I remember something happened and my dad brought a psychiatrist in and the decision was made to institutionalize him. It was obvious something was *very* wrong."

Sandy Bakalar remembers vividly when Dukakis told her. "We were sitting outside of school on a stone wall. He said, 'It's hard for me to tell you.' But I said, 'You'll feel better.' " Then he told her. "He said, 'My brother's really sad. He's falling apart. He's going to have to come home.' Michael cried. It was a sad time for him. We didn't understand somebody losing interest in life. We were so full of life. I think that Michael really loved Stelian." But here, she said, "was one thing that he couldn't do anything about. Michael was just shattered. He was sitting on the wall, the tears were coming down his face, and I just wanted to die."

The event was an enormous blow to the family, and the more so because it was totally unanticipated. Stelian had been an honor student in high school and, like Michael, captain of the tennis team. The motto he chose for his high school yearbook was *Mens sana in corpore sano*—a healthy mind in a healthy body. After graduating in 1948, he had gone to the college both his parents had attended, and he seemed to be doing well. In particular, he was an excellent cross-country runner, "the best two-miler in Maine," Michael remembers. But after his breakdown, Stelian was never the same. He was able to live on his own and to find work. But his condition, according to his mother, "was a concern, always." Virtually his whole adult life, she says, "was a difficult time for him. Why, we don't know."

For Michael Dukakis, or any Brookline High senior with his record, Harvard was the expected college choice, and the headmaster, a Harvard alumnus named Robert G. Andree, told Dukakis, Wool, and another senior that he could guarantee their admission. But Dukakis didn't even apply; he had never been outside New England and wanted some distance from Brookline. He looked at Bates, Oberlin, and finally chose Swarthmore, a small, academically rigorous college outside Philadelphia.

Dukakis entered Swarthmore in a pre-med program, but he switched to political science after a run-in with freshman physics. Dukakis has sometimes said that he flunked the course, sometimes that he got "a charitable D." His transcript indicates the latter is correct. Regardless, he was off the medical track. Dr. Dukakis had hoped that Michael would become a physician, but in 1974 he acknowledged that the course showed Michael "could not be a lab rat for four years." There are others who think that, intentionally or not, the physics grade produced a desired result.

"He needed an excuse to get out of pre-med," says his cousin Arthur. And his roommate for three years, Frank Sieverts, says they both arrived as pre-meds, but "I think we both found ourselves being turned on by excellent political science teaching and excellent history teaching."

A bit of wanderlust struck Dukakis at Swarthmore, and, usually with a friend, he pursued it through the mechanism common to college students at the time—the thumb. Trips to Wisconsin, Canada, and even the West Coast and Mexico were included, not to mention visits home. "I don't think I ever paid a penny to get to Swarthmore or back," he says.

In college as in high school, Dukakis took his politics both ways—as a candidate himself, winning election to the Student Council, and as a campaign worker in 1952, passing out leaflets in Philadelphia for Adlai Stevenson, the Democratic presidential nominee. In fact, Dukakis had plunged into the local political scene in 1951, during the fall of his freshman year, helping the reform candidate Joseph Clark become mayor of Philadelphia. "We went down to the so-called river wards to do some poll-watching," Sieverts recalls. "We thought we were very brave."

In January 1954, before he was even old enough to vote, Dukakis wrote a letter to his state's freshman U.S. senator, John F. Kennedy. It sounded almost as though he were writing to a peer. "I feel its [sic] about time I dropped you a note on a couple of issues now pending in the Senate," Dukakis wrote in a neat but imperfectly typed, three-paragraph letter now on file at the Kennedy Library in Boston. He explained that, although he was studying in Pennsylvania, "I am a resident of Brookline, Massachusetts, and try to do as much for the Democratic Party as possible down here and back home when I am around Boston."

Dukakis mentioned the Bricker Amendment, which would have limited a president's power to negotiate treaties. "You are probably as much opposed as I am," Dukakis wrote, to "what looks to me like an attempt to legislate isolationism, pure and simple." The amendment was defeated a month later. Dukakis also commended Kennedy for his support of the St. Lawrence Seaway, a stand that had more appeal nationally than in Massachusetts. "I think your suggestions on what to do to bolster the New England economy are extremely well-taken," wrote Dukakis.

Dukakis was busy at Swarthmore, playing trumpet in the orchestra, writing about sports for the school newspaper, *The Phoenix,* running cross-country and playing baseball, both at the varsity level, and playing junior varsity basketball and tennis, all in addition to his political activity.

Despite his hapless encounter with freshman physics, he graduated both Phi Beta Kappa (as his mother had from Bates) and with highest honors, an outstanding achievement in a school where virtually all of the students were exceptionally bright. The 1955 yearbook, *Halcyon,* says of Dukakis much that is still true today. Next to his senior picture is the following: "A man of ideals teaching himself how to apply them . . . self-confident . . . wants to see and do things himself . . . hitch-hiker par excellence . . . 14-day round trip to mexico city with schiller by foot . . . distinguished political advisor and campaign manager . . . loves a hot controversy . . . unpopular with local barbers . . . originality . . . natural leadership . . . thrives on greek."

"Local barbers" refers to a story that has become one of the basics of Dukakis lore. Swarthmore was not exactly a racial melting pot—only 2 of 213 in Dukakis's class were black—but the civil rights movement began to stir consciences there nonetheless. When the town barber refused to cut the hair of the black students, Dukakis quickly stepped in and set up his own campus tonsorium, employing skills he had learned as a camp counselor. Soon, the operation became a civil rights symbol, and Dukakis was trimming, not only blacks, but dozens of white students who boycotted the local barber. At 65 cents each, the haircuts gave Dukakis some spending money, providing him, as he remarked later, with a chance to combine public purpose with a bit of private enterprise. As Sieverts recalls, there was only one style of haircut, which resembled Marine Corps issue. "We all ended up looking alike—looking like Ollie North," he says.

One twist, according to Sieverts, is that Dukakis could not cut his own hair, so he went to the most practical place—the barber who had rejected the blacks. The barber, knowing that Dukakis was his competitor, turned the chair around as his own form of protest so that Dukakis could not watch his work in the mirror. Sieverts thinks this part of the story tells something important about Dukakis, who has never liked confrontation or empty symbolism. "He's a solver of problems rather than a creator of issues," Sieverts says.

Dukakis was chairman of the campus branch of Students for Democratic Action, the college wing of Americans for Democratic Action, and in that role ran into some free speech issues. McCarthy was still on the rampage in Washington, and the chill extended to many colleges. "We felt brave listening to Pete Seeger," Sieverts says. A controversy grew around the question of whether the leftist reporter I. F. Stone should be invited to speak on campus. Dukakis helped to resolve the issue by minimizing the ideological aspect, saying that anyone should be allowed to speak. "He was very matter-of-fact," Sieverts says. "He turned down the temperature."

As in high school, Dukakis refused to join exclusive clubs, staying out of the fraternities that were a central part of campus life for some students and declining an invitation to join Book and Key, an honor society. Many of those in Dukakis's circle felt the same way. "We felt it was a selection *in* that selected other people out," says Sieverts. Still, Dukakis was popular, he says— "very much a personality around campus." Sieverts found his roommate to be exceptionally self-assured for a young man in an atmosphere where many of his contemporaries were actively searching for their selves, testing their values. "He was very directed," says Sieverts. "He was orderly, but not fanatically so. He was utterly non-neurotic . . . In an environment where a lot of people were frantic at times, he was not one of those who was rushing at the last minute." Dukakis himself says that, in all his academic life, he never once worked through the night to finish a paper or cram for a test; in fact, he says he has never stayed up all night for *any* reason. Yet the product was exceptional, particularly at Swarthmore. "In the normal course, he turned out absolutely first-class work," Sieverts says.

Howard M. Temin, another classmate, has a similar memory of Dukakis. "He was mature more than most," he recalls. "He seemed to know clearly what he wanted to do. It was unusual." Temin, a biologist who is now teaching at the University of Wisconsin and who won the Nobel Prize in medicine in 1975, also remembers Dukakis as having a good sense of humor and enjoying campus life. Several of Dukakis's friends also stood out scholastically. Sieverts went to Oxford as a Rhodes scholar, and others won Marshall and Fulbright fellowships. But Dukakis chose not to apply. "He had his own things he felt he had to do," says Sieverts.

One of them was to become governor of Massachusetts. It didn't come out quite that baldly, but the pieces took shape at Swarthmore. He knew he wanted to get into public life, and he determined to get the military and law school behind him as quickly as possible. Oxford might have been stimulating, but would have taken time. "I wasn't interested," he says. Dukakis was not only more impatient than his schoolmates, he had a different idea. Late at night, says Sieverts, those interested in public service would talk about running for the U.S. House or Senate eventually, or possibly entering the foreign service. Sieverts chose the latter and is now on the staff of the Senate Foreign Relations Committee. But by sophomore or junior year, he says, Dukakis was focused on running for governor. "Through state government, you can accomplish more," Sieverts remembers Dukakis saying.

Socially, Dukakis was a little more gregarious than he had been in high school, dating fairly often but developing no serious romance. "He played the field," Sieverts says. "Besides, we were the pre-pill generation."

One of the college experiences that proved to be a powerful influence on Dukakis happened more or less by accident. During the summer of 1954, Dukakis was interested enough in his parents' homeland to want to visit Greece, but he failed to win the Social Science Research Foundation grant for which he had applied. An adviser suggested he apply for another fellowship. "The next thing I know," says Dukakis, "I'm hitchhiking down to Miami to save a few bucks to get a plane for Lima."

The $750 fellowship included tuition for a program at the University of San Marcos, the oldest university in South Amer-

ica, as well as enough extra for Dukakis to visit elsewhere in
Latin America, including Bolivia and parts of Central America
and Cuba, then run by the dictator Fulgencio Batista. Dukakis
spoke no Spanish when he was granted the fellowship, but
scrambled to learn it. Buying a dictionary and borrowing records from the library, his father remembered, he picked up
enough to get along, then improved steadily over the summer at
San Marcos, where the courses were all in Spanish. His knowledge of Spanish stayed with him, and it became an asset in his
presidential campaign.

More than the language, however, Dukakis was influenced by
the education he received in Latin American politics. Peru was
ruled at the time by the right-wing dictator Manuel A. Odría,
who was supported by the Eisenhower administration but not by
the people, at least not those Dukakis met. (Odría was voted out
of office two years later.) The University of San Marcos was itself
a hotbed of political activity; it was there in 1958 that Vice-
President Richard Nixon was pelted with stones and insults and
forced to retreat. While at the university, Dukakis stayed in Lima
with Victor and Blanca Nuñez del Arco and their six children.
He was a former lawyer who ran a children's clothing store; she
was very political and supported APRA, the outlawed non-Com-
munist opposition.

"Blanca and I were very close; we really got along," recalls
Dukakis. He says the atmosphere of repression was thick.
"There was no political freedom of any kind." He remembers
seeing militaristic parades, with row upon row of "those troops
with the German bucket helmets," and hearing of dozens of
political prisoners who had been spirited off to an island jail,
where they could not even communicate with their relatives.
Blanca del Arco had known some of these prisoners personally.
In addition, Dukakis says, "it just so happens that 1954 was the
year the United States government overthrew the popularly
elected government in Guatemala"—in late June, when Dukakis
was newly arrived in Lima—an event that was followed closely
in Peru. In fact, Dukakis found that people throughout Latin
America were far better informed on American policy and actions in the hemisphere than most Americans were.

Dukakis has retained an interest in Latin American develop-
ments and particularly in U.S. policy. He has not tried to use his
state offices to affect national policy, but in an interview in June
1984 he lambasted the Reagan administration's policy in Nicaragua, which he said was based on a "trigger-happy, reach-for-
your-gun, Communist-under-every-bed kind of ideology" that
could lead to war. Dukakis said then that his strong views de-
rived from his earlier experiences. "There was incredible poverty in Latin America in the face of tremendous wealth at the
top," he said. "I have never gotten over walking through the
squatters' sections in Lima: people living in shacks and in the
sides of mountains, people literally living in holes." At the start
of his presidential candidacy, Latin American policy was the one
aspect of foreign affairs he was able to speak to with some passion and detail.

In the fall of 1954, Dukakis took a semester at American University in Washington, an exciting time to be in the capital, especially since it was then that Joe McCarthy was condemned by his
colleagues in the Senate. John Kennedy never expressed outrage at McCarthy. In fact, in one of the more controversial moments of his Senate career, Kennedy was the only Democrat not
recorded on the condemnation vote. He was in the hospital,
though some critics questioned his timing. Dukakis says now he
doesn't remember making the connection between the two political figures he says influenced him so powerfully. The fact that
Kennedy lacked his own anti-McCarthy zeal "didn't really trouble me that much," he says.

Dukakis's father spoke proudly in later years of his son's academic success at Swarthmore, but Michael's next move was not
so popular at home. He intended to go to law school and had
applied at Harvard, where he was accepted. But he decided to
get his military obligation out of the way first. When he did not
go directly to law school, which would have given him a student
deferment, he was, as he expected, drafted for a two-year hitch
in the regular army. "His father was terribly unhappy," Mrs.
Dukakis recalls. He thought Michael should go to law school
first, then if he went in the military he could learn some lawyer-

ing in the judge advocate's office. But Michael "wanted to get it over with," his mother says, so that he would be able to leave law school and immediately begin his career.

Much of Dukakis's tour was spent at Munsan, South Korea, helping supervise the armistice that had been in place since July 1953. Living in the Far East did not excite him in the way his summer in Peru had, but he found some utility in it nonetheless, exercising his facility for languages by studying Korean. He was honorably discharged, after twenty-one months, with the rank of specialist third class. In his early campaigns, Dukakis invariably cited his military service in his campaign literature. A flyer distributed when he was running for lieutenant governor in 1970, for instance, lists these attributes: "Endorsed by the Democratic State Convention—Fighter for Low Cost Auto Insurance—Veteran—Experienced Legislator." More recently, Dukakis has referred to his military duty only rarely.

One adventure he has mentioned apparently contributed to the unease Dukakis still experiences in airplanes. As he tells it, a Taiwanese airliner, trying to land in heavy fog, was about to touch down when the pilot—and the passengers—realized the runway was seventy-five feet to one side. A second effort was successful. Dukakis turns the story on himself, saying he should have expected as much, since he chose that airline for its rock-bottom fares.

Completing his tour in 1957, Dukakis went directly to Harvard Law School, the major transitional period of his life, when his attention turned from school to his career, elective politics. His first run came, in fact, at the age of twenty-four, in the spring of his first year. His formal education was completed with competence, but not with the glory he had achieved in high school and college. He was graduated from law school cum laude, seventy-first in a class of 468. But he was not among those with exceptional grades who were asked to join the staff of the *Harvard Law Review*.

Still, the law school offered a variety of stimuli. In his class were Francis X. Meaney, who was for years his closest political friend, and Barry Bunshoft, who conspired with him in their early reform campaigns. Other classmates who have since reached high public office included Paul Sarbanes, since 1977 a Democratic U.S. senator from Maryland, and Antonin Scalia (who *was* on the *Law Review*), a Reagan appointee to the U.S. Supreme Court. And entering Dukakis's class in its second year, following study at Oxford under a Marshall Scholarship, was another son of Greek immigrants who became Dukakis's closest friend, Paul Brountas.

Brountas, who comes from Maine, had heard of Dukakis before he arrived at Harvard but was not impressed. A sister-in-law who lived in Boston and had been delivered by Dr. Dukakis knew that Michael was at the law school and suggested that the two would have a lot in common. "I didn't bother to look him up," says Brountas, who felt that he and the other students would be too cosmopolitan to put much stock in something as parochial as similar Greek roots. "I was sure that I wasn't going to like him," Brountas says. But the two talked at a dinner Sarbanes had organized, and they got along, gradually becoming friends. When they were finishing up their coursework and preparing for the bar exam, the two took a review course together. Their last act as students was a devil-may-care cut of their own planned study session. "The night before the bar exam," Brountas recalls, "we saw the movie *Psycho*."

Both passed, nevertheless, and almost immediately took off on a cross-country car trip that has become the source of countless stories. Piled into Brountas's 1956 blue Volkswagen Karmann Ghia hardtop, the young bachelors spent nearly seven weeks touring the United States and Mexico in what was partially an attempt to see how far they could go on how little. "Mike said, 'Let's take sleeping bags and we'll sleep out,'" Brountas says, but for the most part they ended up staying in dollar-a-night Milner hotels. Before it was over, they had wandered to the Grand Canyon, down to Mexico City and Acapulco, where Dukakis showed off his Spanish and the two lazed by the pool at the El Presidente Hotel—"We knew a couple of ladies who were staying there," Brountas says—and back through the Shenandoah Valley, visiting as many Civil War battlefields as they could.

Starting his presidential campaign in Iowa in 1987, Dukakis

mentioned this trip, saying he had been in the state briefly once before. Brief was indeed the word, because the beginning of the expedition was far from leisurely. They left Boston on July 5 or 6, 1960, and were determined to get to the Democratic National Convention, which opened in Los Angeles on July 11. "We headed west and didn't really stop till we hit the Rockies," Brountas says.

They arrived in Los Angeles in time for the major events, and Dukakis, already with political connections, managed to get them into the hall. He strongly supported John Kennedy, who seemed likely to win the nomination, although some uncertainty remained. According to Brountas, Stelian was also at the convention, working to give Adlai Stevenson a third try as the Democratic nominee, but Dukakis says he has no memory of seeing his brother in Los Angeles. Brountas says he was inclined toward Stevenson initially, but he was persuaded to join Kennedy's camp at the convention. Brountas remembers being in the audience on Wednesday, July 13, to hear Eugene McCarthy give one of the great convention speeches of all time, imploring the delegates not to forget Stevenson, not to "leave this prophet without honor in his own party." Dukakis's memory is that he was in a bar, having a beer and sandwich, and saw the speech on television. Nevertheless, both were close at hand a few hours later when Kennedy, backed by a steamroller campaign—run in large part by men only a decade older than the new law school graduates—rumbled to the nomination on the first ballot.

Between Los Angeles and Mexico, Brountas and Dukakis took a side trip to Las Vegas. They invaded that city of sin in grand fashion, blowing a quarter each to splash in a public swimming pool. In the evening, they tested the rumors they had heard about the casinos' bountiful buffets, to keep their gamblers happy, and came away with the biggest and best meal of their trip, for a dollar apiece. Then Brountas recalls that he wanted to gamble *something,* saying they were in Las Vegas for possibly the only time in their lives, and it had to be done once. Dukakis wouldn't hear of it. "I don't gamble," Brountas recalls him saying. "I finally convinced him. We each got five dollars in quarters and went to the slot machines. Michael put in a quarter and pulled the arm and hit the jackpot. It was unbelievable—probably about twenty-five dollars. He scooped up the money and I said, 'Aren't you going to bet anymore?' and he said, 'No. I don't gamble.' "

Years later, having been persuaded to attend a charity fundraiser at Foxboro Raceway, a track for trotting horses outside Boston, Dukakis was besieged by supporters wanting him to bet on a long shot named Governor the Duke that happened to be running in the first race. Dukakis flatly refused. The horse came in, paying about $20, according to Eddie Andelman, a sportscaster and a friend of Kitty's from school days.

In Las Vegas, Dukakis and Brountas finished off their big day with what Brountas says was the only night they ever did spend out of a bed. "We just weren't going to stay in a Las Vegas hotel," Brountas says. So they pulled his car onto a field and discussed the arrangements. In the end, says Brountas, "he slept in the car and I slept on the ground. That was when I knew he was going to be a better politician than I was."

3. Ambition

"He's got to be reckoned with."

BEFORE HE ENTERED Harvard Law School, Michael Dukakis was already an accomplished campus politician, having been elected president of the Student Council in high school and college and class president twice in grade school. At law school, however, he stepped outside the campus to pursue a political career in the real world. By the time he graduated in 1960, he had already run for elective office three times, had won twice, and had taken over the Democratic party leadership in his home town, ousting established leaders in a dramatic coup. From the first, his tone was moralistic, his cry for reform. In the next decade, Dukakis moved forward determinedly, brushing impediments from his path, whether friend or foe. He earned a statewide reputation and put himself on a track headed straight for the governor's office.

To many who knew him from childhood, his political ambition and success came as no surprise. In the home of Panos and Euterpe Dukakis, politics and success had always been staples. Recounting his family story as a candidate for the presidency, Dukakis said he thought his commitment to public service was inherited from his father, while his identification with the Democrats had been passed down from his mother. Throughout his public career, he has often quoted his father: "Much has been given to you; much is expected of you." At many stops in his presidential campaign, he has drawn a laugh by conceding that his father was on the conservative side and usually voted Republican until 1962, when Dukakis first ran in a partisan election, for the state House of Representatives. Panos changed his registration to Democratic to vote for his son. But Euterpe Dukakis was the family Democrat.

"My dad was pretty conservative politically," he says. "I think I probably almost unconsciously got from him this sense that serving others was the most important thing you could do in this world. I mean he just *loved* medicine and the opportunity it gave him to serve others, to help others, to make a difference in the lives of people for the better . . . Although she wasn't that active politically, I think I probably got a lot of my politics from my mother . . . She was the more liberal of the two."

His parents were hardly his only political influence, however. Stelian and their two uncles, Constantine Dukakis and Nicholas Boukis, kept the house alive with politics. Boukis, a men's clothier who was Euterpe's oldest brother and Michael's godfather, took a healthy interest in public affairs and "was quite an influence" on Michael, Euterpe says. "We were always interested, particularly at election time." Michael remembers him as "a very liberal guy but a great fan of Leverett Saltonstall," a Republican governor and U.S. senator from Massachusetts. Michael's cousin Arthur has a similar memory of the many times the families shared together. Arthur's father, George, a restaurateur in Lowell, was the older brother who had helped Panos through school. For years, most of the major holidays were spent either at George's or Panos's house. "At the dinner table, the talk was always of politics," Arthur recalls. Frequently Constantine, the youngest Dukakis brother, an accountant who lived most of his life in suburban Arlington, Massachusetts, would join the festivities. He took particular delight in goading Stelian and Michael into political debate. "Constantine always took an opposing view just to get Michael and Stelian going," Arthur says. Michael remembers Constantine as a controversial and feisty conservative. In Arthur's view, Michael "always wanted to be a politician from day one," but in this he was again following the lead of Stelian. "I think a lot of the politics may have come from Stelian and rubbed off on Michael," Arthur says.

Dukakis was eager to plunge into Brookline politics after working for Philadelphia's mayor in 1951 and for Adlai Stevenson in 1952. Beginning in 1954, he campaigned energetically in Brookline for Sumner Z. Kaplan, helping him become the first Democrat elected to the state legislature from the town in modern times. Though that was the summer he spent in South America, Dukakis remembers coming home in the fall to help Kaplan. Brookline had been solidly Republican, but in 1954 the first cracks appeared in the GOP. Jackson J. Holtz of Brookline made a surprisingly strong challenge against the Republican congressman Laurence Curtis that year. Holtz lost by fewer than 2000 votes but carried Brookline. His campaign helped push Kaplan to victory, but the crucial ingredient was hard work. Barry Bunshoft recalls the early campaigning for Kaplan, who was re-elected biennially through 1960. "We had brochures, and we were out there at seven in the morning, on the corners, at the streetcar stops. I think Michael and I both learned our politics courtesy of Sumner." Another member of the group, Haskell "Hackie" Kassler, now a Boston lawyer, remembers, "You used to sign up to be at a particular car stop from seven to eight-fifteen or eight-twenty, then you had your option. You could go back to Sumner's house and his mother would cook breakfast for you, or you could go to school or work or whatever."

Kaplan's political style was an innovation for Brookline at the time—a street campaign that included day after day of personal, door-to-door canvassing. The approach was picked up soon after by two young Brookline Democrats, Beryl Cohen and Michael Dukakis.

Cohen was a year behind Dukakis in high school (succeeding him as Student Council president) and was not part of the battle for control of the Democratic party structure in Brookline, as Dukakis was. But he got an early start, running for the Massachusetts House of Representatives in 1960 and winning. According to Cohen, Dukakis succeeded two years later with the same technique. "Michael's campaign was a copycat of mine, and mine was a copycat of Kaplan's," he recalls. "We walked door-to-door." Kaplan "was really the godfather of Michael Dukakis politically," Cohen says. "He brought Michael in—he put him in place."

Dukakis's first try for public office came in the spring of 1958, when he was still a first-year law student. He ran for a seat on the Brookline Redevelopment Authority, and his campaign was an odd amalgam of friends from Brookline and law school, the latter including Paul Sarbanes and Carl M. Sapers, a third-year law student and reform Democrat who had moved from Brookline to Boston. Bunshoft was another supporter who bridged the two camps.

The Brookline Redevelopment Authority was a new body, created because of the town's concern with overdevelopment. Dukakis had a growing interest in development issues, which he explored two years later with Fran Meaney in their major law school paper, on urban renewal in Boston. Four seats were open, and Dukakis, at the age of twenty-four, took a shot. He campaigned hard, going from door to door and pressing his volunteers for a maximum effort. Sarbanes remembers standing at a polling place for thirteen hours straight. Another eager neophyte was Meaney, who was to become Dukakis's political right hand for fifteen years. When the votes were counted on March 4, however, Dukakis had lost, running a close fifth. Dukakis remembers finishing 117 votes short of the fourth seat, demonstrating that his celebrated memory for detail is strong but not infallible: he lost by 127 votes.

As a budding politician in Brookline, Dukakis had little time for extracurricular activities at law school, but he was a member of the Young Democrats Club and received a lesson in political performance when John F. Kennedy spoke to the group. The year was 1958 and Kennedy was a senator running for re-election with token opposition, but it was clear that he was looking toward the White House. Herbert P. Gleason, who was two years ahead of Dukakis, was club president. Gleason, now a Boston lawyer, remembers telling Kennedy that the young law students were more interested in having questions answered than in hearing a long speech. Kennedy marched onto the stage at Harkness Commons, Gleason recalls, "and said, 'My name is John Kennedy, and I'm a candidate for president of the United States. Are there any questions?' " What followed struck Dukakis as "one of the most impressive hours and a half I had ever spent with a political figure." Dukakis still bubbles with enthusiasm when he recalls "the interaction between this guy and the audience—his wit, humor, intelligence, directness, candor. I remember his hands going in and out of his pockets," a mannerism Dukakis employs now when he remembers not to wave them in the air like oak leaves in a gale. "It was brilliant," Dukakis continues, "I mean, Jesus, I had never seen anything quite like it."

The following year, Dukakis won his first public office, one of twenty-one seats as a member of the Brookline town meeting from his precinct, the 12th. "That was the year that Sumner, again, had us all run for town meeting member," Kassler recalls. "There were new districts. Many of us went door-to-door in our own precincts, and we sent out mailings." The effort shocked Brookline, he says, because it challenged the time-honored way of running for office in the town. "You didn't campaign; you were supposed to *stand* for election," he says.

But the big push came in 1960, just weeks before Dukakis was graduated from law school. He and Sapers, along with a number of other young Democrats, had met frequently in the late 1950s to commiserate over what they saw as the dismal condition of their party. They cheered Kennedy's emergence as a national power, but despised the glad-handing cronyism, often resulting in outright corruption, that characterized their state party's established leadership. They were determined to fight the establishment, not only in campaigns for public office, but also by battling for control of the party itself. The group cut its teeth in a 1958 congressional campaign in which, backing John "Jock" Saltonstall, a Democrat, they failed to unseat the Republican incumbent, Laurence Curtis. Then they moved on to more promising endeavors.

Sapers organized a slate to run against the old leadership of Boston's Ward 5, centered on Beacon Hill, and in April 1960 they won. Charlie McGlue, a veteran Democratic elections expert and longtime Ward 5 chairman, was knocked out and Sapers replaced him. On the same day, the slate headed by Dukakis in Brookline also won, and Dukakis immediately took over as chairman. The campaign was "masterfully organized," according to Kassler, with each candidate contacting voters in one part of the town, mostly through tireless door-knocking, then exchanging telephone lists and encouraging voters to back the entire slate—to "vote for Group Two. Group One was the regulars," Kassler says. "They never knew what hit 'em."

Group Two swept all but one of the thirty-five seats on the committee. The *Brookline Chronicle Citizen* called it "the most amazing upset of recent political history in this town." Though most of the insurgents were newcomers at the time, they took firm control of the party. The new committee members turned out to be a virtual *Who's Who* of Brookline politics for decades. In addition to Dukakis and Kassler, the slate included William Sapers, Carl's brother; Joan Hertzmark, a devoted volunteer in all of Dukakis's campaigns and still town committee chairman; Allan Sidd, who would become one of Dukakis's mentors; and Dukakis's own brother, Stelian. This was nine years after Stelian's breakdown, and Michael, who organized the slate, surely must have been responsible for including his brother, but he says now he has no memory of it. Kassler says he does not recall Stelian's being active in the campaign or on the committee. Not long after the election, Stelian moved temporarily to Boston and was not re-elected.

Two months later, at the Democratic state convention at the old, decrepit Boston Arena, Dukakis and Carl Sapers called a meeting to announce the formation of the Commonwealth Organization of Democrats (COD), with a manifesto of reform. Jesse Fillman, a New Deal veteran who was better known than the young insurgents, was named president, and Meaney became an unofficial—and unpaid—executive director. Dukakis went out seeking support for the revolution, which took on a generational tone. On March 16, 1961, he urged young liberals in the Boston College chapter of Americans for Democratic Action to seize control of the Democratic party or face the "uninspired, vacillating conduct of state affairs which has become a chronic condition." Referring to Kennedy's New Frontier in Washington, Dukakis said, "It is ironic that while the nation prepares to send the cream of its youth to assist new nations in the development of their social and economic resources, we here in

Massachusetts have not yet proved we can efficiently govern ourselves."

The establishment politicians in the Democratic State Committee foolishly helped out the insurgents by huffily suing to prevent their use of the word *Democrat* in their name. Under Massachusetts statutes at the time, the insiders in the legislature had given the insiders in the state committee a virtual copyright on the use of the word with a capital *D*. The young reformers gloried in the publicity, fought the move in court, and eventually won. In the meantime, they incorporated themselves under the name COD, Inc., knowing the press would spell out the acronym.

COD is long since defunct. But its impact and reputation were such that many Democrats now claim to have had key roles in its formation—to have been present at the creation. All agree, however, that Dukakis, Carl Sapers, Bill Sapers, Fran Meaney, and Herb Gleason were major players. In Gleason's mind, "It was really Michael's organization . . . He was the brains behind it. He was the mover." The subject of COD meetings, Gleason says, "was mostly what Michael wanted to do next."

Though not strictly a COD effort, Carl Sapers and Gleason scored an early coup for the Democratic youth movement by helping win the 1960 state convention endorsement for secretary of state for Kevin H. White, a newcomer who combined a family background in the rough-and-tumble ward politics of Boston with a Williams College degree and Beacon Hill address. White won the job and went on to become mayor of Boston from 1968 to 1984, during which time his relations with the reformers steadily deteriorated.

As the flirtation with White indicated, COD initially showed more energy than direction. "We did not have a specific program," says Bill Sapers, and they were not prepared to implement a detailed agenda. But the young reformers knew very well what they were *against*. In Brookline, "we didn't think the town committee really represented the party," Bill Sapers says. "We felt that new people should come aboard who were more representative of a new generation of Democrats." In other words, their central goal was more political than substantive:

they wanted to dislodge the established party leaders and take power.

Accordingly, COD members focused for two years on recruiting candidates for the legislature and raising money to support them. Carl Sapers remembers collecting enough to give each of thirteen to fourteen candidates about $1000, a significant sum for a House race at that time. A few incumbents, like Paul C. Menton of Watertown, who had been elected in 1958, were endorsed by COD, but most of its candidates were new. Among the winners was Michael Dukakis of Brookline, whose victory in 1962 began a quarter-century State House career.

But the two years between law school and his election to the legislature were not exclusively given over to politics. During this period he developed two associations of significance to his later life—one with a law firm and one with a woman.

After his travels with Brountas, Dukakis went to work as an associate at the Boston law firm of Hill, Barlow, Goodale and Adams, now Hill & Barlow. Carl Sapers had joined in 1958 and Gleason, in 1959. There was some competition for Dukakis's services, since another Boston firm, Foley, Hoag & Eliot, where he had worked one summer, also offered him a position, but, says Sapers, "we were able to lure him here." Though his heart was in politics, Dukakis was by all accounts a diligent and competent lawyer, doing some work in real estate and some in minor court cases. In 1961 and 1962, he also assisted a more senior partner who represented the Boston Finance Commission, which was investigating city land sales under the chairmanship of Edward W. Brooke. In one of the countless ironies that suffuse Massachusetts politics, Dukakis thereby did some work for Brooke, the Republican who had been defeated by Kevin White for secretary of state in 1960 and who was given the FinCom chairmanship by his fellow Republican Governor John A. Volpe as a consolation prize and steppingstone.

A year later, in October 1961, Dukakis had his first date with Katharine Dickson. Kitty says she knew of Dukakis as a grade-schooler and met him when she started at Brookline High. Then she remembers seeing him in the fall of 1961, waiting in line for rush tickets at Symphony Hall. (Dukakis remembers none of this.) Sandy Bakalar, a classmate and occasional date of Dukakis's in high school and later a close friend of Kitty's, was the matchmaker, suggesting that Michael call Kitty. She was busy the first time, but he called again.

One bit of evidence suggests that Kitty was not entirely unknown to Dukakis, or at least that he had some reason to try to impress her. Why else would he spring for such a fancy date? They went first to dinner at Maître Jacques, one of the pricier French restaurants in Boston, the kind of place that would usually have the frugal Dukakis grumbling about inflated prices and unnecessary waste, if he found himself there at all. Then it was off to see an Italian film, *Rocco and His Brothers*. "We both hated it," Kitty recalls. The movie dramatized the difficulties facing a family that moved from the depressed south of Italy to bustling Milan, and to that extent it paralleled the story of Dukakis's parents. But the comparison ended there. Luchino Visconti's movie was about disorientation, while the Dukakises had succeeded in large part because of their unwavering sense of direction. "We left halfway through," says Kitty, adding that she has since kidded her husband regularly about leaving a show he had already paid for. "We went back to my apartment and talked a lot about politics."

Dukakis was already running for the House seat he would win a year later, and he had plenty to talk about. Kitty had a lot to say as well. Like Dukakis, she had been born and raised in Brookline and had gone to college in Pennsylvania. But her history was dramatically different from Dukakis's and included her own fascinating parents, three grandmothers, a failed marriage, and a three-year-old son.

Her father, Harry Ellis Dickson, was born into a Jewish family in the diverse, blue-collar Boston suburb of Somerville. He had a passion for music, and was studying violin when he met Jane Goldberg in Berlin in 1932.

Jane's upbringing might seem bizarre now but was not unique in her day. Her mother, Margaret Fielding, was deserted by her husband, an Irishman named James Byrnes, soon after Jane was born. At her wit's end but still resourceful, Margaret Fielding struck a bargain with a wealthy Jewish couple, Mabel and Harry Goldberg, by which the Goldbergs adopted Jane and Fielding joined the household as governess to her own daughter. The arrangement took. In fact, Kitty and her younger sister, Janet Peters, knew Margaret Fielding well as children, but were unaware that she was their real grandmother until they were in their teens.

Jane Dickson grew up in an active and intellectual family, living in New York City and New Rochelle and studying in France and Germany. She was surely influenced by the example of her adoptive mother, Mabel Goldberg, who often used her maiden name, Williams, and went to Columbia when she was in her fifties to pursue a Ph.D. in social work. Taking a similar path, Jane was a social worker in New York for two years after she returned from Germany, in 1933, when Hitler was coming to power. Harry Dickson came home the same year. He sought Jane out and they were married in 1935. Kitty was born on December 26, 1936.

For virtually all of his adult life, Dickson has been something of a celebrity as well as one of the leading professional musicians in Boston, standing out especially for his ability to attract new audiences. He founded the Boston Youth Concerts and was for many years associate director of the Boston Pops Orchestra. He was also a violinist in the Boston Symphony Orchestra for forty-nine years.

Kitty grew up in a home where her parents attracted musicians, actors, and other people from the arts; she was named for Kitty Carlisle, a school friend of her mother's. Nevertheless, Kitty describes herself as a shy child who considered turning to acting, or dancing, partly as a means of expression. Indeed, she has taught dance on and off for much of her life. But by the time she walked out of *Rocco* with Dukakis, she was a twenty-four-year-old with a lot of life behind her. As a high school student, she showed some interest in public affairs and had some success in participating. She was a freshman class representative and, at seventeen, president of the Brookline Girls' League. In this capacity she attended a conference at which Eleanor Roosevelt spoke, an experience that she says was an inspiration.

Two people who knew both Kitty and Michael before they knew each other are Kassler and Bakalar. Kassler was his friend in high school and political comrade-in-arms in the Sumner Kaplan campaigns. But in between, when Dukakis was off at Swarthmore, one of the people Kassler dated was Kitty Dickson. Even then, he says, she was "very much of a stand-up, outspoken person" with a keen interest in politics and human issues.

After her high school graduation in 1954, Kitty went to Pennsylvania State University, where she fell in love with John Chaffetz, a student she had met at camp during the summer between high school and college. Kitty left school in 1956 and on March 17, 1957, married Chaffetz, who was then in the air force. The following years were hectic, with moves to San Antonio; Panama City, Florida; and San Jose and Point Hueneme, California. In San Jose, their son, John, was born on June 9, 1958. But the marriage was not working out well. Kitty had started taking diet pills in 1956, a practice that she feels contributed to two miscarriages and that became a habit, continuing for twenty-six years. Kitty divorced Chaffetz and stayed for some months on the West Coast, then decided to return to Massachusetts.

With three-year-old John, Kitty moved into an apartment on Everett Street in Cambridge in September 1961 and registered at Lesley College, determined to complete her college education. Working part-time, juggling day care, babysitting, schoolwork, and, gradually, a social life, Kitty managed to cope with her years of single motherhood. Dukakis, making up his mind with a speed similar to his father's, decided Kitty was the girl for him soon after they began dating in 1961. Kitty, burned once, was more cautious.

Dukakis was a persistent suitor. "From the beginning, it was clear that he was very much enamored," Kassler recalls. And if Kitty was not eager to consider marriage right away, she was moved by the unusual combination of determination and domesticity she found in him. "He had such strong feelings of wanting to help others," she says, and "an incredible intellectual capacity to absorb," yet also "he had patience. I don't have that." In particular, Kitty was warmed by his immediate and complete acceptance of John. Early on, Dukakis gave him a baseball glove and would often play with him or take him for a walk when his mother needed to study. John remembers that it was Dukakis who taught him to ride a bicycle: "I remember that very vividly." As a treat, Dukakis would give John a ride on his Vespa. Before long, without his ever proposing formally, Kitty and Michael were talking marriage.

The match was not necessarily an obvious one. Then as now, both were stubbornly opinionated. Michael likes to save money; Kitty likes to spend it. Michael is cool; Kitty is emotional. Michael is a morning person; Kitty is an evening person. Michael exhibits extraordinary self-control; Kitty is continually losing a lifelong battle to quit smoking, which Michael treats with open disdain. At the same time, as Kassler puts it, "she kids the hell out of him for being so cheap." And often in public. There are scores of stories portraying Michael as a skinflint, and about half of them include Kitty calling him on it. When they were traveling in Greece, he offered to buy soft drinks for the party, a move in keeping with the exuberant generosity of most Greek people. Kitty delivered a characteristic needle: "Come on, Michael, we've been in Greece for two days now and you haven't cashed a single traveler's check yet." Perhaps the best measure of how seriously Kitty took Michael's parsimony comes from her father. Sitting in his Brookline home one afternoon, Dickson smiles as he motions toward the second floor and says, "For a while, much of her clothes were hanging in my closet up here."

"You could look at it as oil and water," Kassler says, "but it's not. They became such a natural so quickly." Bakalar also says she was well aware of their personality differences when she suggested that Michael and Kitty date, differences, she says, that have turned out to be complementary. "She has what he doesn't—she exudes passion," Bakalar says. "He feels it but doesn't show it. She acts out what he can't."

Certainly, the Dicksons were pleased. "Immediately, I said, 'What a wonderful guy this is,' " recalls Harry. Kitty says that her mother called Michael "the saint," referring to his willingness to put up with Kitty. Michael could do no wrong in Jane's eyes. Harry's memory is that Jane also referred to Michael as "Jesus Christ." When Michael fought with legislators during his

first term as governor, Dickson says, she became so annoyed that
she told him the State House crowd wasn't good enough for him
and he should resign from office and become a judge. Still,
there was a hurdle to cross on Rangeley Road. Dukakis's parents, especially his father, felt strongly about traditional values
and Greek customs. He knew that Michael was independent and
stubborn, and he had grown to accept that. Kitty's being Jewish,
not Greek, was of little concern; many of Michael's friends and
dates since high school had been Jewish. But "the fact that I had
been divorced, and had a child, was difficult for his dad," Kitty
remembers.

Nevertheless, Michael and Kitty were married on June 20,
1963, five months after he entered the state House of Representatives and a few weeks after she earned her bachelor's degree.
It was a small, ecumenical service, with only family members
present, in the Dicksons' apartment on Amory Street in Brookline. The couple settled in Brookline, but not in the comfortable,
relatively homogeneous South Brookline neighborhood where
his parents lived. Instead, they found an apartment at 93 Perry
Street, in what Ira Jackson calls "the funky Coolidge Corner
section" of the town, a neighborhood with town workers and a
variety of ethnic groups, close to the Boston line. It also was in
the district of the Lawrence School, which had a strong reputation. "We had a mixed marriage," Kitty says, "and we wanted a
school that had some diversity to it."

On December 30, 1963, after living on Perry Street for six
months, the Dukakises purchased the building—containing six
apartments—for $55,000. Dukakis is not only frugal but also
conservative with his money, and this is perhaps the one substantial financial risk he has ever taken in his life. He signed two
mortgages totaling $51,100 to buy the building, so he had an
equity of only $3900 and faced high mortgage payments. His
salary as a legislator was only $5200 a year, which was augment-
ed by about $5000 from his position at Hill & Barlow. However,
the investment was similar in some respects to that of his uncles
Nicholas and Adam Boukis, who half a century earlier had
bought the apartment houses they lived in in Haverhill as soon
as they could scrape the money together. The Dukakises' real

estate judgment turned out to be just as good. The apartments had reliable tenants, and the value of Brookline property was rising. In 1971, they turned the six units into condominiums and sold them for a total of $81,000, making a profit of $26,000. Earlier that year, they bought 85 Perry Street, half of the side-by-side brick duplex next door, for $25,000 and moved in. They live there still.

As has happened often in Dukakis's life, the period of great happiness and promise right after his marriage was accompanied by loss. Kitty became pregnant early in 1964, but did not feel well. German measles was widespread that year, and Kitty now thinks this was a factor. At the time she checked with her mother, who reported that Kitty had already had them, but Kitty now believes that "I obviously had them during my first trimester and didn't know it." The day after a checkup during her seventh month, Kitty went into premature labor. The baby, a girl, lived only twenty minutes. As it turned out, she was anencephalic and would have been gravely handicapped had she survived. The loss was hard for both parents, although Kitty says she was steeled somewhat by having had two miscarriages in her first marriage. It was hardest of all, Kitty says, on Michael's father, who was at the hospital and distraught at the fate of his first grandchild.

By early 1965, however, Kitty was pregnant again, and a healthy girl, Andrea, was born on the morning of November 10. Kitty had gone into labor the afternoon before and called her husband at the State House. He was hurrying home on the subway when the lights went out—it was the night of the great Northeast blackout. Dukakis ran the rest of the way home, about two miles—part of it along Beacon Street, retracing a fragment of the Boston Marathon route he had raced fourteen years earlier. He scooped up an anxious Kitty and sped to the hospital, where full power returned well before Andrea's delivery at 7:00 A.M. Another healthy girl, Kara, followed on November 4, 1968, the eve of Dukakis's last election to the House.

Dukakis's political career, meanwhile, was progressing nicely. It has often been remarked that he is a lucky politician—a charge to which most candidates would gladly plead guilty. In Dukakis's case, the truth is that he has had some good luck and some bad, and his own idiosyncrasies have contributed to both. But fortune has helped at many key points from the beginning.

Sumner Kaplan did not seek re-election to the House in 1962, thereby opening a door for his protégé at the very moment he was ready. Dukakis did not hesitate. Throughout the 1960s, Brookline was represented by three members in the House, all elected townwide in what was called a triple district. In 1962, the veteran Republican Freyda P. Koplow was considered a shoo-in, and Beryl Cohen, the Democrat who had won a surprise victory in 1960, was also seeking re-election. The third seat, being vacated by Kaplan, was wide open.

Dukakis campaigned as he had been taught, going from door to door, marshaling volunteers, using the resources of the Democratic Town Committee (of which he was still chairman) and of COD. Over and over, from beginning to end, his themes were change, youth, new blood, and reform. Dukakis's determination was evident to his cousin Arthur, who was married in Lowell just nine days before the primary; Michael attended the wedding, then hurried away from the reception to campaign. On September 18, 1962, Dukakis actually topped the ticket in the Democratic primary, beating Cohen by 71 votes out of the 27,000 cast. In the general election on November 6, Dukakis ran third—250 votes behind Koplow and just 2 behind Cohen—but it was enough to send him to the State House. In the re-election campaigns of 1964, 1966, and 1968, Dukakis topped the ticket in all three primaries and all three finals.

In every campaign, and into his first term as governor, Dukakis was bolstered by an extraordinary relationship with the most memorable figure in Brookline politics, longtime town treasurer Allan Sidd. Ten years Dukakis's senior, Sidd was an enormous man with enormous appetites—and a heart to match. In person, he and Dukakis were a Mutt and Jeff act. Sidd smoked, drank, and swore copiously; Dukakis, almost never. Sidd was an overweight, garrulous glad-hander who enjoyed the company of backroom politicians; Dukakis was a trim, stiff reformer. Yet they were united in their passion to make government work and in a glowing affection for one another. "They were opposite personalities, but Allan Sidd absolutely loved Michael," says Mike Alexander, a Democrat who has been active in Brookline politics since the 1950s. "Allan was one of the great protagonists," says Martin A. Linsky, of Brookline, a former Republican colleague of Dukakis in the House. "He was a very tough campaigner, but he loved it—he loved the game and he loved people who loved the game." Kitty Dukakis says that Sidd also gave her husband candid criticism and humor. "I think Allan was always concerned that Michael didn't have as much political sense as he should have," she says. Yet "he was very much a part of the family . . . Allan made politics fun."

Like everyone who entered the House in the class of 1962, Dukakis faced a baptism by fire. Endicott "Chub" Peabody had won the governor's office for the Democrats that year with a promise of reform, and his first move was to try to dump the notorious House speaker, John F. Thompson.

"The Iron Duke," as he was known to all, was a coarse, swaggering, bibulous man whose nickname described how he had consolidated his control over the 240-member House. Dukakis was soon to take on the natural nickname "the Duke" himself, but the Iron Duke stood for everything that the freshman hated and had campaigned against. Even so, Dukakis's course of action was not obvious and is still the subject of controversy. On the very day that the new legislature was sworn in, January 2, 1963, the first order of business was the election of the speaker. It was a donnybrook that lasted two full days and six long roll calls and divided House Democrats for years afterward. Peabody's candidate as Thompson's challenger was Michael Paul Feeney of the Hyde Park section of Boston, an eight-term veteran who had delivered a key bloc of delegates to Peabody at the 1962 state Democratic convention. Peabody was supported in this effort by the state's new U.S. senator, Edward M. "Ted" Kennedy, the president's brother. A second challenge was raised by one of the outstanding House orators, Cornelius F. Kiernan of Lowell, who had been Thompson's floor leader.

Neither Feeney nor Kiernan was pure enough for Dukakis, who voted for Paul C. Menton of Watertown, a liberal reformer whose campaign had been backed by COD. Dukakis had little company; in fact, his was the *only* Menton vote on the third ballot. Some liberals, including Beryl Cohen, still feel that the Iron Duke could have been deposed if Dukakis and a few others had been more pragmatic, though the roll calls make this hard to prove. On the sixth ballot, Thompson prevailed.

For the next eight years, Dukakis put together a legislative record that earned him a reputation as an effective, substantive reformer. But his style did not appeal to all of his colleagues. To some, his self-assurance often came across as arrant cockiness. And of course many of the most powerful members of the legislature felt sure that his rhetoric of reform included them as targets. The legislative leaders did appoint Dukakis chairman of the Public Service Committee for most of his third term, but he was never an insider. Had seniority been the criterion for selecting committee chairmen, rather than the House speaker's personal choice, Dukakis would certainly have finished his years in the House in charge of one committee or another. As it was, he ended his legislative career as vice-chairman of the Insurance Committee.

Dukakis left his mark in the House, however. He was a persuasive debater, one of a small handful of representatives who could change a vote on the floor. He was not loved by most of his colleagues, but he was widely respected—so much so, in fact, that in 1967 his fellow House members voted him the outstanding legislator in a survey conducted by the *New Bedford Standard Times*.

Dukakis's voting record was consistently liberal, though some activists noted then—and more would later—that the issues on which he really worked and showed originality tended to be matters of process dealing with governmental reform and the structure of institutions. Dukakis did push the legislature to enact several bills encouraging the construction of new low- and moderate-income housing, some of which used innovative incentives. For the most part, however, direct attempts to improve benefits for poor people would be likely to get his vote, but not his active participation. Among his major efforts were the drives to reduce the size of the House and to eliminate the Governor's

Council, an eight-member body that injected political bargaining into a number of gubernatorial functions, including the selection of judges. The House cut was eventually approved, and while the council was not abolished, its powers were reduced. Dukakis also worked to limit campaign expenditures and to regulate billboards and was a leader in the successful effort to stop new highway construction close to Boston.

His role in the civil rights movement of the 1960s was typical of his approach. A number of his acquaintances, including his close friend Haskell Kassler, plunged into the effort vigorously. Kassler joined a small group of lawyers traveling to the South to help defend civil rights protesters who had been arrested. But Dukakis never went south, didn't march or carry banners. Instead, he worked in the legislature to create the Massachusetts Commission Against Discrimination (MCAD) and to give it strong enforcement powers. He was true to the assessment of his college roommate, Frank Sieverts, spurning confrontation, seeing issues as problems to be solved by reason.

As a legislator, Dukakis's crowning achievement was the passage of the nation's first no-fault auto insurance bill, a reform that eliminated thousands of minor accidents from litigation and saved Massachusetts motorists many millions of dollars in insurance premiums. Perhaps the best indication of the law's success was the eventual adoption of similar laws in numerous other states. As it played out, the issue showed a lot about Dukakis. First, it was a reform, pitting consumer interests against those of politically powerful forces, namely, the doctors and lawyers who were pushing up insurance costs with expensive court cases. Second, it was a rational approach to the problem—a solution advanced, in fact, by two academics. Third, stubborn persistence through six years of defeats was needed, and Dukakis had it.

Even the climax was instructive—doubly so. When the bill finally passed both branches of the legislature in 1970, Dukakis was appointed to a conference committee to iron out the differences, but after wrangling among the participants threatened the whole bill, a new conference committee was appointed, and Dukakis was not among those making the final changes. A few days later, however, he took the microphone in the House to address any final concerns before the bill was sent on to become law. For two solid hours, Dukakis answered questions calmly and in detail, drawing from a deep well of knowledge to describe the bill's intricacies and implications. When the last question had been answered, his colleagues rose in applause, an extraordinary tribute rarely seen in the chamber.

The no-fault debate was typical of Dukakis in yet another way: when it was finally resolved, in 1970, he was already a candidate for lieutenant governor. It was not the first time the young reformer had sought higher office. Almost from the moment he walked into the House, his ambition for statewide office was clear. The state Senate seat that included Brookline became available during his first term in the House, but Dukakis already had his sights set higher. He deferred to his more experienced colleague Beryl Cohen, who made the run and was elevated to the Senate in a special election in April 1964. But it was not long before Dukakis showed his hand. Late in 1965, after only three years in the House, Dukakis decided to run for attorney general, showing not a speck of deference to his elders. Former Governor Foster Furcolo, former Lieutenant Governor Francis X. Bellotti, and Lester Hyman, a Ted Kennedy protégé, were among those already running, but when the thirty-two-year-old Dukakis announced his candidacy on January 4, 1966, he derided the party veterans. "At a time when some of the same tired voices solicit our party's nomination for attorney general," he said, "I hope that my candidacy for this office will offer Democrats a choice for reform and progress."

His own record was short, so he tried to turn the others' political experience against them. The job of attorney general, he said, "is a demanding one and cannot be treated as a political way station," though of course that is what it would have been for him too, had he won. Dukakis could claim little experience as a lawyer, none as a prosecutor, and almost none in law enforcement of any kind. In addition, he opposed the granting of subpoena power to the attorney general, a move that some of the candidates were trying to turn into a stance against crime. But he tried to make the most of what experience he had. His relatively brief participation in Hill & Barlow's work with the Boston Finance Commission was described in a campaign brochure as: "Associate Counsel, Boston Finance Commission, Investigation of City Land Sales, 1961–1962"—a clear attempt to turn a bit of back-up work in the law firm into a shining example of fighting corruption.

As has happened continually during his career, the Dukakis campaign hit hard, pointing fingers at alleged wrongdoing in high places. In his earliest years as a legislator, Dukakis had already attracted attention as an opponent of corruption. Given his position, the only weapon he had was rhetoric, but he used it to effect. In June 1965, when he was about to embark on the campaign for attorney general, the *Saturday Evening Post* ran a story on the political underbelly of Massachusetts that was then being exposed by various investigations. The story included a picture of Dukakis. "Men like young Rep. Michael Dukakis," it said, "may save the scandal-ridden legislature."

When the time came for Dukakis to make his presence felt in the campaign for attorney general, assistance came from Beryl Cohen, Carl Sapers, and Fran Meaney, in his customary position as campaign chairman. Cohen, by this time, was on a special commission established by the Senate to investigate various state contracts, and the probe was turning up some apparent connections between campaign contributions and construction jobs. "Michael got interested, and we shared a lot," Cohen recalls. In the spring, Dukakis began to use the information, "all stuff that I fed him through the work of the commission," according to Cohen. On May 2, 1966, for instance, Dukakis charged that, four years earlier, eleven architects had given Governor Volpe campaign contributions that "paid off handsomely" with design contracts. The next day, Volpe, then running for re-election, challenged Dukakis to back up his charges. Two days later, Dukakis released a list of eighteen projects, including the enormous University of Massachusetts Medical School, at Worcester, that substantiated his charge. The story thus stayed in the headlines for several days. Sapers, a strategist for the campaign, remembers that other information "was fed to the papers over three or four months."

At the Democratic convention, however, Dukakis was overmatched in votes and strategy. The delegates met in Boston's new War Memorial Auditorium on June 11, and when the first roll call was completed, Bellotti was a few votes short of the majority he needed. "For a few minutes there we were euphoric," remembers Fran Meaney. The Dukakis tactics were based on the assumption that Bellotti's support would peak on the first ballot. If that support fell short of a majority, Dukakis would have an excellent shot at the endorsement. But Bellotti wasn't stopped. The presiding officer kept the roll call open, and Bellotti's floor operatives went to work. Soon, enough delegates had switched their votes to give Bellotti the endorsement. "We weren't geared for that," Meaney says. But he and Dukakis learned an important lesson—the value of the gavel in controlling a convention. Overall, Dukakis's performance was given high marks. He came in second, with 369 votes to Bellotti's 824. Dukakis's presence at the convention, at which Cohen both led his floor operation and delivered his nominating speech, was noted by many delegates. Some Democrats still consider the event "the fortune cookie convention" because of the thousands of fortune cookies Dukakis's organization distributed with messages such as: "In your future is a great new attorney general— Mike Dukakis." The fact that he outscored four other candidates, including Furcolo and Hyman, impressed other Democrats. And even Bellotti—who was surely one of those Dukakis had in mind when he spoke of "tired voices" five months earlier—took a new view of the young legislator when, immediately after the vote, Dukakis folded his tent and announced his full support for the nominee. As it turned out, Bellotti lost the election to the Republican, Elliot L. Richardson, but he came back to win the job in 1974 and held it for twelve years, including Dukakis's first two terms as governor. Starting early in their first terms, Dukakis and Bellotti began building a political alliance that would strengthen over time, and, eventually, prove crucial to the careers of both men.

The 1966 convention defeat only whetted Dukakis's appetite for statewide office. For the next two years, he worked with growing influence in the House and continued at Hill & Barlow, but all the while he pointed toward another attempt at the attorney general's office in 1970.

Ambition stirred also in Beryl Cohen, Dukakis's friend and cohort. Cohen remembers running into Dukakis in 1968 when the two were campaigning in Coolidge Corner for re-election, he for the state Senate and Dukakis for the House. Both were candid about their intentions of running statewide in 1970, but Cohen was preparing to try for lieutenant governor, and the only question was whether there was room for two Brookline liberals on the same ticket. They thought there was. In fact, the prospects for both of them seemed quite bright. "We resolved it," Cohen says, "on the basis that my running for lieutenant governor and his running for attorney general would not be a problem—that we would both be supportive of each other."

But it was not to be. In one of the most controversial moves of his life, Dukakis decided to run against Cohen, a man who had helped him at important junctures throughout his career. But Michael Dukakis's ambition precluded any action based on mere sentiment. He would run against his friend and supporter, and he would beat him.

The situation developed unexpectedly. Since there were no elections for state office in Massachusetts in 1968, the political landscape was thought to be stable. When Richard Nixon won the presidency, however, Attorney General Richardson became undersecretary of state, and, as specified in Massachusetts law, the vacancy was filled by the legislature. In a flash, the Democrats who dominated the House and Senate handed the job to House Speaker Robert H. Quinn of Boston. Dukakis was angry—"absolutely enraged," Meaney says—that Quinn had jumped squarely in his career path, but he was powerless to prevent it. He was then faced with the choice of challenging Quinn, a sitting Democrat who was certain to try to keep the office, or of looking elsewhere.

Not far into the next year, a knock came on Cohen's door one night at about nine or ten o'clock, as he remembers it: "It was Michael. He came to my house to inform me that he was going to run for lieutenant governor." Cohen was thunderstruck. At first he couldn't believe it. He sputtered for a minute, then blurted out: "But Michael, *I'm* running for lieutenant governor." Dukakis was not there to discuss it, however. His mind was made up, and he was there to let Cohen know.

In Brookline, news of the challenge produced differing reactions. Kassler remembers that "there really wasn't any great conflict." But even Dukakis partisans like Ira Jackson say there was "a shock when Michael leaped over him. It was a traumatic event in Brookline." Some people thought Dukakis had every right to make the race: he was a year older than Cohen and had started to establish himself as a political power in the town even before Cohen, although Cohen went to the legislature one term earlier. Others felt that Cohen had political seniority and so had a claim on that race. They wondered how Dukakis could run against a man who had been his friend, his political ally and supporter. They wondered how Dukakis, who was still breathing the rhetoric of reform, could turn away from challenging an old Boston regular like Quinn in favor of a race that one outstanding Brookline liberal was sure to lose.

Cohen knew Dukakis well enough to understand that, from his point of view, there was nothing personal about it. "It has to do with his ambition, his single-mindedness, notwithstanding our relationship," Cohen says. Plain and simple, "he had made the judgment that he couldn't run against a former speaker at a Democratic convention." It was a cold calculation of cold realities. The man Cohen had seen as putting principle over pragmatism in the great speakership fight of 1963 was now putting pragmatism first. Cohen confesses that he himself could not divorce it entirely from personal feelings. "Frankly," he says, "it colored my future relations with him."

The campaign itself, however, was positive and devoid of acrimony. As earlier, when he challenged Bob Wool for the class presidency at Brookline High, and as would happen again, Dukakis saw no reason why friends could not compete politically. To both men, the key to the campaign was the Democratic convention, scheduled for June 1970 in the western Massachusetts college town of Amherst. Though it was possible to challenge a candidate endorsed by the convention in the September primary, Dukakis and Cohen both expected to abide by the convention's choice. Night after night and week after week, both men toured the state, talking to small groups of delegates. Cohen was confident as June approached, and many Democrats thought he had a right to be. He had worked hard, and he enjoyed the added advantage of relatively strong ties to the legislative leaders. Dukakis was still considered an outsider, a bit of a maverick, by most of the regulars in the legislature. Since it always exerted a strong influence on Democratic conventions, Cohen was optimistic. "I thought I could win—that I was going to win," he says.

What happened in Amherst is still remembered in Massachusetts. On Friday night, June 12, the convention endorsed Senate President Maurice A. Donahue for governor. Donahue had little statewide reputation, and he appeared wooden to people who didn't know him, but he enjoyed the affection of most who did, including state legislators, who made their presence felt in the balloting. Donahue turned aside a challenge from Boston Mayor Kevin White, though White left the auditorium committed to a primary fight against Donahue.

Cohen had good relations with Donahue, and on Friday he thought his own prospects for victory brightened even further with the Donahue endorsement. But when Cohen approached the hall the next morning, he was beckoned under some stairs by an aide of Donahue's. "He said, 'You're not going to win,' " Cohen recalls. "It was just like the scene from On the Waterfront where Marlon Brando is told, 'Champ, this ain't your night.' " Cohen says he exploded, protesting the move, but to no avail. As Cohen understands it now, Donahue and his handlers had decided they needed more balance on the ticket. They didn't want another senator, or a representative, either. The strategy was to stalemate the voting for a couple of ballots, then bring in a new candidate, preferably an Italian American. Donahue says now he never authorized an attempt to scuttle Cohen, whom he personally favored. But the man who was then Donahue's majority leader in the Senate, Kevin B. Harrington, says Donahue asked him and another senator to inquire whether Frank Bellotti would be interested. When Bellotti declined, Donahue stayed more or less neutral in the contest, but a lot of his supporters, according to Harrington, put up a fight against both Cohen and Dukakis. Many of the most vehement, Harrington says, were lawyer-legislators "who hated Dukakis with a passion because of no-fault" insurance. As it happened, the strategy worked with Cohen. "I was much more of an 'in' pol than Michael," he says.

"I tried to stop the flood, but they took my votes away." It was a different story with Dukakis. "They couldn't deal with his votes, he had such a hold on them," Cohen remembers with admiration.

That Dukakis's delegates remained stubbornly with him is not, at least in retrospect, surprising. Throughout his nearly thirty years in politics—with the exception of one election—Dukakis's supporters have been among the most unswervingly devoted anywhere. To them, Dukakis represents everything that is right with government and public service. His natural ability to lead was established long ago, and he exudes the sort of strength and certainty that inspire confidence. During his career he has nearly always been the smartest candidate, the cleanest candidate, the candidate without a hidden agenda, the one whose appeal was to make government work better. It is said that his style is not inspiring, but many of his supporters have, somehow, been inspired.

At the convention, Dukakis received a bit of help from a budding political alliance. Harrington says that after he left Bellotti, he learned later, "Bellotti calls Dukakis and says, 'The Donahue people are trying to cut your throat.' " Much more important than this tip, however, was Dukakis's dogged campaigning, which had locked up the convention before the regulars knew it. "He had done the work," Donahue says. "The vote could not have been changed."

Dukakis won the endorsement for lieutenant governor on the first ballot, 697 to 428. Cohen still talks with wonder of Dukakis's ability to turn a convention against the wishes of Donahue, the man the delegates themselves had endorsed for governor just twelve hours earlier, and his supporters. "He more than beat me, he beat *them*," Cohen says. The result points to a continuing Dukakis strength. "He's a great retailer," says Harrington, who was once Dukakis's most bitter antagonist and is still no fan. "There is probably no one in the country better in someone's kitchen or living room." Adds Cohen: "He's got to be reckoned with. He won't be derailed by any kind of last-minute deals or shenanigans."

True to his word, Cohen did not challenge Dukakis in the

September 15 primary. Four other Democrats did, but Dukakis won his first statewide election easily, amassing nearly twice as many votes as his nearest competitor. Donahue did not fare as well. Kevin White won a clear victory in the primary, so two of the state's brightest young Democrats—White and Dukakis, who had been part of the same reform insurgency a decade earlier— were paired to run against the incumbent Republican, Francis W. Sargent, and Donald R. Dwight, a Holyoke newspaper executive whom Sargent had picked as his running mate.

On paper, the Democrats' chances seemed good. White, nearing the end of his first term as mayor of Boston, was one of the smoothest and most charismatic politicians the Democrats had. And Sargent held the governor's job more by accident than design. He had been elected lieutenant governor in 1966, and was only a fill-in for that role. Elliot Richardson had preceded him as lieutenant governor, but since he was viewed as a much stronger vote-getter, he was asked by party elders to run against Bellotti for the more important job of attorney general. Richardson did so and won. Sargent, a former state natural resources and public works commissioner with no elective experience, glided into the lieutenant governor's office behind Governor Volpe in 1966. But when President-elect Nixon recruited Richardson late in 1968, he also asked Volpe to be secretary of transportation. This left Sargent with the job of running the commonwealth. But as the election of 1970 approached, he was still technically the acting governor, with few political credentials.

Sargent, however, turned out to be a masterful politician. Tall, friendly, voluble, with a great kidding sense of humor, he had all the assets of the Yankee Brahmin he was, but without the stiffness. Though a Republican, he was moderate to liberal on most issues, and he relished the give-and-take that were an essential part of relations with the Democratic legislature. Most important, the voters loved him.

The White-Dukakis team was stronger in theory than in reality. From the beginning, the campaign had problems. White was hounded in Boston for wanting to move up and out of the mayor's office before he had finished even a single term. Early in October, he was stricken with a perforated stomach ulcer that required surgery, which gave Dukakis an opportunity to stand as the ticket's single voice. He made the most of it, impressing voters with his crisp style and familiarity with the issues. Dukakis wanted to debate Sargent in White's place, but Sargent wouldn't agree to it—and neither, according to Meaney, would White. In the end, the cause was futile. Boston's machines delivered the news early on election night: Sargent had even beaten the mayor in his home city. Ultimately, White and Dukakis lost by more than a quarter of a million votes—1,058,623 to 799,269.

The defeat was bad enough, but far worse was the tragic death hours later of one of Dukakis's closest aides. Late at night following the election, Dukakis went to Channel 56 in the Dorchester neighborhood of Boston for an interview. Several campaign workers, including John F. Nason, Jr., of Melrose, accompanied him. When Dukakis headed home, Nason drove away from the station moments later and was hit by a truck. He was rushed to Boston City Hospital, where he died.

Two Metropolitan District Commission police at the accident scene arrested the driver of the truck and charged him with drunk driving. They also sought in court to charge him with manslaughter, but a judge refused to do so.

The driver, who came from a politically active family, went on trial in Dorchester District Court, which was presided over by Judge Jerome P. Troy, a man who symbolized the corrupt political system Dukakis so vigorously opposed. Troy picked a judge to preside at the trial. During the proceeding, three police officers testified that they believed the driver was drunk on the night of the accident. One person, a neighbor and family friend of the driver, said he had been with the man that evening and had not seen him drink. The judge believed the friend, and found the driver innocent of drunk driving.

The verdict was greeted with outrage in the press, but to no avail. All Dukakis could do was grieve over his dead friend, set up a fund to help the family, and wait for the day when he would take on the political establishment.

While out of office, Dukakis split with the Sapers brothers. Carl, who had moved back to Brookline, was campaigning in 1971 against Hackie Kassler for an open seat on the board of select-men. According to Bill Sapers, who had been Dukakis's leading fund-raiser in 1966 and 1970, Dukakis at first indicated he would support Carl, then that he would stay neutral, but he ended up helping Kassler. "I was less than happy," says Bill Sapers. Although this campaign was the immediate reason for the break, Sapers says there had been other frustrations with Dukakis. One was his desire at one point to limit contributions to one hundred dollars. The effort seems curious now, since Duka-kis's presidential campaign has set records for raising maximum contributions from thousands of people across the country. Then, it wasn't that Dukakis himself felt compromised by larger amounts, but he worried that contributors "will think they own me," Sapers says. "Here was a very brilliant, good, solid guy with a crazy sense of what the world is all about. Anybody who thinks somebody owns them for a hundred dollars is dangerous. We had to turn him around," he says. "It took a long time."

In addition, Sapers says, "Michael had a way of not knowing how to say thank you to anyone. He was a good man, and any-body who thought he was a good man should be with him. He didn't owe them anything." Sapers believes this attitude has changed in Dukakis, though it took a traumatic defeat to do it.

In 1971, Dukakis was out of the political spotlight for the first time in a decade, but he had no intention of staying away. And his goal was clearly to make a comeback at the state level. His reputation for political organization had already begun to circu-late widely, and Senator Edmund Muskie of Maine offered him a top political job in his 1972 presidential campaign soon after the 1970 election, but Dukakis turned it down. He then orga-nized a research group and assigned teams of young volunteers to scrutinize state agencies. Referred to variously as "the Dukakis Diggers," "the Dukakis Raiders," and "Mike's Marauders," the groups turned out reports criticizing the state Insurance Depart-ment, the Outdoor Advertising Board, and the Massachusetts Port Authority. The work was patterned on the efforts of Ralph Nader's "Raiders," with one exception: no one thought Nader was running for office, whereas no one doubted Dukakis was. And the reports were directed at his most likely political target:

Sargent. In December 1970, Dukakis went back to Hill & Barlow, where he had left his associate's job to campaign. Now, he was offered, and he accepted, a partnership. In addition, he took on the role of moderator on the public television show *The Advocates*. This served three purposes: it kept him in the public eye; it kept him abreast of public issues; and it honed his TV skills. When the time came to make his next move, he was more than ready.

Exactly what that move would be took some figuring out. Dukakis wanted to be governor, but Attorney General Quinn indicated that he might seek that job. According to Meaney, a complicated set of maneuvers produced a decision by Dukakis to go for attorney general if Quinn was firmly committed to the governor's race. Quinn was told in effect that the choice was his, Meaney says. But Quinn was not sure and vacillated long enough so that Dukakis, by early 1973, decided to wait no longer: he would run for governor. "It's the job I really want," he said at the time. When Quinn finally made the same decision, Dukakis was already off and running.

Just as this campaign was being organized, however—the one that would give him the job he'd wanted since college—his family suffered a sudden, wrenching loss that ended more than two decades in which the family's close affection had been mixed with frustration, worry, and pain. Michael's brother, Stelian, was killed.

It was a Saturday night, March 17, 1973, and Stelian was riding his bicycle on Winchester Street in Brookline, near his home at 198 St. Paul Street. The bicycle was his only means of transportation, and he had ridden it without incident for years, but that night, he was struck by a car. It was a terrible accident—his mother still remembers that "the bicycle was sort of doubled over, it was so bad"—but the driver did not stop, and was never found. Stelian had severe head injuries and was taken to Beth Israel Hospital in a coma. Night after night, Panos, Euterpe, Michael, and Kitty went to the hospital to be with Stelian, wanting to help. But they could only sit in anguish as he lay dying. They were unable to do anything then, as they had been through twenty-two years of trying to figure out how to help Stelian Dukakis.

For Stelian had been disturbed, had experienced periods of odd behavior and unbalanced emotions, ever since his breakdown in 1951. After Stelian went home from school that spring, he was institutionalized for three or four months at Baldpate Hospital in Georgetown, a private facility north of Boston, where, according to Dukakis, he got the basic recognized treatments for mental illness at the time, insulin and shock treatment. He responded, returned to Bates, and graduated in 1953 with a major in government. His yearbook notes that he was called "Duke," that he was a classical music lover, that he was on the cross-country and track teams and a member of the International Relations Club for his first three years, and that he "took a short vacation." Stelian received psychiatric treatment for much of his adult life, but his recovery from the original trauma was sufficient that he lived on his own, working as an assistant to the city managers in the suburbs of Waltham and Medford, and teaching at North Attleboro High School and at Boston State College, among many jobs.

John J. McGlynn, who was mayor of Medford when Stelian worked there in the early 1960s, remembers him as "a very gentle person, very, very circumspect." McGlynn says they occasionally spoke about Michael and that Stelian never expressed anything but "great affection for his brother."

Friends who knew him well before his breakdown say that Stelian was never the same afterward. "He was a very popular guy in high school," remembers Carl Sapers, who was a year behind him. "But he went a little crazy. He never quite found himself after that." Beryl Cohen describes him as "a good guy— one for whom you'd have a fond feeling." And Arthur Dukakis, Stelian's cousin and contemporary (he was born just eight days after Stelian), knew him as a hearty companion who, more than Michael, might be expected to instigate a prank or a bit of mischief. "Stelian enjoyed a good laugh," he says.

After Stelian's breakdown, situations began to arise in which he seemed to compete with Michael's record—and usually fell short. In 1958, seven years after Michael ran the Boston Marathon, Stelian entered the race, but dropped out after 16 miles. In 1960, Stelian was at the Democratic convention in Los Angeles supporting Adlai Stevenson; Michael was there favoring John Kennedy. Later, Stelian's political efforts became more personal.

In the most bizarre and hurtful episode, Stelian went around Brookline one evening, dropping off leaflets that urged people to vote against his brother. The details are sketchy; no copy of the leaflet apparently survives. There is even some uncertainty about when the incident occurred, though Meaney is sure it was during Michael's first campaign for re-election to the House, in 1964. According to Dukakis, Meaney, and Cohen, the leaflet was not simply supporting another candidate. It was clearly from Stelian and it argued against Michael. Meaney believes that Stelian asserted in the leaflet that he intended to run against Michael himself. When word of the flyers got out, Dukakis's supporters quickly followed Stelian's trail, trying to retrieve them before they were read. Meaney says, "I got a call from Kitty. She was very upset, as you might expect." He believes Dukakis was not available—he was either out of town or tied up in Boston—so the campaign volunteers rallied as much help as they could find, including Cohen's campaign. Though Cohen doesn't remember who called, his own campaign workers were soon on the street: "My people were responding at ten or eleven at night and pulling them out of the mailboxes." Meaney says Stelian had even managed to get into Longwood Towers, a venerable, 285-unit luxury apartment complex not far from Michael's home. "We looked in, and—damn it—there was a leaflet in every box," he says. "But we talked our way in and took them right out, every one." Carl Sapers refers to this incident as one of the points in Stelian's later life when "he was absolutely, uncontrollably aggressive . . . aggressively hostile to Mike."

In between, in the fall of 1972, Stelian, now registered as a Republican, ran for the state representative seat Michael had vacated. He won the nomination, finishing third in a four-way race for three spots in the primary, but then came in last of the six candidates in the general election.

Exactly what troubled Stelian is uncertain. But it is clear that his competition with his brother became unhealthy and was at least an effect of his problem, if not a cause. Kassler, for one, thinks Stelian's switch to the Republican party may have been a way of forcing his parents to choose between their sons. Both Panos and Euterpe did change their registration to vote Republican in 1972, though this did not involve a choice against Michael, who was not running that year. Cohen says he's not sure whether Stelian's late political efforts came from "competing or jealousy or just wanting his own career." Meaney says he did not know Stelian well enough to make a judgment, but the speculation at the time was that "Stelian just couldn't handle his brother's success . . . Michael eclipsed him in every area." Even Bakalar, whose affection for Michael and Kitty is enormous, says, "I think it must have been tough for Stelian. Would *you* want to have Michael Dukakis for a brother?"

Arthur Dukakis says, "There was always this competition among the boys," and it produced frustration. "Stelian wanted to be in politics," he says, "but I think things didn't come as easy to Stelian as to Michael. Stelian would have liked to be where Michael is today."

For his family, Stelian's problems were a torment. Stelian estranged himself from the family for a while, according to Dickson. He says that beginning in the early 1960s, he and his wife would go to Panos and Euterpe's home for holidays such as Thanksgiving, Christmas, and Greek Easter. During all these years, Dickson says, he never remembers Stelian's being there.

Panos and Euterpe found Stelian's condition unfathomable. "My folks couldn't understand it," Michael says, and they spent some time blaming themselves. Michael says he has come to believe that the condition may have been physiological, the result of some kind of chemical imbalance that is not uncommon and that can now be treated in many cases with drugs not available thirty years ago.

When he is asked about Stelian, Dukakis frequently mentions the increased public understanding of youthful depression. "In those days," he says, "we were, I think, less open about this kind of thing. These days you have [groups] led largely by the parents of children that have had this problem. I remember a group of them coming in to see me, and I was so impressed by the fact that they were very open about it, they weren't blaming themselves." Now, Dukakis does not shrink from questions about his brother, but there is much he doesn't remember, including Stelian's presence at the Los Angeles convention, his role as a member of the Democratic Town Committee in Brookline, and even, so he says, the very fact of his suicide attempt. And there are a number of intimate friends who say Dukakis has never shared such details. Even Don and Merna Lipsitt, a psychiatrist and his wife who had been close to the family for twenty-five years, were kept in the dark. Merna believes that, since Stelian was very close to Michael, "possibly he has repressed that because it's so painful that he really doesn't remember." Don says that frequently, while Stelian was still alive, "Michael would ask me questions of a professional nature." He says Michael wished for improvement in Stelian so earnestly that he was somewhat unrealistic. "He thought you should be able to go to a physician and it should be fixed up," Don says. "He had a tendency to want to diminish the seriousness."

Dukakis now talks of this part of his life, including the leafleting, with stoicism. "We had to live with it," he says, "and be as supportive as we could."

Stelian died on July 29, 1973, four months and twelve days after the accident. He never regained consciousness.

4. Governor

"This is not a plot on the part of
a cigar-smoking, old-line, conservative
Irish-Catholic Democrat to try and pull you down.
You've done this yourself."

IN THE AFTERMATH of Watergate, Michael Dukakis was ideally positioned to be elected governor of Massachusetts. He had a reputation for integrity, and he was a liberal on such issues as civil rights, women's rights, and protection of the environment. But he was also a man on whom the rhetorical coat of fiscal responsibility—the signal that he would not shower tax dollars on every imaginable social cause—was nicely tailored. In the primary, Dukakis was a squeaky clean reformer, well organized at the grass-roots level against Attorney General Quinn, who relied on sedentary public officials barely able to deliver their own votes, never mind anyone else's. And in the general election, he was a reform Democrat in a Democratic state against an incumbent, Frank Sargent, who happened to belong to the party that had been disgraced by Watergate. And it was a time of recession, of the oil embargo—a time when the political tides were sweeping Republicans out of office.

Dukakis announced his candidacy on October 1, 1973, and proceeded to travel throughout the state day and night, building an organization at the town, ward, and precinct level that would become one of the best Massachusetts had ever seen. His campaign was not just an effort to win public office, though, but a crusade, an attempt to crack the very foundation of Massachusetts politics—the spoils system by which politicians used government programs, policies, and jobs to take care of themselves and their supporters. It was a classic patronage system that Dukakis characterized as "a cancer" on state government, a system that "must be destroyed."

"The mood is angry, the mood is unhappy," he said during an interview in January 1974. "I think the governor is there for the taking."

His campaign literature said that Dukakis "represents a new kind of politics in Massachusetts," that "throughout his career Mike has been a leader in the fight for governmental reform and an end to waste and inefficiency in state government." Perhaps the most ironic statement in this material was his claim that "I get more guidance from small community and neighborhood meetings than I do from any other source. These meetings give me a chance to listen to all kinds of people from all parts of the state, and that's how I learn." If only it had been true, he might well have saved himself some painful times four years later. Dukakis was trying to sound humble and in touch, but his bumper stickers gave a truer reflection of his attitude: MIKE DUKAKIS SHOULD BE GOVERNOR. The slogan itself was controversial. Some people found it presumptuous, even a bit arrogant. But Fran Meaney, who was managing what was to be his last campaign for Dukakis, thought it fit the campaign and the candidate perfectly. "Our strategy was to run against Sargent from day one," he says. "That very self-confident slogan conveyed stature, inevitability." It focused the campaign on the office, not on the primary, and in Meaney's view it carried a key message about Dukakis: "This is not just another pol running for office."

During the campaign, Dukakis made sure to touch all the liberal bases. He pledged to bring more women into state government. He made public his state and federal income tax returns from the previous five years. And he won the endorsements of the state's two most active liberal organizations, Citizens for Participation in Political Action (CPPAX) and the Massachusetts chapter of Americans for Democratic Action (ADA).

Dukakis campaigned hard, often referring to his shepherding of the popular no-fault auto insurance law through the legislature, a success that showed he was on the side of consumers and proved he could be effective. Dukakis demonstrated the strength of his commitment to winning by taking out a personal loan of $10,000 to prime his campaign budget.

But in 1974, Dukakis also made sure to carve out a fiscally responsible agenda, saying that if elected he would reduce the state's unemployment, balance the budget, deliver social services at lower costs—all without raising taxes. It was a message with an oddly Republican ring.

In contrast, Quinn did not present himself as an antidote to the turbulent and corrupt politics of the times. He ran a safe, uninspiring campaign in which he was seen, at the outset, as the favorite. To regular Democrats, including Quinn, the notion that a Greek could beat an Irishman in a Democratic primary in Massachusetts was ridiculous. But as the campaign progressed, it became clear that Dukakis's message had tapped into widespread frustrations throughout the state; that Quinn's image was mushy, whereas Dukakis stood for the brand of reform voters wanted.

Quinn was the perfect establishment foil for Dukakis's rock-the-boat primary style. His campaign was inept. Even when Dukakis moved ahead in the polls, Quinn was unwilling to face him in debate. Near the end of the campaign, Quinn attacked Dukakis on the divisive issue of abortion. Nick Zervas remembers many Dukakis advisers urging a counterattack. But Dukakis, who had largely ignored Quinn in the primary, said, "No way. This is an admission of defeat [by Quinn]. We don't have to say anything." Dukakis was correct. In the end, he beat Quinn with ease, 444,590 to 326,385.

Sargent was now on the defensive. He had to contend, not only with Watergate and its backlash against Republicans, but also with running for re-election in a state whose unemployment rate was well above the national average. It was a remarkably uncomplicated campaign, much the same as the primary had been. Dukakis's position was simply too strong for Sargent ever to overcome. Sargent could not undo Watergate, nor magically re-

duce unemployment and inflation. As a result, Dukakis began—
and ended—the general election as the acknowledged front-
runner.

During a series of debates, Dukakis repeated his reformist
themes and his no-tax pledge. "Without a new governor," Dukakis said during one debate, "we will be doomed to another
dreary round of tax increases." He pledged that, in his administration, "there will be no exchanging of jobs or favors."

The central campaign issue, though, became the fiscal condition of the state. Dukakis would come to rue the day he promised that he would not raise taxes, but it no doubt helped get
him elected. The pledge came just a couple of weeks before the
election, when Dukakis was attacking Sargent's record on fiscal
matters. During a speech at Suffolk University in Boston, Dukakis said he would not raise taxes, and he charged that Sargent
would raise taxes by as much as $150 million. He told the stu-
dents that he could cut the state budget through the elimination
of patronage and better cash management. Afterward, Dukakis
told reporters: "I will guarantee there will be no new taxes next
year if I am elected." A *Globe* reporter asked him if that was a
"lead pipe guarantee." Dukakis said it was.

It was an odd campaign, in a way. Sargent, who was surely one
of the most liberal if not *the* most liberal Republican officeholder
in the nation, would talk during the debates about compassion
and decency in government while Dukakis, a cool technocrat,
talked about efficiency and budget-cutting.

Riding high, Dukakis became a bit sanctimonious. In a letter
to Sargent concerning debates, Dukakis wrote that if their re-
spective campaign managers were unable to work out the details, Dukakis himself would be willing to meet with Sargent,
"but not at the State House and not on the public's time." In an
election day story, the *New York Times* called Dukakis "earnest,
brisk, businesslike, serious, and, to some observers, righteous."
Dukakis overwhelmed Sargent at the polls that day, winning the
election 992,284 to 784,353. Sargent chalked the loss up to "the
price of hamburg." Michael Dukakis knew better—knew the
vote had been at least as much for the young reformer as against
the personable veteran. Meanwhile, he had achieved his fondest

dream. He had been elected the sixty-fifth governor of the Commonwealth of Massachusetts.

On election night, Dukakis appeared before five thousand cheering supporters jammed into the ballroom at the 57 Hotel in Boston. "This is the greatest moment of my life," he said. "We will give this state the best government it has ever had."

Dukakis took over a state whose economy was suffering a major trauma. It was an overstatement to describe Massachusetts, as some had, as the Appalachia of the North, but the phrase nonetheless hinted at the outlines of an economy whose thriving mills had become a home for field mice and spider webs.

To understand what Dukakis faced in the fall of 1974, it is necessary to dig back to the roots of the problem, roots buried deep in the rocky soil of the 1920s. Back then, the bedrock industries that provided the people of Massachusetts with jobs and whatever measure of prosperity they had were textiles, shoes, apparel, and leather. These industries aged rather gracefully until the 1930s. Yet when the Depression hit they were in desperate need of modernization, of investment capital to pay for more efficient plants and equipment. But during the Depression, investment money was harder to find than work, and the sprawling shoe mills of Haverhill, the vast woolen mills of Lawrence, and similar others went into a sharp decline.

World War II brought something of a comeback, providing more work than most communities could handle. Old plants, no matter how outdated their machinery or production methods, were pressed into service. In Lawrence, for example, one of the largest woolen mills on earth began churning out army blankets by the hundreds of thousands. Throughout the war, Massachusetts companies provided the War Department with metalwork, electronics, and research. As Ronald F. Ferguson and Helen F. Ladd pointed out in May 1986, in a study for Harvard's Kennedy School of Government, "Defense spending has always been vital to the Massachusetts economy, dating back to the contracts for development of interchangeable parts for rifles before the Civil War."

But far from saving the state's bread-and-butter industries, the boom times of the war period merely delayed the day of economic reckoning. When the war ended, the executives of the cotton, wool, textile, leather, and related industries recognized that most of their plants were twenty or more years old, and a number of companies were operating out of nineteenth-century structures. These managers knew that to compete in the postwar era they desperately needed significant reinvestment. Tired of unions, they looked to the South and liked very much what they saw: weak unions or, in many cases, no unions at all; workers who were paid less than half the wage they earned in Massachusetts. The decline of these industries was hastened in 1948 and 1949 by a severe recession, from which New England wouldn't recover for nearly thirty years. As it struck, major businesses began leaving the state in large numbers and suddenly Massachusetts was plunged into a state of economic despair.

The state had grown accustomed to economic hardship. Since the turn of the century, its manufacturing wages had been lower and unemployment higher than the national average. But this crisis in the late forties was unlike anything it had experienced since the Depression.

It was during the state's leanest years, however, that seeds for a bountiful economic future were planted, and many of those seeds found fertile soil in Cambridge, at the Massachusetts Institute of Technology (MIT). Without this remarkable university and its visionary students and faculty, Massachusetts quite likely would never have recovered as it did. MIT's initial contribution to the state's economy was not widely noticed when it occurred. In 1946, Karl Taylor Compton, MIT's president, and General Georges F. Doriot, a Harvard Business School professor, founded one of the first venture capital companies in the United States, American Research and Development. Even before its establishment, and long before it would help fund some of the most spectacular high technology successes in the world, there were indications that technology might well become a key part of the state's economy. While the mills were in decline, the high tech sector, with MIT at its center, was slowly beginning to grow in importance. The electrical machinery industry was already the state's third largest employer by 1923, with 26,400 workers, and that number jumped to 60,000 in 1947, stimulated by wartime production.

In 1957, the Russians launched Sputnik, thus beginning the frenetic space race between the U.S. and the USSR. The National Aeronautics and Space Administration (NASA) was born, and it smiled on Massachusetts, among other states. Huge amounts of money for research began flowing into the state, principally to MIT, and by the 1960s the school was at the heart of an effort that would put Americans on the moon.

Harvard and other institutions in the Boston area were also critical to rebuilding the state's economy, but the intellectual driving force behind the recovery was MIT. Lester Thurow, a prominent economist and dean of MIT's Sloan School of Management, says that bright engineers flocked to MIT, working for less than they might have been paid elsewhere, eager for the experience of being able to work with the best minds at MIT, the Mitre Corporation, and Lincoln and Draper labs, which were closely affiliated with the school.

The year 1957 marked another turning point in the Massachusetts economy, when Kenneth H. Olsen, a young engineer at Lincoln Laboratories in Lexington, quit his job to start a new company. Olsen believed he could make digital computers smaller and more efficient than the machines then in use, so, with a $72,000 investment from Doriot's American Research and Development, he started the Digital Equipment Corporation.

Olsen was a symbol of the future of eastern Massachusetts, particularly on Route 128, the circumferential road around Boston completed in 1951 which today features signs reading "America's Technology Highway." It provided access to cheap land for thousands of burgeoning companies and thereby had an enormous impact in enlarging the state's economic geography. MIT was nearby, as were the financial, service, and insurance industries of Boston. Route 128 became a magnet for thousands of other people—many of them, like Olsen, products of MIT—who possessed the entrepreneurial spirit, the brainpower, and the vision to see how academic research could be used commercially. They created companies such as Teradyne,

Apollo Computer, Biogen, and Lotus Development Corporation.

With the introduction of the microchip, much smaller, faster, and less expensive machines—minicomputers—could be manufactured, and companies like Olsen's were poised to take off. Before, only major companies and institutions had been able to afford the enormously expensive computers. And ironically, one of the important elements of high tech's success was that, in contrast to the 1950s, cheap labor was now more available in the North than in the South, for enormous economic growth in the South had pushed wages and benefits higher than they were in the North.

Thurow says the high technology boom in Massachusetts began during the 1960s but went unnoticed for a number of years because the shoe and textile industries were in the final stages of crashing. By the mid-1970s, says Thurow, "all the bad things that could have happened had happened, and we had nowhere to go but up."

But while high tech in general and the fledgling minicomputer industry in particular were beginning to lay a new foundation for the economy of Massachusetts, other factors—most of them having to do with state politics—were militating against economic recovery.

When the mills went south in the late forties and fifties, leaving behind low-income jobs and high unemployment, the Massachusetts legislature was dominated by Democrats who had grown up worshiping at Roosevelt's New Deal altar. These were men who believed in an activist government, who saw social programs as the solution to economic ills, and who had no qualms about raising the taxes necessary to pay for such programs. This trend did not sit well with the business community. In the words of James H. Howell, the chief economist at the Bank of Boston, the state's politicians "set about systematically to pursue policies of income redistribution [creating] what was beginning to be a welfare state in Massachusetts. They passed practically every conceivable law dealing with problems of the welfare state, and that pushed taxes up significantly. This all happened in '60 to '70. By 1970 Massachusetts had the highest tax burden as a percent of income in the United States." In the period from 1963 to 1973, state and local taxes increased from 9.6 to 14.8 percent of personal income—15 percent higher than the national average.

"Between 1959 and 1971, elected officials made 14 changes in the tax laws," according to Ferguson and Ladd, "including 13 tax rate increases and the enactment of a sales tax. Yet, with the 1974–75 recession, the state government was near bankruptcy in 1975," when Dukakis took over. Spending fed on itself, creating its own demand.

Unfortunately for Massachusetts, while state spending was rapidly expanding, federal investment in the state was contracting. The Vietnam War forced NASA to make sharp cutbacks, triggering a protracted period of unemployment among high tech firms. In 1972, the state Department of Employment Security set up an unemployment office on Route 128 for engineers and other professionals who were out of work. It was a bewildering time, for it appeared that technology, which had been seen as transforming Massachusetts into the promised land, had encouraged false hopes.

When Dukakis took office in January, the unemployment rate in Massachusetts was 11.2 percent, among the highest of any industrial state. He took over a state with what he would soon find out was a mind-boggling budget deficit and a tax burden well above the national average. "The decline in military spending, plus dramatic increases in the price of oil on which the state was highly dependent," wrote Ferguson and Ladd, "made a national recession in 1973–74 into a depression in Massachusetts.

"The structure of the Massachusetts economy had changed radically in the postwar period," they continued. "By 1975, the state economy was quite well diversified . . . The potential for growth of this more diversified economy, however, was not well understood in 1975. Instead, with high unemployment, state government near bankruptcy, rising oil prices, and declining defense spending, the economic future of Massachusetts looked bleak."

But the word *bleak* could not begin to describe how desperate the state's short-term financial future would be.

*

Jack Flannery, Sargent's chief of staff who died in December 1987, recalled that very soon after the election, two senior members of Dukakis's transition team, Fran Meaney and Dolores Mitchell, visited him in the governor's office. Flannery conceded his bias, but he says that during the transition the Dukakis staff people—with the exception of Meaney—were "very uptight, humorless, and self-important. They had the attitude that 'we are going to save the state government.'" Flannery vividly recalled Mitchell's demeanor when she and Meaney arrived for a meeting to learn how Sargent's office had run. "She came in as if detecting a bad odor," he said. "She looked at us with disdain and made it very clear that the first thing she was going to have to do was fumigate the place. They were the most holier-than-thou people I have ever met in the business."*

Still, a sense of mission and an attitude of complete self-confidence were passed along to Dukakis's top people from the man himself: he was an avenger atop a white steed, a brilliant young man who knew what was *right* and who, through the force of his own will if need be, would *make* things right in Massachusetts. Initially, he took steps that pleased those voters attracted by his rhetoric of reform. Continuing to condemn patronage, he denied job requests from dozens of his campaign supporters who were eager to work in the administration and instituted a lottery to take the state's summer jobs away from the politicians. He gave four of his ten cabinet posts to women, meeting a target that had been set publicly by his wife, though he denied she was the driving force. One of the cabinet jobs even went to a former president of one of the state's most active reform groups, the League of Women Voters. Dukakis also put his modest lifestyle and his support for public transportation on display by using the trolley for his daily 15-minute commute to the State House.

Moral righteousness, however, was not the best style with which to approach the most severe fiscal crisis in the history of Massachusetts. Signs that danger lay ahead had begun appear-

---

*Mitchell objects to Flannery's characterization, saying there was no attempt on her part to be "anything other than kind and professional."

ing many months before Dukakis was elected. Shortly before fiscal 1974 ended on June 30, the Sargent administration discovered that the Department of Public Welfare was about to run out of money. Within a matter of days, administration officials and legislative leaders won passage of a deficiency budget of $91.8 million (of which $89.8 million went to the welfare department), so that instead of the state's ending its fiscal year with a surplus of $117 million, its surplus was $24.9 million. By late spring or early summer, it was clear that something was going terribly wrong with the state's finances. Much of the trouble—the 1973 Arab oil embargo, the national recession, and double-digit inflation—was well beyond the control of the Sargent administration. Even the state's jobless rate, which had pushed past the national level and reached 12 percent, seemed beyond the ability of a governor to control to any great degree. Climbing unemployment swelled the welfare rolls. But even as demand for state funds was rising, unemployment and the sagging economy cut into tax revenues, which were running far shy of projected levels.

"Mainly what happened was, there was a welfare explosion and a deep recession," says Edward Moscovitch, who served as budget director under Sargent and held the same position for a number of months in the Dukakis administration. "It wasn't reasonable to think that anyone could have anticipated it . . . In any case, it *certainly* wasn't Michael's fault."

Apart from the cause, however, it is difficult to believe that both Sargent and Dukakis were unaware long before election day that whoever won would face a serious budget deficit. Certainly senior officials within the administration as well as Democrats in the legislature knew of the problem. Moscovitch says that it was clear to him in "May or June of 1974 that the situation was bad. Here were two candidates running for governor both saying they didn't need taxes and I knew perfectly well they did."

Moscovitch was not the only one. An official at the conservative, business-oriented Massachusetts Taxpayers Foundation saw that new taxes were inevitable, too. He was Charles E. Shepard, a respected state fiscal expert and former secretary of ad-

ministration and finance in the Sargent administration. He
wrote a memo to Richard A. Manley, head of the Taxpayers
Foundation, on July 10, 1974: "Assuming that an all-out effort is
going to be made to conserve funds already appropriated, it
would still seem to be impossible to avoid tax increases during
FY 1975." But, during the course of the campaign, neither candidate said much about it.

For Sargent to acknowledge the looming crisis would have
invited criticism that his administration had precipitated the
problems. For Dukakis to acknowledge it would have made his
"lead pipe guarantee" ludicrous. Dukakis's only concession to
the state's fiscal trouble was his contention that unless Sargent
"makes a serious effort to cut expenses, the people of the commonwealth will be hit hard by an increase in state taxes next
year." That view, offered on October 24, makes it clear Dukakis
believed that whether taxes rose was up to Frank Sargent. But
his position soon changed. For many months to come he stubbornly clung to the notion that, although Sargent had not made
significant cuts, he, Michael Dukakis, would prevent taxes from
rising.

On November 18, thirteen days after the election, Dukakis
reported that the state faced a $300 million deficit. On Decem-
ber 4, he said at a press conference that the fiscal problems in
the state were so severe that drastic cuts in state spending might
be required in order to bring the budget into balance without
new taxes. A reporter asked Dukakis about human service programs, which accounted for about half the state's spending. If
new taxes were to be avoided, the reporter wondered, might a
scalpel be needed to cut those programs?

"He's generous when he's talking about a scalpel," Dukakis
replied. "It might be a meat cleaver."

Criticism of this comment came swiftly from Richard Row-
land, the director of the Public Welfare Council, a poor people's
advocacy group, who said that "the meat cleaver approach to
slashing human services is not creative leadership. I hope that
the governor-elect would show greater sensitivity to human services and not punish the poor for being poor and the sick for
being sick."

Dukakis's comment upset other liberals, including some in the legislature who had worked hard for his election and who saw him as one of their own. But it was already clear well before he took the oath of office that his liberal friends in the House were as determined to see taxes raised as the governor-elect was to avoid them. During the second week in December, two liberal Democratic representatives, Barney Frank of Boston and James Smith of Lynn, proposed a tax package that would raise $50 million in new revenue. Dukakis wouldn't hear of it. He would balance the budget his own way. He would cut "deadwood," he said, as well as "trim off the duplicate layers of fat."

But few State House insiders believed he could pull it off. The legislative leaders, House Speaker David M. Bartley and Senate President Kevin B. Harrington, made it clear to Dukakis that they believed he had no alternative but to raise taxes. "Everybody in America knew except him that he had to raise taxes," says Frank.

Shortly after Dukakis was elected, Harrington says he and James A. Kelly, Jr., chairman of the Senate Committee on Ways and Means, went to see the governor-elect. Harrington recalls that he told Dukakis there were "tens of millions of dollars in unpaid bills and there is no way you can avoid taxes, so you better bite the bullet before the situation gets very bad and gets out of hand." Harrington suggested that Dukakis "come right in and say, 'I made a promise in the course of the campaign and I was telling the truth,' but that 'we have uncovered a terrible fiscal situation and I have no alternative but to confront it head-on.' "

But Dukakis had no interest in such an approach. "He said he was going to balance the budget by cutting programs, and economizing," Harrington says. "We told him we didn't think he could do that."

"It was common knowledge" that new taxes were needed, says Bartley. He says that soon after the election he met with Dukakis and told him the deficit was "spiraling"; "there was no question in my mind that new taxes should be the number one priority for 1975." One scheme Bartley considered was calling the legislature back into session before Dukakis was sworn in, passing a tax bill, and presenting it to Sargent. "It was a very serious idea," Bartley says, and one he believes might have worked if Dukakis had gone along with it. But he did not.

"There was no question the legislative leadership was ready to pass a tax bill," says Moscovitch, the budget director. "It was all over the State House that he could have had it." The word at the time was that leading legislators told Dukakis to blame the mess on Sargent, raise taxes, and get it over with. New taxes were inevitable, they argued, and the longer Dukakis waited to raise them, the more likely the people would blame him for the increase. In addition, they said, delay would deepen the crisis.

The governor-elect would not budge. "I think he had it in his own mind that he was just a hell of a lot smarter than I was," says Sargent, "and he could take that budget home and spread it out on the kitchen table and he and Kitty could figure it out. But it was tougher than he thought."

"He thought that there was a lot of fat in the budget," Moscovitch says, "and that when he got in with his own cabinet secretaries they would help him find it."

The meat cleaver, a tool of slaughter, became the symbol of the liberal, reform-minded governor. He seemed to take a certain pride in it, for in his office, on a cabinet near the window, sat a stainless steel cleaver, mounted on a base bearing the message "Go to it, Mike"—a gift from the Russell Harrington Cutlery Company of Southbridge, Massachusetts.

Barney Frank believes Dukakis couldn't bring himself to raise taxes for three reasons. First, he had made the "lead pipe" promise; second, he thought he could squeeze fat and waste out of government; and third, as Frank puts it, "He did not mind nearly as much as I thought he would cutting back on poor people." Dukakis had been "enormously successful" to that point in his life, says Frank, and "I think he thought failure was weakness. He had not a lot of sympathy with failure." Bartley's view was that Dukakis would not break his no-tax promise because he truly believed he could balance the budget without taxes. "That was still his messiah complex period," says Bartley, a time when Dukakis "believed if he just willed it to happen it would happen."

In his budget message to the legislature on January 22, 1975, Dukakis said the deficit could be as high as $350 million, "far in excess of even the most pessimistic predictions." But no, it was not time for new taxes. He continued:

"I suppose some would say, 'Why go on?' Why not simply concede that there is no hope; that the dreary cycle of expenditures beyond our means followed by tax increases followed by further expenditures is becoming a Massachusetts tradition; and that it was all the fault of the outgoing administration anyway?

"That is the easy way out—but it is not the way of this administration. I do not know if we can close our current budget gap and balance next year's budget. So it would be perfectly possible to throw up one's hands in despair; to blame it all on somebody else; and to recommend a vast new tax program which, so the reasoning goes, will have long since been swallowed and forgotten by 1978.

"But before I recommend that we impose still more tax burdens on citizens who are desperately trying to cope with the twin problems of runaway inflation and job insecurity, I believe that you and I must make a Herculean effort to reduce expenditures; to eliminate waste; to re-examine old programs and priorities; and to do everything humanly possible to match expenditures with revenue."

Liberal activists were growing angrier by the day. They believed they were being betrayed by a man they had always seen as sympathetic to their causes, as one of them. Liberals concerned with issues such as women's rights or the environment or government reform had nothing to complain about. His anti-patronage, "good-government" efforts still had appeal, but many of the people most attracted by this aspect of the new administration were the same people most outraged by its social policy. It was on the question of the poor that Dukakis took the most heat.

On January 29—he had been governor for less than a month—the Massachusetts Advocacy Center, a nonprofit organization that specializes in promoting human services programs, announced it would sue Dukakis to end a budget freeze he had imposed, which the group said would hurt programs for chil-

dren. It characterized Dukakis's cuts as "morally unconsciona-
ble." This sort of rhetoric might not have been surprising for a
liberal human services group to use on a conservative Republican governor, but aimed at a man who had long been a liberal
Democrat, it was harsh stuff, indeed. But Dukakis proceeded
with what he saw as his mission—to rein in runaway state spending and to put the state on a sound financial ground.

The state constitution at the time required that the governor
submit a budget by the fourth Wednesday in January for the
fiscal year beginning the following July 1. But amid the fiscal
chaos of the moment, Dukakis submitted only the broadest possible outline of how he saw the state's financial condition. During the last week in January, Dukakis said that Massachusetts
had "the largest current budget deficit of any state in the nation
and an economic base that is stagnant and eroding." He said the
situation would be so bad by early February that there was a
possibility the deficit could surpass $1 billion in the next eigh-
teen months.

In February, Dukakis said that to balance the budget without
new taxes, there would be no cost-of-living increases for state
employees or welfare recipients. Those affected, pointing out
the 14 percent inflation rate, howled in protest. In addition,
Dukakis proposed to pay for part of the deficit by borrowing
money over five years, but bankers and other financial professionals frowned, pointing out that it was precisely this practice
that had brought New York City to the brink of financial ruin.

By spring, the news only got worse. State officials found that
welfare department bills going back five years had literally been
stacked up in shoe boxes. Something on the order of $90 million
worth of bills had simply not been recorded on the state ledgers.
On April 28, Dukakis announced that the deficit for the current
fiscal year, which a month earlier had been estimated at $300
million, was now somewhere between $400 million and $450
million—an extraordinary amount for a state whose total budget was $3 billion. Dukakis felt he had no alternative but to go to
the bond markets and borrow $450 million to pay the state's
operating debts. It was a bitter moment for the new governor,
for there could be no borrowing without his breaking his "lead

pipe guarantee." Dukakis sought and the legislature approved increases in the state meals, liquor, gasoline, and cigarette taxes, amounting to $110 million a year, which would allow the state to pay off the bond issue over five years.

Paul Brountas remembers a phone call he got from the governor when he reached this point, a call that shocked Brountas because of Dukakis's emotional tone. "He said, 'Paul, I'm going to have to raise taxes. I'm going to have to go back on my word.' He was down, despondent, really questioning himself, what he had done," Brountas says. He adds, with hindsight, "He should have done it sixty days prior."

In mid-June, five months after the constitutional deadline for the new budget, Dukakis proposed a fiscal 1976 spending plan that called for removing 18,000 employable men and women from the general relief rolls and laying off at least 1000 state employees. When he took over as governor, he said in the budget message, "what we found was appalling. We found that this state was in worse financial shape than any other state in the union—and that if immediate and drastic steps were not taken, we could rapidly become the New York City of state governments . . .

"In February, I told the Legislature that we simply could not afford a cost of living increase for state employees and welfare recipients. In April, I asked the Legislature to approve reductions in our welfare program totaling $311 million."

In all, he had proposed cuts of more than $500 million. But there was still a huge gap. "So you and I will have to come up with $687 million in new taxes to make up the difference," he said.

By the end of the month, the legislators had signaled that they were in no mood to approve the governor's request for nearly $700 million in new taxes. As a result, Dukakis said, more cuts would be required.

That was it for Hubie Jones, an associate professor of urban planning at MIT and chairman of the Massachusetts Advocacy Center. Jones had long been one of the leading activists in Boston's black community and, to him, the proposed new cuts were simply going too far. Jones wrote in the *Globe* on August 10:

"Make no mistake about it, the governor is on a mission to redefine the fundamental role and responsibility of state government in relation to human needs.

"His orchestrated actions are designed to create a governmental role based on an economy of scarcity rather than on legitimate human needs. In essence, we are being asked to replace the governmental philosophy which has evolved in this state and country since the Great Depression with a new form of Social Darwinism that embraces individual responsibility for one's own survival."

Jones was prophetic in a sense. Ten days after his column appeared, Dukakis signed legislation cutting between 15,000 and 18,000 people from general relief and reducing medical care for those remaining, as well as for welfare recipients on Medicaid. The legislation repealed the state's guarantee of assistance to the needy not eligible for federally reimbursed welfare programs by striking from the law the promise that "the Commonwealth . . . shall assist . . . all poor and indigent persons residing therein, whenever they stand in need of such assistance." How remarkable that a state known for its liberalism and compassion—a place where people took as an article of faith Roosevelt's dictum that we must help those unable to help themselves—would pass a law reneging on such a sacred promise.

By late October, pressure had mounted on the legislature to act or to face the possibility that the state would be plunged into fiscal chaos. Senate President Harrington warned that the state would go bankrupt within six months unless a budget including a tax increase was passed quickly. Bankruptcy, Harrington said, would mean that state institutions would shut down, state workers would not be paid, and welfare checks would not go out. "You'd have chaos and anarchy in Massachusetts," he said.

At the same time, officials from the First National Bank of Boston told Dukakis and legislative leaders that $120 million in state housing bonds would be in default unless a budget with a tax increase was swiftly enacted. Default would come on December 11. The messages from Harrington and the bankers created near panic in the State House. Dukakis's chief counsel, Daniel A.

Taylor, says that only a few of the governor's close advisers were aware of how grave the situation was. Taylor recalls asking his wife several times during the crisis, "What would it be like to be the chief counsel to the first governor of the first state in the history of the union to actually default and declare bankruptcy?"

Harrington was determined to avert the crisis, even if it meant bending—or abusing—the legislative process. When Dukakis's budget proposal, including major increases in the income and sales taxes, reached the floor of the Senate toward the end of October, Harrington quickly found that it lacked the necessary votes for passage. As the session pushed late into the night, Harrington convened a caucus of the Democrats, who held an overwhelming majority in the forty-member Senate. (The Republicans, in fact, lacked the eight members required to demand roll call votes.) Harrington explained that the state faced a serious crisis unless they passed the budget. His idea was to gavel the bill through, in effect, by calling for a voice vote, which he would interpret—no matter what he actually heard—in the affirmative. That would get the budget passed and permit the many senators with objections to it to avoid being on record as supporting it. Such a maneuver was commonplace for minor pieces of legislation, but unheard of for anything as significant as a budget bill. During the private caucus, Harrington asked, "Supposing I take the responsibility of putting it through" on a voice vote. "I asked them would they sit in their chairs and not force a roll call." The Democrats agreed. Harrington returned to the Senate chamber and, in a rapid staccato, asked that "all in favor say aye; opposed, no; the ayes have it."

Naturally, the Republican senators were furious with this autocratic approach and objected vehemently, but their numbers prevented them from undoing the vote. Their attacks, however, did prompt Harrington to make a speech on the floor of the Senate to defend his actions. Privately, Harrington had been critical of Dukakis for some time, but he had generally avoided going public. That changed, however, when he spoke in the middle of the night of October 23. In his own defense, Harrington outlined the state's fiscal crisis that year and said he had felt compelled to do what he had done because "the Legislature is apparently confronted with a chief executive who is unable to govern effectively."

Within an hour or two, Harrington received a call that the governor wished to see him. Harrington walked down the hall to the governor's office and found Michael Dukakis "white-faced with rage," he says. "If I wasn't six-foot-nine and about two hundred and sixty pounds, I think he would have taken a swing at me. He was really savage. I didn't know what it was about because I had just risked my entire political career to put through *his* tax package. He was savage about that comment, that someone would suggest he was not competent enough to handle the problem. We had some very harsh words. He started by saying, 'I'm the governor, I rang the doorbells, I got the votes.' I said, 'I respect that. You are the governor and no one is taking anything away from you.' I said, 'Who turned [state Senator] Alan Sisitsky against you? He was your western Massachusetts coordinator. He hates you.' I went down a list of people who had turned against him, people who had been great, great Dukakis supporters he had totally alienated. They were out to cut his throat. I was trying to make the point that 'this is not a plot on the part of a cigar-smoking, old-line, conservative Irish-Catholic Democrat to try and pull you down. You've done this yourself.' "

Both the House and Senate had passed budgets, but the two versions differed significantly. A House-Senate conference committee was appointed to work out a compromise and reached agreement on November 5, one turbulent year to the day after Dukakis had been elected governor. The package included $362 million in new taxes—the largest increase ever in Massachusetts—and cuts in medical programs for the poor that actually went beyond what Dukakis wanted. The new revenue would come from a 7.5 percent surtax on the state's income tax and an increase in the sales tax from 3 to 5 percent. Welfare was cut sharply, as were programs for state colleges and medical assistance to the poor. To become law, the compromise proposal still needed to pass the full House and Senate.

The next day Dukakis went on television and radio seeking public support. He said that without the budget and tax increase Massachusetts "faces the peril that has already struck New York City." New York Mayor Fiorello La Guardia, he noted, "used to say that when he made a mistake 'it was a beaut.' And I suppose every politician at one time or another makes mistakes which later come back to haunt him. I'm afraid that's the case with my campaign statements about new taxes. I felt at the time that we could avoid new taxes if we had the courage and the will to clean up the waste and inefficiency in state government . . . Quite clearly, I was wrong. I'm only too well aware of the deep feelings aroused by the no new taxes pledge. And I sincerely regret it." He said that "in good conscience" he could not cut any more from the budget. Taxes were absolutely necessary.

On November 7, the legislature approved the budget and sent it to Dukakis, who signed it on November 8. "We have had to make deep and sometimes damaging cuts," he said at the signing ceremony, "and we will have to pay new taxes at a time when we are already reeling under the twin blows of high unemployment and rising inflation." But, he added, "the Commonwealth quite simply has been speeding into bankruptcy, and we had to apply the brakes before it was too late."

The new budget affected every single Massachusetts resident. Education cuts meant that student-teacher ratios increased; medical benefits to welfare recipients were reduced; and social services were squeezed. And consumers and businesses had to pay higher taxes.

Barney Frank later wrote an article on this period for the *Real Paper,* an alternative weekly newspaper published in Cambridge, in which he asserted that "at the height of the worst recession in 40 years, Michael Dukakis reduced the real incomes of all welfare recipients, and initiated and pushed through legislation to cut off the long-term unemployed from any public assistance whatsoever . . . While some human service cuts were inevitable in the situation Dukakis inherited in 1974, by his own conscious, deliberate choices he exacerbated that situation and inflicted social damage far beyond what had to occur . . ."

Dukakis, looking back over thirteen years, has a very different

view of that period. He says that when he took office he believed
that with budget trims in the right places he would be able to
balance the budget without taxes. By no means was it obvious to
him in January 1975 that new taxes were needed, he says. "We
had a plan for some modest cuts . . . which we thought would
carry it through, and about every two weeks we'd come up with
another $50 million or another $100 million [in debt]. I mean,
the lack of information at the time was appalling . . . There was
a massive lack of information. 'Have you paid your bills or
haven't you paid your bills? Well, how many months of Medicaid bills did you *not* pay?'

"We ended up that first year with not only the deficit we inherited but with negative revenue growth, and I don't think that
had ever happened except maybe in the Depression. I mean we
literally had less money coming in my first year than we had had
the previous year. I remember coming back from a vacation we
took with the kids in April, when Jack [Buckley, the secretary of
administration and finance] and I really kind of thought we had
worked this thing out in a way that was going to work, and I got
this memo under the door this Sunday night when I got back. It
said, 'Well, I think it's a lot worse even than we thought it was.'
. . . There was nobody managing the state's debt. I mean *nobody*.
And of course the pension system wasn't funded at all. And then
you had these twelve-month notes that had been rolled over for
twenty or twenty-five years to pay for public housing. Somebody
should have turned them into long-term bonds years previously.
Financing the short-term notes was one of our big dilemmas.
We almost went belly up a few days before Christmas in '75. It
wasn't one event or one moment in time. It was just a constant
struggle . . ."

If he had known in January what he knew the following November, would he have raised taxes sooner? "I probably would
have done it or recommended it in the spring. Although it was
very important—and I would hate to have to go through what
we went through by way of cuts—but there was a lot of water to
squeeze out of the system, and that had to be done at the same
time. But the fact is that we didn't know and it was a process of
rather painful discovery."

"It's hard to exaggerate the wrenching change that all of this represented," he says. "I mean we had just been kind of sailing along in the sixties and seventies, just doing our thing, and expectations were very high, and suddenly Dukakis comes along and says, 'There's no money there, guys. In fact, we're swimming in red ink and we're just gonna have to stop.' "

Jim Howell of the Bank of Boston agrees that Dukakis did the right thing: "I suspect we would not have had the revitalization we had or not the scope we had because we would still have been left with the tax problem."

The harsh rhetoric from friends like Barney Frank and other liberals was tough to take, says Dukakis, but he's not sentimental on the point. "It was also true that in their desire to be helpful to people, and compassionate and caring, they had paid very little attention to the fiscal side of the ledger and somebody had to come along and straighten the mess out, and I was the governor, so that was my job. And while the cuts were painful and going through that process was painful, I really believe that our willingness collectively—because the legislature was involved in this as well, obviously—to bite the bullet and to finally get that fiscal mess straightened out—and to begin to build a good strong fiscal foundation for the state—was an absolutely essential precondition for the kind of economic development effort we put together. There was no way you were going to persuade people you were serious about rebuilding this state's economy when you couldn't pay your bills."

For all practical purposes, the first half of Dukakis's term was dedicated to coping with financial woes. But once the fiscal condition of the state had improved enough so that it was not, of necessity, a gubernatorial obsession, Dukakis was able to turn to a number of other issues. He worked hard to reform the auto insurance laws and to institute a requirement that some people work for their welfare checks. He also tried to reform the sprawling court system and to hammer together an urban strategy that would revitalize the state's older cities.

Dukakis went at auto insurance reform with relish. Massachusetts had long operated under a system whereby the insurance commissioner, a gubernatorial appointee, would by fiat establish the rates companies would be permitted to charge. In 1976, however, Dukakis's insurance commissioner, James Stone, proposed a change that became law. Though Dukakis had developed a reputation among business people as an excessive regulator, Stone's system would permit companies to set their own rates, allowing consumers to shop for the best insurance buy. With the new system in effect, rates declined overall, but many city residents, particularly young people, found their rates soaring. In some extreme cases, drivers under the age of twenty-five in major cities received insurance bills of $2500.

Legislators were furious with the governor and demanded action. The situation was so bad that on April 21, 1977, a meeting in Watertown was disrupted by three hundred angry demonstrators demanding lower rates.

Competitive rates were a failure, and they angered both voters and the insurance industry, which saw Commissioner Stone as a knee-jerk consumer advocate. Dukakis's banking commissioner, Carol Greenwald, similarly irritated bankers. Her determined pro-consumer efforts, combined with a style that could be abrasive and heavy-handed, made her, in her own words, "almost a nationally hated symbol to bankers across America."

Stone and Greenwald, whatever the merits of their work, came to represent what many saw as Dukakis's anti-business attitude. Invariably, when business people complained about the Dukakis administration, the first two names out of their mouths were Stone and Greenwald.

Dukakis managed to alienate both ends of the spectrum. He was unpopular among business leaders, and his work on another controversial issue during the second half of his term further eroded his crumbling liberal base. The issue was workfare, and it foreshadowed a program he instituted during his second term that brought him national recognition and served as a model for other states. But at its inception, it did little more than deepen his problems within his own political party.

Workfare was part of an effort by Dukakis to get jobs for welfare fathers. Aimed at the hard-core unemployed, men who had been without work for years while relying on welfare, it was never expected to employ more than about two thousand fathers. The plan would have required able-bodied men on welfare who could not be placed by the state in private or federally funded Comprehensive Employment and Training Act (CETA) jobs to work in other public jobs or at nonprofit agencies three days a week, a minimum of ninety-six hours a month, to earn their welfare checks. Families in which a man refused to accept the assigned work would, under the proposal, lose his share of the household welfare check for three months. After three months, the person would be offered another job.

Though abhorred by most liberals, workfare fit comfortably into Dukakis's view of the way one ought to live one's life. He was the son of a man who had worked six and a half days a week for nearly fifty years. Dukakis and his brother had been required to do chores around the house. He received no allowance as a child and gave none to his own children. And throughout his adult life Dukakis had worked extremely hard. He had always believed that work was basic to personal betterment.

Dukakis believed that if these men on welfare were given work experience, they would eventually find better-paying jobs in the private sector. Liberal critics of workfare, and there were many, charged that the program constituted "slave labor," by forcing men to work for less than the minimum wage, and that it did not provide the one thing most desperately needed by the hard-core unemployed—training. Critics also claimed that the plan was punitive, motivated by Dukakis's desire to appeal to conservative elements in the state. Dukakis defended the plan as an opportunity for thousands of welfare fathers to find work that could pull them out of poverty.

The reception to Dukakis's proposal was vehement. During a hearing on the plan at the State House on July 1, 1977, opponents became so agitated that the Capitol Police called for reinforcements. "I understand something about politics and the mood against the poor in our country today," Barney Frank said at the hearing. "But today we're talking about a governor who, since the day he came into office, has been waging war against the poor. This workfare program is a disgrace." Said Senator Sisitsky: "Workfare appeals to the popular prejudice that most welfare recipients are black, poor, and don't want to work. It serves no useful purpose other than for his re-election campaign."

Opposition built throughout the rest of 1977, and some legis-

lators claimed that under federal welfare regulations the proposal was illegal. By early December, it appeared doomed. The
Senate president, without whose support it would almost surely
not get past the Senate, pronounced workfare dead. A drastically scaled-down version of the original idea—it was little more
than a training program for a small number of welfare fathers—
was put into effect.

Throughout his first term, Dukakis designed a number of
policies to try to stimulate growth in the commercial centers of
the state's older cities. Pushed by the governor and his chief
planner, Frank T. Keefe, state agencies were required to rent
office space downtown, even if it was not always the most practical site. A variety of incentives—including an elaborate series of
urban heritage parks—was put in place to encourage private
investment in the urban centers. State regulators often used
their powers aggressively. In the most controversial case, the
administration opposed the construction of a new shopping mall
outside Pittsfield, in western Massachusetts, arguing that it
would suck the last bits of life from the downtown retail district.
When the developer pushed ahead, securing the land and all the
other permits, the state Department of Public Works refused to
allow curb cuts off the state highway, denying access to cars. The
state also took strong action in Lowell, Worcester, and several
other cities. By the time the term had ended, Dukakis and Keefe
felt their policy was a success.

The initiative Dukakis emphasized most during his first term
was court reform. He believed he could bring a chaotic judicial
system, plagued by waste, delay, poor management, and court
backlogs, into the twentieth century. As violent crime increased,
backlogs grew, and prison overcrowding reached new levels.
Dukakis's notion was that court reform would put judges where
they were needed and provide speedier, more even-handed justice. Dukakis adopted the proposals of the Governor's Select
Committee on Judicial Needs, headed by Archibald Cox, a Harvard Law School professor and the former Watergate special
prosecutor. The committee's report declared that the "administration of justice in Massachusetts is on the brink of disaster."
Because of its intricacy and lack of sex appeal to the public,

court reform was the sort of issue that put other politicians to sleep, but it brought Dukakis to life.

The proposal that the committee ultimately offered and that Dukakis endorsed called for sweeping changes in the judiciary. A new chief administrative justice would manage state courts and have broad flexibility in transferring judges to courts with the heaviest caseloads. The bill also suggested raises for virtually all court personnel.

It was a difficult challenge for Dukakis, since similar proposals had failed in the past, and it was clear from the beginning that he would face well-organized opposition from some trial lawyers, judges, and county court officials resistant to change. In trying to sell the reform package, Dukakis pointed out that the system as then established wasn't working. As in his political campaigns, he traveled throughout the state, pushing for the legislation. He blamed the court system for rising crime, the turtle-like pace of the courts, and lenient sentencing. "There's a feeling that our system just isn't coping," the governor said in February 1977, "that government isn't working for the people."

But Dukakis had political problems that interfered with his ability to get his package passed. Sisitsky, chairman of the Senate Judiciary Committee, complained that though his committee would pass judgment on the proposal, "the governor hasn't even bothered to speak to me about it. He hasn't indicated a readiness to negotiate."

When the legislature failed to move on his court reform proposal by the close of the 1977 session, Dukakis called its inaction "disgusting" and, in a gesture symbolizing how important the issue was to him, personally walked down to the House Clerk's office in January 1978 to refile the bill.

In the months that followed, Dukakis worked the House and Senate far more effectively than he had the year before, and it paid off. When the legislature adjourned for the year on July 12, it had passed and sent to Dukakis a court reform bill. On July 18, 1978—barely two months before the Democratic gubernatorial primary—Dukakis, terming the occasion "momentous," signed the court reform bill into law.

5. Reform

---

*"You've been a pretty good governor,
but I'm not voting for you."*

F OR A TIME, it seemed that Dukakis's political troubles were
behind him. During the early part of 1978, there were
clear indications that much of the damage from his first
three years in office had been repaired.

The most fortuitous event—from the perspective of Dukakis's
public image—was the once-in-a-century blizzard that began on
February 6, 1978, dumping nearly three feet of snow on the
region and paralyzing most of Massachusetts for a full week.
The storm was so bad that driving was prohibited in the eastern
part of the state for five days, and the only connection many
people had to the outside world was their radio or television.
After a day or two, most areas had their electricity restored and
people were able to watch the tube, where, hour after hour, they
saw their governor in action. Dukakis established a headquarters
in the Metropolitan District Commission building near the State
House and ran the blizzard-battling operation. Wearing a turtle-
neck shirt and crew neck sweater, he came across on television as
calm, understanding, and in charge. It was the kind of sustained
positive publicity that politicians dream about.

Soon afterward, an advertising man who had created commercials for Gerald Ford's 1976 presidential campaign assessed
the political fallout from the storm. Malcolm MacDougall, who

was a principal in the Boston firm of Humphrey Browning Mac-
Dougall, said that Dukakis's performance amounted to a "very,
very valuable political advertisement, one that money couldn't
buy." A rough estimate of the worth of such exposure, MacDougall said, was a minimum of $2 million, more money than Duka-
kis spent on his 1974 campaign, and would spend on his 1978
campaign, combined.

And there was other encouragement for Dukakis concerning
the toughest issue of all, the state's fiscal health. Throughout the
first two years of his term, there was little in the way of good
fiscal news, but by the beginning of 1977 a turnaround had
begun. On February 17, 1977, Dukakis went to New York City,
where he met with officials from Chase Manhattan Bank and
the major bond rating houses, Moody's and Standard and
Poor's. He talked about the "bloody" fiscal period, when he cut
services and raised taxes, but he assured them that "Massachusetts's fiscal house is in order."

He was well received in New York, but the cutting wasn't over
yet. In July 1977, Dukakis ordered his cabinet secretaries to reduce the state workforce by three thousand people during the
ensuing year and to exact higher productivity from the remaining employees. The cut was needed, he said, because the total
state workforce had increased by three thousand since late 1975.

The best news of Dukakis's term came on July 28, 1977, when
Jack Buckley announced that for fiscal 1977, which had ended
on June 30, Massachusetts had a budget surplus of $69.2 mil-
lion. Weeks earlier, administration officials had predicted a surplus, but they had estimated that it would be something on the
order of $12 million. But it seemed that where fiscal matters
were involved, whatever the Dukakis administration did got the
governor in trouble. For Buckley didn't merely announce the
surplus, utter platitudes about superior management, and leave
it at that. Instead, he talked about the following year's budget
and said he might come up with a surplus then, too, which he
said he would "hide . . . in a different drawer next year."

The notion that Buckley had been less than honest with the
administration and with the legislature in reporting on the
state's income—that he had tucked nearly $70 million aside so
he would have a year-end surplus—angered not only legislators

but members of Dukakis's own cabinet, who felt Buckley had forced them to squeeze their budgets, knowing full well he had money available. Some of them complained publicly. By early August, Buckley's estimate of the surplus had climbed to nearly $100 million.

An upbeat Dukakis announced in March 1978—a month after the blizzard—that the Massachusetts economy had been "born again" and that Massachusetts and New England were "probably better equipped to meet the future than many other areas of the country." In a speech at Boston College, Dukakis said that "our economy today has a better balance, a better mix, than it has had for many, many years. It has a competitive resilience and maturity. It's a lot more resistant to the pressures that plagued it for years."

In the spring of 1978, polls showed Dukakis with leads of thirty-plus percentage points over his current political rivals. A survey published by the *Boston Globe* in May indicated that, largely as a result of his blizzard publicity, Dukakis appeared virtually unbeatable. The survey of 998 voters showed Dukakis with impressive support among various segments of the electorate and massive leads over both Democratic and Republican opponents. Sixty-seven percent of those polled said they had a favorable opinion of the governor, while 30 percent said they had an unfavorable view of him. Though the 30 percent negative rating is a bit uncomfortable for most public officials, it is not unusual for an executive, and the 67 percent positive rating could hardly have been better, and, in fact, it seemed astonishing, given the turbulence of much of Dukakis's term. Just four months before the September primary, Dukakis's ratings were incomparably better than those of either of his Democratic opponents. Barbara Ackermann, a liberal and former mayor of Cambridge, was rated 26 percent favorable and 9 percent unfavorable. Edward J. King of Winthrop, a conservative and former executive director of the Massachusetts Port Authority, received ratings of 24 percent favorable, 8 percent unfavorable. In both cases, nearly two thirds of those polled didn't know Ackermann or King well enough to have an opinion of them, or had never heard of them at all.

The only encouragement Dukakis's opponents found in the

survey was a hint of softness in his support. It seemed that he had a sizable number of backers in large measure because they knew so little about his rivals. But as the primary approached, Dukakis appeared to be in very strong shape. He—and the legislature—had brought the state back to fiscally solid ground; he had three years of experience from which he had learned a great deal, he said; he had given a strong performance during the blizzard; and he was facing apparently weak primary opponents. Ackermann had been defeated the previous year in a race for Cambridge City Council, and King had never run for political office before.

Perhaps most important was Dukakis's perception that his performance had improved markedly during his term. In an interview in November 1977 with Eleanor Roberts of the *Boston Herald*, Dukakis said he had changed personally since winning the governorship. "I'm a great deal more patient now," he told Roberts. "That's one of the big changes . . . I'm more willing to listen—to reflect . . . I also am more willing to acknowledge my mistakes than before." It certainly *sounded* good, but in retrospect the changes were mostly in Dukakis's imagination.

In personal terms, Dukakis's first administration contained strong cross-currents. Despite the fiscal crisis of the first year and persistent friction with legislative leaders, Dukakis was throwing his energy and single-mindedness into the job he had always wanted. He earned a reputation in Washington and in the National Governors Association as one of the more effective state leaders. When Jimmy Carter's staff drew up a list of potential vice-presidential candidates in 1976, Dukakis was one of the four highest-rated governors. He gained attention as chairman of the committee drafting the party's platform that year. And he was discovered by a number of commentators from the national press, some of whom identified him and California's governor, Edmund G. "Jerry" Brown, Jr., as leaders of a new pragmatic, technocratic wing of the Democratic party.

Dukakis even acquired a bit of international experience, traveling in 1976 to Caracas for energy talks, to Ireland with a delegation of governors, to Greece, and, in 1977, to Israel for two weeks' vacation. In Ireland, challenged to a foot race by other governors, Dukakis slipped on wet grass at the American ambassador's baronial residence in Dublin and tumbled head over heels, snapping his collarbone. After being placed in a shoulder harness at St. Vincent's Hospital, Dukakis returned for dinner, but Kitty knew he was in pain when he asked for two aspirins. "He never has taken more than one aspirin at a time," she said.

Especially in his State House office in Boston, Dukakis's spirits seemed to soar after the first year. Though pomp and history were not his specialties, Dukakis gloried in the example set for him by the crusty firebrand Samuel Adams, whose portrait he had chosen to hang over his desk, and in July 1976 he rode in an open limousine with Queen Elizabeth II to the Old North Church as part of the nation's bicentennial celebration. His persistent optimism flagged only slightly in the buffeting of 1975; after that, his self-confidence was abundant. He clearly thought that his ambition from undergraduate days had been right: that he fit the job of governor, and the job fit him, perfectly.

Dukakis was buttressed as well during this period by the routine he had established in his home life. Although there were many demands on his time, Dukakis insisted on a schedule that allowed him to leave the State House at five-thirty so that he could be home, most days by subway, for dinner at six. Usually, he would be driven to functions later at night, but the dinner hour was nearly inviolable for the whole family. And Sundays were kept clear as well for tending the front yard tomato patch and other domestic chores.

John Dukakis says the dinners were "a compressed hour" when Michael was governor, but time the family "took for granted." John remembers being at a forum once with other political families and hearing that some of them barred political discussion from their family gatherings. But "politics was everything" in the Dukakis house, he says. "If we had had that rule, we would have had silent dinners every night."

The relationship between Michael and John strengthened through these years. Although Michael has never adopted him legally, John has treated Michael like a father for most of his life and started using the name Dukakis as a small boy. In 1976, he took the name legally.

John, Andrea, and Kara all went to the Lawrence School—

when he was governor, Dukakis would usually start his day by walking the girls there on his way to the subway—and then to Brookline High. John says his father had high expectations for them scholastically but was not overbearing. "He had difficulty at times understanding anything less than an A," says John, "but he got better over time."

In fact, all three children did well in school, well enough so that John and Kara both went to Brown and Andrea to Princeton. When John was a freshman at Brown, however, a passion for acting, which began in high school, was intensified when he had a chance to play a minor part in *Jaws II*. He wanted to leave school for Hollywood, and, after talking it over, Michael supported him completely. This seemed unusually flexible, given the familial value placed on education. But John says he was not surprised, for two reasons: "One is that he has always been fascinated by things he doesn't know very much about," and the other is that "he recognizes and admires commitment." John had commitment and some talent as well, finding a number of roles in motion pictures and on television shows, ranging from soap operas to public television dramas, including one with Vanessa Redgrave. After several years, though, he abandoned acting and went into politics, working in Washington for Senator John F. Kerry of Massachusetts before signing on with his father's presidential campaign.

Yet these years also contained a great deal of loss for Dukakis— loss that was certainly far deeper than he showed, that may have had a deeper impact than he realized at the time. Stelian's death, in July 1973, came just two months before his formal announcement for governor. Then, during his first year in office, two uncles who had meant much to him in his youth, Constantine and George Dukakis, both died. And Kitty's mother, Jane Dickson, died in December 1977.

In addition, Dukakis also lost the advice and support of the five men who, arguably, had been most crucial to putting him in the governor's office. One, Allan Sidd, died unexpectedly. The other four—Stephen Kinzer, J. Joseph Grandmaison, Sumner Kaplan, and Fran Meaney—split with Dukakis over personal and political differences.

Sidd was only fifty-three years old when he suffered a massive heart attack and died on February 21, 1977. He had been hospitalized for a minor surgical procedure, yet he was apprehensive enough to ask his friend Hackie Kassler to draw up a new will. True to his exuberant self, Sidd directed that at his death, there should be a memorial service of celebration, complete with Dixieland music. Dukakis spoke, and for once, showed his emotion. Brountas remembers, "He tried to fit into the atmosphere of celebration and happiness, and everybody started weeping . . . It was the first time I'd ever seen that kind of open emotion from Michael. It was very moving."

It was considered a great loss to Dukakis. Dave O'Brien, a columnist for the *Boston Herald,* said, "If any one person deserved credit for inventing Michael Dukakis, it most certainly was Sidd." The following year, Dukakis's supporters would lament the loss of Sidd's ability to see political situations as they were, not as Dukakis wanted them to be.

The breaks with his four other friends had none of the public emotion that Dukakis displayed after Sidd's death.

The least traumatic separation involved Kinzer, a young Brookline High graduate, who had been a disciple of Dukakis's from 1970 through 1974, working day and night, traveling methodically and incessantly back and forth across the state with him, laying the groundwork for the 1974 campaign. Kinzer, now a reporter for the *New York Times,* stayed with Dukakis for about nine months, into his first year as governor, but left, at the age of twenty-five, with a sense that there was no government job in which his abilities would be crucial to Dukakis.

The break with Grandmaison was sharper. He had labored doggedly as Dukakis's campaign manager in 1974. The relationship between the two men was helped by their compatible views of campaigns, which stressed intensive local organizing. Grandmaison was a former Nashua, New Hampshire, alderman who had run George McGovern's dramatic New Hampshire primary campaign in 1972. He took over Dukakis's campaign in August 1973, more than a month before the formal announcement. One of their few disagreements was over the issue of fund-raising. Grandmaison thought Dukakis was a little too finicky in going over virtually every contribution to ensure that no money was accepted from lobbyists or state workers. But, on the whole, the campaign went very well, and, though they had some differences, the two men became a close-knit team during the fifteen-month effort.

About two weeks before the primary, according to Grandmaison, Dukakis "asked me if I would be interested in staying on as his chief secretary," the top job in the administration. Grandmaison remembers responding that that might be terrific, but that they needed to concentrate on the two months of hard campaigning left to go. On the day after the election, he says, "Meaney called me in and said the governor-elect would no longer be needing my services, but wanted to give me a bonus." Grandmaison was furious, but to no avail. He took a job—no thanks to Dukakis—in the office of federal-state relations in Washington headed by Lieutenant Governor Thomas P. O'Neill III, a son of Speaker of the House Thomas P. "Tip" O'Neill, Jr. But Grandmaison stayed only six months before quitting, with hard feelings, and returning to New Hampshire.

Dukakis shrugs off the Grandmaison incident. "Joe had been a hell of a campaign manager, but he's a pretty strong-willed guy, and it just seemed to me at the time that he probably wasn't the person who would be the best chief of staff for me."

Grandmaison, who is now chairman of the Democratic State Committee in New Hampshire, acknowledges that "I am a terribly aggressive person" and says that, in several disputes with Dukakis over the years, "more often than not I blamed me." Despite everything, he adds, "we continue to be friends, or at least at this moment we are friends—it's a fluid state."

The break with Kaplan was even sharper than that with Grandmaison. Kaplan had been Dukakis's first political mentor and also his trailblazer: his decision not to seek re-election in 1962 opened the seat for Dukakis. Kaplan stayed active as a practicing lawyer and in Brookline politics, including a stint as chairman of the board of selectmen. When a judgeship opened up in Brookline District Court in 1977, Kaplan seemed a natural. But Dukakis didn't appoint him. The reason Dukakis gives is that the Judicial Nominating Commission he appointed, a panel whose task was to recommend people for judgeships, did not propose Kaplan for the job. Dukakis sent the list of prospective judges back to the commission and asked for another list, but, again, Kaplan's name was not sent up to him. Dukakis could have made it clear to the commission that he wanted Kaplan, but this would have run counter to the hands-off attitude he had enunciated in establishing the commission.

Dukakis maintains that he does not know why Kaplan wasn't proposed by the commission, saying only that "based on their review and the interview [with Kaplan] they weren't prepared to recommend him ... I wasn't happy with the situation but I knew they were very good people who spent a lot of time working at their job, and if they did not see their way clear to recommend somebody they had done so for good and sufficient reason."

In the end, Dukakis's old friend was left hanging. A complete and bitter break between the two was the result. Kassler, who knows both men well, believes the problem stemmed from a misunderstanding within the commission, but there is no denying the personal enmity that resulted. "It was really unfortunate for both people," Kassler says. In one of the many ironies of Massachusetts politics, Dukakis's nemesis, Governor Edward J. King, as one of his final acts in 1982, appointed Kaplan to the Probate Court.

If Kaplan was Dukakis's godfather, Fran Meaney was his first political brother. Ever since law school, Meaney had been at Dukakis's side—his campaign manager, chief strategist, fund-raiser, and organizer in every campaign. From COD through the legislature and on to three statewide campaigns, the two were comrades-in-arms in a fifteen-year crusade that landed Dukakis in the governor's office. Meaney headed the transition operation in late 1974, but then returned to the major Boston law firm where he was a partner, Mintz, Levin, Cohn, Ferris, Glovsky & Popeo. He preferred his behind-the-scenes connections with the administration, such as coordinating a management task force of private-sector volunteers who recommended ways to streamline the government. Suddenly, in the fall of 1976, his relationship with Dukakis fell apart. For some time Meaney's law firm had been seeking work as bond counsel for public entities, mostly school building authorities and cities and towns. This was shortly after New York City almost went bankrupt, and the work was increasingly demanding and lucrative. In September, state Treasurer Robert Q. Crane selected Meaney's firm as counsel on a $116 million bond issue. "We were ecstatic," Meaney says. But Dukakis asked him not to accept the work.

Dukakis was adamant about appearances. He felt the work might be viewed as a favor to Meaney and his firm. "I was absolutely flabbergasted and taken aback and frankly resentful," Meaney says. He and his senior partner, William M. Glovsky, went to talk to Dukakis. They pointed out that in Massachusetts the treasurer is a separately elected constitutional officer. In this case, Crane had been elected long before Dukakis, in 1964 originally, and had no special tie with the governor. Meaney said that since no one thought Dukakis was clearing his judicial appointments with Crane, why should anybody think Crane was clearing his bond counsel assignments with Dukakis? In addition, if there was a political connection, it would be seen as coming primarily through another of Meaney's senior partners, Robert Popeo, who was much closer to Crane than Meaney and who had no connection to the governor. Dukakis wouldn't budge. But neither was he in a position to make his wishes stick. The work was Crane's to give, and Mintz, Levin took it. "There was no reason to accede to his request," Meaney says. "To this day, I don't know what bad there was."

At the time, Meaney was just as blunt. "I have given a great deal to the governor and to public service over the years," he said. "In the past two years, I have worked without pay for eleven hundred hours discharging my responsibilities to him. I feel badly used by him. I am not a satellite to Michael Dukakis."

Even some lawyers close to Dukakis have mixed feelings about this incident. Paul Brountas says, "I do think it was more firm business than Meaney business," though "Michael felt very strongly about it." Kassler believes that though this was well into the second year of the gubernatorial term, it was still early enough so that Dukakis's passion about the appearance of clean government was a legitimate factor, and thus that he "may have

Above, left: Michael in the costume of the *evzones*, elite Greek ceremonial guards, at age six. *Above, right:* Michael and his brother, Stelian, at about eight and eleven years old, when sports was their passion. *Below, left:* Panos Dukakis with his sons in 1944. *Below, right:* Euterpe Dukakis.

Above: The 1951 Brookline High School yearbook pictured the "most brilliant" seniors—Dukakis and Marilyn Tanner. "Most popular" were Bob Wool, one of the few people ever to beat Dukakis in an election, and Sandy Cohen, his sweetheart in school and one of his closest friends afterward. *Below, left:* April 1951: finishing 57th in the Boston Marathon. *Below, right:* Dukakis in 1952 with his Swarthmore roommate, Frank Sieverts, who became a Rhodes Scholar.

MIKE DUKAKIS
for LT. GOVERNOR

- Endorsed by the Democratic State Convention
- Fighter for Low Cost Auto Insurance
- Veteran ● Experienced Legislator

Above, left: A brochure from the 1970 campaign for lieutenant governor: Andrea is smiling at John; Kara, at the camera. *Above, top right:* Allan Sidd, a close friend of Dukakis's and a legend in Brookline politics. *Above, bottom right:* Haskell "Hackie" Kassler, a friend since high school. *Below:* Moderating *The Advocates* in Boston's Faneuil Hall for public television.

Above, left: With Beryl Cohen at the 1970 state convention, where Dukakis beat his old friend for the nomination for lieutenant governor. *Above, right:* Joe Grandmaison, Dukakis's campaign manager in 1974. A week after this picture was taken, Grandmaison celebrated victory with Dukakis, then was dismissed. *Below, left:* When Dukakis did not appoint his friend Sumner Z. Kaplan to a judgeship, their friendship was over. *Below, right:* Fran Meaney, Dukakis's closest political sidekick, until their split in 1976.

Above, left: Riding the "T" to Boston with Kitty the morning after being elected governor. *Above, right:* With Kitty in front of the Acropolis in 1976. *Below, left:* His unruffled command during the blizzard of 1978 made Dukakis unbeatable for re-election. Or so it was thought. *Below, right:* At one point Dukakis was so angry with Kevin Harrington, the Senate president says, that "if I wasn't six-foot-nine and about two hundred and sixty pounds, I think he would've taken a swing at me."

Above: The symbolic meat cleaver. *Below, left:* The fiscal crisis took its toll. *Below, right:* ". . . a public death."

Above, left: Ed King, Dukakis's nemesis in two elections. *Above, center:* Paul Brountas, Dukakis's closest friend since law school. *Above, right:* Bob Farmer, friend and fund-raiser. *Below:* John Sasso in the governor's office. His departure from the presidential campaign was a major blow to the candidate.

Above, left: On his first trip to Iowa, the candidate milked no cows, petted no pigs. *Above, right:* As a presidential candidate, his message was too simple for some but effective with many. *Below:* The family picture on the mantel of the governor's office. The children, from left, are Andrea, John, and Kara.

been hurt" by what he saw as Meaney's putting him in an awkward position.

The dispute drove a wedge between two men who had been inseparable politically for a decade and a half. Now, Meaney speaks highly of attributes he thinks would make Dukakis "an excellent president," and he has contributed the maximum amount to Dukakis's campaign. But to this day, there is almost no communication between them.

More than eleven years later, Dukakis's position on the Meaney affair is unchanged. "I just didn't think it was appropriate given his closeness to me . . . [It] seemed to me this was pretty fundamental. Fran had been chairman of the committee, very close to me personally and politically, and I just thought it was something he and his firm should not do and I told him so."

Dukakis's splits with these close colleagues demonstrate as much as anything the self-sufficiency that has been a hallmark of his career from the start. Most public officials would have gone to great lengths to retain the support and counsel of one such political intimate, never mind four, especially when the official was a first-term governor whose effectiveness had come under question. But Dukakis allowed these relationships to be severed with no apparent sense of loss. If he felt weakened as an administrator or pained as a friend, he didn't show it.

"There's always a sense of loss when things happen that are troubling or disappointing or unhappy," he says now, "but once I came into this office in '75 I had to be . . . fully engaged in what was going on around here . . . That first year, year and a half, was difficult, but I think the difficulty had a lot more to do with the burdens and pressures of the office and the necessity of having to deal with some very difficult problems . . .

"I was just so totally engaged in what I was doing that while there was certainly a loss . . . there wasn't much time to think about it, to ruminate on it or be terribly introspective. I mean, I'm not a particularly introspective guy anyway."

It was a disconcerting time politically in Massachusetts. The fiscal crisis was still a haunting memory in the minds of many politicians, and members of the House were edgy over a task they were required to carry out that year, cutting their own membership by a third, from 240 to 160, a reduction mandated by a ballot referendum in 1974.

Morale in the State House, which had been poor ever since Dukakis's election, continued to sink as the reality of the House cut approached. By the end of 1977, Dukakis had managed to patch up his tattered relationships with many members of the legislature, but his ability to deal with others had deteriorated badly. A trip Dukakis made to Washington in April 1977 indicated the depths to which his relations with other politicians had sunk. The governor had scheduled a meeting with Tip O'Neill, but was kept waiting outside the office for more than half an hour. Such an affront was virtually unheard of—this was, after all, the governor of O'Neill's home state. An infuriated Dukakis finally left without seeing the Speaker.

The speaker of the Massachusetts House, Thomas W. McGee, with whom Dukakis had never gotten on, reached a point where he didn't want to be in the same room with Dukakis, so much did he loathe the governor. Once, McGee made a frantic call from the House chamber to the office of his majority leader, William Q. "Biff" MacLean. Dukakis was about to enter the House for a ceremonial function, and McGee told MacLean to come take the gavel. The speaker couldn't stand to share the rostrum with the governor. Halfway through Dukakis's term, McGee made it clear that Dukakis didn't play by any political rules he had ever heard of. He said, "I don't really understand him. For example, if you came to me for a job and it was between just you and some guy I'd known for twenty years, I'd probably give the job to the guy I knew. That's human nature, right? Not Dukakis," said McGee. "If you went to him for a job and one of his friends also wanted it, I'd bet you'd get the job."

As a legislator, Dukakis's cool style did not hinder his effectiveness. And he started his term as governor with a rhetorical bow to the lawmakers, noting that he was himself a product of the legislature. In addition, his two top deputies, Chief Secretary David Liederman and his secretary of administration and finance, Jack Buckley, were both former members of the House, as was his lieutenant governor, Tom O'Neill. But it wasn't enough. His aloofness, his tendency to lecture legislators in a didactic fashion, combined with his refusal to grant patronage, wrecked his relations with the legislature. A "perfect ingrate" was how Barney Frank described Dukakis. Representative Paul Means, who had been one of the Dukakis campaign's first three paid staff members in 1974, was elected to the legislature at the same time Dukakis became governor. Means recalls that he was ecstatic, thrilled at his own good fortune. There he was in the House, with his pal Mike down the hall in the corner office. Means had it made—or so he thought. He soon learned what other Dukakis supporters would also learn—that Dukakis didn't do political business. He would not help his friends with jobs, even as his opponents found other sources of patronage. As Means put it years later: "I couldn't get the time of day" from Dukakis. James Segel, a Brookline Democrat who occupied the seat that had once been Dukakis's own, remembers the same phenomenon. "We all joked about it in the legislature," he says. "If you wanted something, you had to oppose him."

Dukakis's attitude toward patronage, of course, had been a theme of his 1974 campaign and had been made clear in the early days of the administration—excessively clear, according even to some loyal supporters. Brountas, for instance, says that campaign workers were excluded from state jobs almost across the board: "That's how rigid he was in those days—their participation in the campaign foreclosed their participation in government."

There were other reasons for hostility toward the governor. One was his stubbornness on certain issues, a quality that often seemed to carry with it disdain for opposing views. In the spring of 1976, Dukakis—the philosophical opponent of superhighways, the strap-hanging advocate of public transportation—decided to refuse $51 million in federal funds for highway improvements. The money was not for new roads, but for widening and safety improvements on existing highways. Labor leaders said it would produce four thousand jobs. Politicians said that, as a federal grant, it was basically free money for the state. Dukakis said that didn't matter. He had a well-known dislike for the orange barrels set out by road crews; he thought they were dangerous and expensive. He called the projects "Mickey Mouse" and "a waste of the taxpayers' money." The political leaders erupted. The state House of Representatives voted, 219–1, against the decision. Dukakis's own lieutenant governor, Tom O'Neill, battled him privately, then openly. The state's congressional delegation howled. "If it were a question of funding for safety for footraces, I'm sure he would approve it," said Joseph Early, a Democratic congressman. Finally, after a two-week storm in which he was virtually alone, Dukakis relented. The money was spent, but memories of his resistance remained strong at the State House.

Among liberal legislators in particular—men and women who had ardently supported his election in 1974—there was open dislike of the governor. Some remained furious over the welfare cuts. Others were angry that he had signed the legislative redistricting bill, which established the new districts for the 160-member House and nakedly gerrymandered a liberal member out of a North Shore district.

As his colleagues attacked Dukakis inside the State House, a variety of groups assaulted him outside. It seemed that wherever he went, he was dogged by demonstrators—state police who believed they were drastically underpaid, welfare recipients living on reduced benefits, car owners angry about insurance costs. Kitty Dukakis recalls that "every time we went someplace publicly there was a group picketing. And that was a *year* before the election."

The Dukakises were even hounded at home. Worst of all was a demonstration by some two dozen protesters who marched to the governor's house in December 1977 the day after Kitty's mother had died of cancer. Jane Dickson's long illness had been emotionally draining for everyone in the family, especially Kitty. And here, the day after her death, was a flatbed truck with banners and a loudspeaker pulling in front of the house to protest workfare and a cut in unemployment benefits. Dukakis, arriving home by car, confronted the protesters briefly, then went inside, saying only, "It's unbelievable, unbelievable." One of the protesters told reporters, "We would have made a bigger stink out here if it hadn't been for his family tragedy." Another said,

"We've got to pray for the dead and fight for the living."

During 1977, political opposition to Dukakis built as a number of potential opponents explored the possibility of running against him. A measure of the contempt some politicians felt toward him came in the fall, when one of his most passionate early supporters, the volatile Alan Sisitsky, said he was seriously considering challenging Dukakis. "The governor turned his back on human services right after he took over as chief executive. That's when my disillusionment with him began," the state senator said. "And it got worse as he continued to waffle on his commitments in this area."

As Sisitsky was deciding whether to run, another Democrat, Ed King, who now headed the New England Council, a business organization, announced his candidacy. At the same time, Senate President Kevin Harrington hinted that he was likely to run as well.

The most formidable challenger, although it was difficult to tell at the time, was King, a hulking former Baltimore Colt lineman, who came at Dukakis from the right. King supported nuclear power, including New Hampshire's controversial Seabrook plant, favored offshore drilling for oil and gas, and wanted highway projects that had been blocked by community groups to go forward. His political message was frank: "We have to increase our business . . . Those who control capital—who decide whether to come here or not, whether to expand here or not, whether to stay here or not—these people do not have confidence in the state." Businessmen, he said, perceived Dukakis as antibusiness.

That the governor was in for a dogfight could be discerned in a quotation from Winston Churchill that hung in King's office: "Never give in. Never, never, never, never. Never yield to force and the apparently overwhelming might of the enemy. Never yield in any way, great or small, large or petty, except to convictions of honor and good sense." King announced his candidacy formally on October 25, 1977.

As others were preparing to run against him, Dukakis also went through the motions of getting ready. He set up a campaign office and hired a young transplanted New Yorker,

George Bachrach, who had just managed a successful congressional campaign in Boston's northern suburbs. But Dukakis, who had risen to power partly by controlling his local Democratic party in Brookline, ignored his own example, failing to consolidate his strength within the Democratic State Committee or to take control of the nominating process. Bachrach became increasingly frustrated at trying to get Dukakis's attention away from his policy advisers at the State House, and he finally quit. "At the end of a year, I just found myself to be irrelevant," Bachrach says.

Nonetheless, Dukakis's political fortunes soared with indications that a strong economic recovery was under way in the state. During 1978, more than 100,000 new jobs were created, and the unemployment rate, for the first time in more than five years, dropped below the national average. "Having come through that '75–'76 business, we were starting to feel very good about the state, about what we were doing," says Dukakis. An improved economy, new fiscal stability, and his performance during the blizzard combined to give the governor a markedly improved level of support among voters. He seemed as popular with the people as he was unpopular with political insiders.

Even so, it appeared that Dukakis might well have one or two Democratic challengers in addition to King. The one most talked about, Harrington, was a smart, intimidatingly tall politician who smoked huge cigars and took pleasure in wielding the considerable power of his office. The Senate was his private reserve; to give it up would be difficult. Yet Dukakis's perceived vulnerability among insiders convinced Harrington that he could become governor. He intended to declare his candidacy formally at the end of January, and in the months preceding, he signed on people to raise money, take polls, and create advertising.

Suddenly, though, during the first week in January, Harrington's candidacy collapsed. It was revealed that a corporate check for $2000 from a New York consulting company that had paid bribes to two state senators had been made out to Harrington. The New York firm of McKee-Berger-Mansueto (MBM) had overseen the construction of the University of Massachusetts campus in Boston. During that time, the firm bribed the senators to alter the contents of a report critical of the firm's work. Both senators were convicted of extortion and sent off to prison. One of them, Joseph J. C. DiCarlo of Revere, had been hand-picked by Harrington as his successor. The other was a young Republican, Ronald C. MacKenzie of Burlington. The two senators' trial had received so much publicity that the name MBM was synonymous with bribery in the minds of many Massachusetts voters.

Harrington said he didn't remember receiving a check from MBM. He said he customarily used his middle initial, B., when signing his name. The check was endorsed with a signature Harrington conceded looked like his own but without the middle initial. It was cashed in a bank in Harrington's home town of Salem, where he is extremely well known. The notion of some-one other than Harrington negotiating the check at a bank in Salem seemed rather farfetched. Given the improbability of Harrington's explanation, his candidacy died.

A liberal candidate eventually did enter the race on the last day of March in the person of Barbara Ackermann, fifty-three years old and a former mayor of Cambridge—hardly a menacing threat to Dukakis. Conceding the hopelessness of her task, Barney Frank said the real point of Ackermann's campaign was to show Dukakis that there was "a price to be paid for hurting poor people."

"It is clear that many people in this state want a new governor," Ackermann said in announcing her candidacy. "The present governor has not cut the cost of government; he has cut essential services." On the heels of her announcement, a human services organization published a study supporting her point of view. The study was done by the Massachusetts Advocacy Center, the same group that had criticized Dukakis's initial fiscal moves. It charged that the spending and hiring freeze imposed by Dukakis early in his term "had the single most destructive impact on Massachusetts citizens of any official action in recent history." At a fund-raising event for Ackermann, Frank joked about the governor. It was terrific that Dukakis rode mass transit, he said; "the only problem is that he gets off at the State House."

Dukakis was not attacked only from the left. He angered conservatives in June by claiming that the state's "fiscal house is in order" and that Massachusetts had no need for a property tax–cutting measure such as Proposition 13, which had been passed in California. The governor conceded that Proposition 13 was a clear signal that voters were fed up with rising property taxes, but he said that Massachusetts was already preparing to reduce the burden, and the people knew it. "I think," he said a bit smugly, "the citizens of this state study referenda questions very carefully." A Republican gubernatorial candidate, state Representative Francis W. Hatch, said it was clear that Dukakis was "out of touch with reality," and King said it was irresponsible of Dukakis to hold such a view. Dukakis also found himself opposed by right-to-life groups, the insurance industry, state employees, labor leaders, and bankers. In fact, so angry were bankers with the Dukakis administration's tight regulation of their industry that fifteen cooperative banks in eastern Massachusetts wrote to employees and customers, asking them to change their registration from Republican to Democrat so that they could vote for King.

In retrospect, Dukakis's biggest problem in the election was not his opposition but himself and the remarkable overconfidence of his supporters, who simply refused to take Ackermann and King seriously. When the governor announced on June 23 that he would seek re-election, few of his supporters believed he could lose. They shared their candidate's view, as he outlined it in his announcement speech: "Today the outlook for Massachusetts is much, much brighter" than it had been when he took over the state. He said he had given Massachusetts "honest, progressive, and hard-working government."

After the announcement came little in the way of aggressive campaigning. Dukakis hired Richard A. Giesser, a friend and Newton resident, to manage his campaign. It seemed a curious choice, for Giesser was a businessman with almost no political experience. Nonetheless, polls throughout the summer showed

Dukakis holding leads of twenty and thirty points and more, yet he cautioned his supporters against overconfidence. He said his supporters often advised him to take a vacation because, as he put it, "you have no troubles in this election."

One indication of Dukakis's belief he would win was that just days before the primary, he appointed his friend Gordon N. Chase, an expert in health planning and policy, to the position of secretary of human services. Another indication of his own confidence was that although he could have raised hundreds of thousands more dollars, he permitted King to outspend him by more than two to one on campaign advertising. King spent $105,000 on broadcast advertising compared with Dukakis's $50,000.

Most of Dukakis's supporters saw no need to work hard against King, but George Papalimberis was an exception. A resident of Winchester, he owned a barber shop on Brattle Street in Cambridge known as "George the Greek's." Papalimberis had first met Dukakis on a blistering summer day at Carson Beach in South Boston. It was 1974, and in spite of temperatures in the nineties, Dukakis was out campaigning. He shook hands with Papalimberis on the beach and said he was running for governor. Papalimberis recalls, "I said to myself, if the guy wants the job this bad, he'll probably do okay."

Papalimberis knew about Dukakis because Panos Dukakis had delivered several of his nieces and nephews. He volunteered and helped Michael's campaign in the Allston-Brighton section of Boston, where he was living at the time. In 1978, he again volunteered to help. This time, nobody responded until a week before the primary, when a campaign worker called and said he could help if he wanted, but victory seemed assured. This worried Papalimberis. "I'm hearing in the barber shop that it's going the other way," he says, but he assumed the campaign people knew better.

Nowhere was Dukakis's overconfidence more on display than in the only live television debate of the campaign, held fewer than three weeks before the September 19 primary. At every opportunity King attacked Dukakis, aggressively hammering home his pro-business, pro–tax cut, pro–capital punishment messages, even when they weren't related to the question being asked. Dukakis, so cool he was nearly laconic, didn't fight back. Where King was sometimes clumsy and aggressive, Dukakis was composed and relaxed enough to seem smug.

He emphasized that he had saved the state from bankruptcy. Under his administration, Dukakis said, the state had gained two hundred thousand new jobs and increased local aid enough to make a property tax cut possible that year. King replied, "If everything is as rosy as Dukakis says, why are our taxes so high?"

King continually made clear his support for a tax cut similar to Proposition 13 and his opposition to state-funded abortions. He emphasized his belief in capital punishment, mandatory sentencing for drug pushers, and raising the drinking age from eighteen to twenty-one. In an unadorned rhetorical style, King told viewers: "If you like my platform, I hope you vote for me. If you don't, vote for Dukakis."

Barney Frank, writing in the *Real Paper*, was explicit about his opposition to Dukakis: "It ought to be beyond dispute that the severity of the cuts imposed by the governor went far beyond what was fiscally necessary. In 1977, a few weeks after Dukakis opposed spending $7 million to provide AFDC recipients with a 3 percent increase in fiscal 1978, his secretary of administration and finance, John Buckley, announced gleefully that the administration had produced a $70 million surplus by lying to the public and the legislature about the true state of our finances. This past November, the governor told an angry coalition of mental health supporters in his office that he could not respond fully to their needs because he feared a deficit in the total budget; six weeks later he kicked off his re-election campaign by pointing proudly to an expected $135 million surplus for the year. The likelihood is that the surplus will in fact exceed $150 million, and it will have come out of the hides of the poorest, most vulnerable people in our society."

A few days before the primary, Dukakis said that he was sensing some problems on the campaign trail. "There's more than apathy out there, there's real anger," he said at the time. "I don't want to overestimate it, but the anger is real." He was concerned about an amorphous kind of negative reaction, recalling a woman he'd recently met while campaigning in Dedham. "This woman said to me," he recalled, " 'Yes, you've been a pretty good governor, but I'm not voting for you.' She didn't say why."

At midday on September 19, primary day, Dukakis seemed at ease, relaxing at home in shirtsleeves. He said he was not taking the nomination for granted—"there's nothing sure about anything"—and he acknowledged that he had detected "disquiet, a lot of concern," among the voters. But, he said, there is "not the kind of gloom there was in 1974." On the whole, 1978 had been a good year, he said, adding, "I think one of my strengths is that people say, 'At least he's trying, he's making the effort.' " Dukakis refused to predict victory, but said he felt his urban strategy would have an impact at the polls. "I think I'm going to do better than '74 in a lot of the older cities," he said. "If we do that, we're not going to have any problems."

Around three or four in the afternoon, Dukakis was still at home with his wife. He was napping in their bedroom, as she recalls, and she was resting with him. The phone rang and Kitty answered it. Jack Cole, a reporter at Boston's NBC affiliate, Channel 4, said, according to Kitty, " 'I hate to do this, but I think you ought to know.' " He told her that things looked very bad. "He said, 'The exit polls are clear, definitive; it's a pattern.' " Kitty got off the phone and told Michael.

6. Rejection

"It was horrible . . . horrendous . . .
It was like a public death."

T HAT NIGHT, Dukakis delivered his remarks at the 57 Hotel in Boston to an audience of several hundred loyalists
who were just as stunned as he. Many of them cried,
some quietly, others more openly, as he entered the room. Kitty,
who was sick with a fever of 102, looked as though she had just
seen her house burn down. Dukakis was obviously in shock
when he approached the microphone, but his tone was measured, emotionless. There were plenty of tears, but none were
his. "I learned something a long time ago, in the early days of my
political career, that you had to be able to win and you had to be
able to lose," he said. "And I've had some experiences with both
phenomena. And I regret to have to report to you that despite a
long and hard and vigorous campaign which not only I and
Kitty, but so many thousands of you literally across the state,
worked so very hard, we are not going to win renomination. I
regret that, obviously. I am personally disappointed . . ."

Disappointed was hardly the word. The defeat was an episode
of horror, the kind from which one would awake and, recalling
the details, shudder. It was nightmarish, but it was no night-
mare. There was nothing in his past to prepare Dukakis for the
pain of this experience. It was true that he had lost elections
before, but he had never been turned out of office. It was crush-

ing. He had achieved his lifelong dream—he was governor of Massachusetts—and now it was gone, rudely, swiftly ripped away from him.

How could it have happened? He had led in the polls throughout the campaign, comfortably in most of them. On primary day, he seemed relaxed as he happily tended to his cherished vegetable garden and pruned his rosebushes. A neighbor, concern visible on her face, came by to tell him she had spent the morning urging people to vote for him. He breezily remarked on the beauty of the day.

If Dukakis had any hint of what was to come he didn't show it, although he certainly should have known something was up. His own campaign poll late in August had shown him falling under 50 percent for the first time, which alarmed some of his advisers. All of the momentum then seemed on King's side. But Dukakis seemed oblivious to the brewing storm until late afternoon, when Jack Cole called. He was shocked. The sickening knowledge that he had run a one-horse, complacent campaign became all too clear. He knew that he had angered some voters with his substance, put off others with his style. He had blown it. He would later characterize it as "the worst day of my life."

So great was the pain of the defeat for Kitty Dukakis that almost seven years later, during an interview with a reporter from the Associated Press, Kitty said, "Oh, it was horrible. It was just horrendous. That was terrible, I mean, it was like a public death." Her husband became so depressed, she recalls now, "that at one point I was really worried about him."

"It was a terrible loss," she says. For two or three months after the defeat he went through what she describes as a "period of mourning," when "he was quieter at home, preoccupied more than usual." He didn't know what he would do in the short run and was by no means sure that he would ever again seek public office.

Euterpe Dukakis recalls that after the loss her son "didn't say very much about it. I suppose he and Kitty talked about it, but not with his father and me." And she never asked him about it; that just wasn't how the family operated. Life went on. Shedding some light on the source of Dukakis's toughness, she said,

"When the boys would fall and hurt themselves, they would pick up and brush off and go on. They didn't dwell on it."

Andrew Sutcliffe, Dukakis's appointments secretary at the time, recalls the governor's being "very dejected . . . He would spend long periods sitting in his office, introspectively staring off into space."

Normally, Dukakis was the most optimistic man around the governor's office, always looking on the bright side. But there was no pretension now that there *was* a bright side. Alan Johnson, who was deputy chief of staff and had been one of Dukakis's closest aides since 1970, describes Dukakis as being "depressed and sullen . . . He was stunned. We were all just incredulous . . . For the several months afterward, a lot of that time was just sort of a painful blur. We had been the crusaders, the righteous heroes, in '74 and '75, and it was inconceivable that we could possibly lose."

Although Kitty and others worried at times that he would become seriously depressed, Dukakis says he didn't seek professional counseling. In fact, he says he has never consulted a psychiatrist, not after his defeat, not after Stelian's breakdown or death.

Dukakis says of himself that he is not very introspective, and most of his responses to the defeat were brief, but there were times when he did air his personal thoughts in public. Dr. John E. Mack, a Brookline neighbor and distinguished psychiatrist, remembers Dukakis's speaking to the International Society of Political Psychology some months after the primary. "It was a rare event," Mack says. "He was reflecting out loud on his own pain, his own hurt, his own mistakes . . . He was still trying to grow from it—not just as a shrewd tactician but really taking it in . . . I recollect being very moved."

Don Lipsitt, also a friend and psychiatrist, says that the process of recovery was a slow one, partly because the setback was such a stunning surprise. "He was grieving," says Lipsitt.

What made the loss even more painful was that he had been beaten by a man for whom he had no respect. Dukakis had discussed with King the job of running the MBTA, Boston's transit system, at the start of his first term, but the two could not get along personally. Dukakis saw King as a beefy Irish pol: a man with instincts for base emotional appeals on divisive issues such as capital punishment and abortion; a man with little ability as a public manager. Whatever regard there had been between the two evaporated in the 1978 campaign. To lose was one thing; to have been beaten by King was all the more stinging.

And worst of all was the specter of rejection—the knowledge that he had been turned out of office by the people he thought he had served well. "I thought it was a personal rejection," he says. "One of the reasons it was so painful was, there you are and people basically said, 'We don't want you, Dukakis. See you later.' "

Ironically, the very flaws in Dukakis that made defeat possible prevented his anticipating it. Never feeling in real danger of losing, Dukakis hadn't campaigned much. Overall, he spent only $75,000 on advertising, compared with $280,000 by King, and at least one TV spot that had been filmed was never aired. In addition, Ackermann siphoned liberal votes away from Dukakis. On top of that, Senator Edward W. Brooke, the first black senator since Reconstruction and a favorite of Massachusetts moderates and liberals for more than a decade, was in a tough primary fight against Avi Nelson, a conservative radio personality. In the state's open primary system, many independents asked for a Republican ballot to help Brooke, who told them he was in trouble, rather than voting Democratic for Dukakis, who gave no danger signal. The final vote was: King, 442,174; Dukakis, 365,417; Ackermann, 58,220.

Ackermann, clearly, did not attract enough votes to deny Dukakis the victory, even if he had won them all. And the Brooke factor can be overemphasized, too. Though it is true that the Republican turnout in 1978 was larger than usual, the Democrats also had a lively primary campaign for the Senate. Overall, 903,249 persons voted in the Democratic primary—93,401 *more* than voted in the 1974 primary, when Dukakis beat Quinn. But, despite the larger turnout, Dukakis received 79,173 *fewer* votes against King than against Quinn.

Kitty Dukakis had another, darker explanation for the loss. Little more than a month after the defeat, she told a Jewish group: "Unfortunately, it was a mistake to assume that anti-Semitism would not be a factor in a political campaign."

Dukakis has discounted this view, but there may have been some truth to it. Though there was no overt anti-Semitic campaign, one of King's campaign workers explained his man's victory over Dukakis this way: "We put all the hate groups together in one big pot and let it boil." On primary night, the raucous mob scene at King's campaign headquarters had an ugly undercurrent. When King, in his victory speech, mentioned Dukakis, the crowd erupted into vigorous booing, which King tried to quell. There was spiteful talk about the *Globe,* which the King people saw as representing the sort of liberalism they despised. Democrats in Massachusetts had been divided along class lines for a number of years, and nowhere was that division more clearly defined than in the Dukakis-King rivalry: in the open pleasure taken at the old-line pols' trouncing of the darling of the suburban good-government types; in the chants of "Dump the Duke," which had a distinct echo of the bitter divisiveness caused just four years earlier by court-ordered busing in Boston.

It is clear that King rallied voters with particular interests far better than the Dukakis campaign realized at the time. Among them were opponents of abortion; supporters of capital punishment, an increase in the drinking age, and mandatory sentences for drug pushers; and tax minimalists, who, stimulated by the passage of California's Proposition 13 on June 6, bought King's incredible—and ultimately hollow—pledge to roll back property taxes by $1.3 billion in three years.

Most voters, though, were not motivated by these issues. They didn't know King nearly as well as they did Dukakis. Even more than in most such elections, the vote was a referendum on the incumbent—a rejection of the stewardship that Dukakis felt so good about. Some voters were angry enough to want Dukakis punished by banishment from his office. Others were simply annoyed; never thinking that he might actually lose, they stayed home or voted Republican or threw a vote to Ackermann in order to send him a message.

Dukakis lost much of his 1974 base in the 1978 primary. Many human services advocates, for instance, were still so upset over the 1975 budget cuts that they worked on other issues, bypass-ing the gubernatorial election. Also, there was a return of ethnic voting in 1978; many of the predominantly Irish precincts that had picked Dukakis over Quinn in 1974 now turned around and voted strongly for King. And the vote seemed to repudiate one of the centerpieces of the Dukakis administration: the urban strategy. Though Dukakis had skewed the state government's role heavily in favor of downtown urban areas, thirty cities voted against him; he won only nine. Even Pittsfield, for whose resi-dents he had taken a decisive stand against suburban retailers, went for King. Worst of all, so did Lowell, the old mill city whose rebirth was one of the emblems of the urban strategy and which had a large Greek population, besides.

With the benefit of nine years of hindsight, Dukakis's own view is that his loss resulted from a number of factors: "Some people were angry about taxes, other people didn't like my style. I think there was an interesting sense that I was going to win it and they wanted to give me a message. And I was the subject of a long and consistently negative campaign and I wasn't going to respond. No question, King and his people in a very skillful way took three or four key issues and went at them and at them, and at them, and I was doing nothing to respond or combat it or counteract it in any way . . . You just can't sit there and take it, you've got to deal with it."

While these factors no doubt contributed to the loss, at root Dukakis was defeated by his own overweening pride and the missed opportunities it bred. He failed to communicate his own successes as governor, believing—naively and arrogantly—that the merits of his work would reveal themselves to voters.

On primary night, Patrick J. "Sonny" McDonough, a veteran member of the Governor's Council, said that Dukakis's loss "doesn't surprise me at all. You can't spit in people's faces. And that's what he's been doing, spitting in people's faces. Oh, he's an arrogant one, he is."

The defeat was not only a political rebuff but a personal rejec-tion as well. True, voters saw him as honest and efficient, but too many also considered him self-righteous, unfeeling, conde-scending. He never laughed or cried. He never bled—or if he did he never showed it. He had also been—in his term as governor—a bad political strategist and tactician, unskilled in the profession in which he had paradoxically advanced so far. This was unfathomable, for Dukakis had always been a very good politician. He had proved it with the results of his campaigns for state representative, by securing the nomination for lieutenant governor, and by his election as governor in the first place. But he was unable to bring the acumen that had helped get him elected to the business of governing. His interest was in the programs and policies that made up a government. All the while, though, he neglected the personal negotiation so essential to political life. Not long after the election, Andy Sutcliffe said that the governor "definitely recognizes his shortcomings. He knows that being governor means being a governmental leader and being a political leader. He knows that he was a disaster in the second."

This all took some time for those around Dukakis to realize. Following the defeat, there was a clamor among a handful of his staff and supporters for him to run as an Independent candidate in November. Within twenty-four to forty-eight hours, the pressure to mount a sticker campaign began. Michael Widmer, who was assistant chief secretary to Dukakis, said that hundreds of people thought the primary result was basically a mistake and that it could be rectified quickly. After the initial rush of excitement, however, it became clear to Dukakis and those around him that such an effort was doomed. Dukakis didn't want to risk another loss so soon, but perhaps more important, as he told Paul Brountas, he desperately needed time to think about what had happened to him and why. Brountas was among those pushing the sticker campaign. "He listened to it all," Brountas recalls, "and said, 'No. I'm a Democrat, and I lost.' He was able to look at it far more objectively than we were."

At noon on January 4, 1979, Michael Dukakis left the State House quietly, a beaten man. "I was hurting," he says. "I really thought I had blown that election. I was very upset with myself for having done so . . . I wasn't really feeling good about myself."

Yet he was able to take some solace from the fact that the state government he turned over to King was in better condition than the one he had inherited. Dukakis's legacy had some impressive aspects. As he left office, he said simply, "I tried to provide leadership and the best and most honest government we could possibly have." In many respects, he succeeded. He left behind a budget surplus, and he took with him an unsullied reputation as a man who had run a notably principled government. His hallmark was, and remained, honesty.

But he also left state government amid jeers from the business community and a sniping, sometimes hateful legislature. If business people were happy to see a man they considered hostile to their professions and overeager to regulate them leave the governorship, more than a few politicians were ecstatic to see a holier-than-thou colleague suffer defeat. The sentiment of some politicians was reflected in a comment from Executive Councilor Joseph Langone, as Dukakis attempted to win confirmation of his final nominations to the state bench on his last day in office. Langone said bitterly that Dukakis "shouldn't get nothing."

That day, Michael Dukakis suspected his political career was over. "I doubted very much that I would run for political office again," he says. "I didn't think it was likely . . . You rarely get a second chance in this business . . . I got beaten and another guy came in, and I kind of assumed if he did a half-decent job it would be very difficult to beat him."

Even after Dukakis had been out of office for nearly a year and a half, it was clear he did not yet subscribe to the notion that his problems had sprung from pride or arrogance.

"People are so burdened and troubled by inflation, the cost of energy, skyrocketing costs of housing, and so many other things," he said in an interview, "that no incumbent, no matter how strong he's perceived to be or no matter how hard he's working his job, can take anything for granted . . . I certainly think that, in retrospect, was a major problem in 1978. There just wasn't a sense of urgency or an appreciation of the fact that early poll numbers or public perceptions will not last very long unless an incumbent governor or anyone else runs a full-scale campaign which has to include, in this day and age, extensive media advertising as well as extensive organization. I'm not an isolated example of this problem, obviously."

He still didn't get it. He still did not understand that he had lost largely because of himself, that he had been his own worst political enemy. But the lesson would come soon enough, and when it did, it would be the most important lesson he had ever learned. He would come to see, according to his intimates, that he needed to humble himself as he never had before in his life. Paul Brountas says that after he had worked the defeat through "he realized that thousands of people . . . thought him cocky and arrogant. He learned a degree of humility."

Nick Zervas says Dukakis took full responsibility on himself: "He didn't blame anybody else. It took him quite a while to get through the tremendous pain and humiliation and guilt. He felt he'd let people down." Zervas called the defeat "the single most influential thing that ever happened" to Dukakis. Meaney has a similar view: "It is the single greatest event that makes it possible [for him] to be a candidate for president of the United States." Richard E. Neustadt, the presidential scholar and a friend of Dukakis, agreed. So crucial was this period in his life that, in an article in the *Economist,* Neustadt compared Dukakis's loss to King with Franklin Delano Roosevelt's polio as a chastening and character-building preparation for leadership.

If he had been a man who cared about the trappings of public office Dukakis would surely have been depressed by his decision to move to a teaching position at the John F. Kennedy School of Government at Harvard. The man who had presided over sixty thousand–plus state employees, whose lobby was filled each day with people eagerly awaiting a few minutes with the state's leader, was now assigned to a glorified cubbyhole. He biked to work each morning, clipping his pant leg to avoid getting his trousers caught in the chain. Some days he arrived with a brown bag. Like everyone else, he waited in line at the school cafeteria. But the asceticism suited Dukakis. It was also appropriate for the time, since he had come to this place to teach and mingle with the best and brightest students and teachers of government and politics.

Dukakis quickly found himself surrounded by like-minded students and faculty whose lives were dedicated to the public sector. These were not corporate lawyers and lobbyists who peddled the most sought-after product in Washington and all state capitals—influence. This place was different, purer in a sense, for those who pursued power here—for the most part, anyway—seemed propelled by motives loftier than greed. Dukakis discovered that while the classes he taught were demanding, requiring long hours of preparation, he still found time to reflect, to consider what had happened to him and why. He wondered about the perception of arrogance. He questioned his own ambition.

His moving to the Kennedy School had by no means been a foregone conclusion, although he had thought, years before taking the job there, that he might like to teach at some point: "I had kind of decided back in '73, when I decided to run for the governorship, that whatever I did I probably wouldn't go back to practicing law . . . I just decided that, win or lose in '74, I was probably going to do something else, and I always had this notion in the back of my head that I might want to teach public policy, so when I got defeated I went to three, or four, or five of the major schools in the Boston area . . . I think I talked to Northeastern and BU and MIT and maybe Tufts, just kind of exploring. And it just so happened, fortunately, that the Kennedy School had begun to think very seriously about taking state and local government and management a lot more seriously, and I walked in.

"Now there were real concerns about another politician coming in. This wasn't a Kennedy fellow thing. I mean, I was talking and they were talking about a faculty appointment and a full teaching load and taking responsibility for major expansion of the state and local program and the senior executive program for senior state and local managers . . . They had some reservations about another guy coming in off the street from a political background. But they seemed to be interested and were good enough to bring me in."

By the spring he was himself again, he says, but he began to feel good only after months of mental anguish. "For the first few months you kind of rerun the race a million times. I mean, how could I have been so stupid to do this and do that and not do this, and what could I have been thinking of? Then, after a while, you get tired of rerunning the race, and it's time to get on with your life." Even as difficult and painful as his first few months out of office were, Michael Dukakis, true to his lifelong form, never doubted his own abilities. "I'm always a guy that has had a fair degree of confidence," he says, characteristically.

Still, his ego was battered, and it would have been soothed some had the Kennedy School deans implored him to join them. Had they said, Your blend of wisdom and practical experience is precisely what we need on our faculty, it might have restored a bit of the pride King had taken away. But they did no such thing. His move, in fact, was far from automatic—on either end. Dukakis had his own doubts about what to do. The Kennedy School had a reputation in some quarters as a warehouse for defeated candidates. And not everyone in the school's administration and faculty felt they would be exactly blessed by this visitation.

"There were some people who didn't think Michael was that smart," says Ira Jackson, then an associate dean at the Kennedy School. "They said, 'What has he written? Has he had an original thought?' " For some, his past academic achievements were not impressive. Thomas C. Schelling, Littauer Professor of Political Economy and one of the most venerated members of the faculty, said there was no blanket opposition to "an active politician using his off-season at the Kennedy School." The worry, he said, "and I shared in it, was that a defeated politician who had not had time to think or to write anything would probably teach in an exceedingly anecdotal way, and run out of anecdotes before the semester was up."

The proposal to give Dukakis a faculty appointment as lecturer in public policy ignited a smoldering feud in the school between the academics and the practitioners. "There was a real debate over whether he was an appropriate faculty member," says Hale Champion, who was in Washington at the time but returned a year later to become the school's executive dean. Of the skeptics, Champion says he responded, "They're crazy. He's a good politician and smarter than many of them, though I didn't tell them that." In the end, he says, it was the new Kennedy School dean, Graham T. Allison, Jr., who "carried the day" on the appointment.

Allison says that, in addition to the new emphasis on state and local government, "one thing we wanted to do was to take elective politics seriously." On top of this, two or three interviews convinced Allison that Dukakis wanted to work, not just decompress. "I became persuaded it was a very high-risk venture, but something we should do," he says. "I was a new dean and wanted it to happen."

So it did. Dukakis, however, was unsure of his own ability. Before going to the Kennedy School, says his wife, "he was very concerned about whether he could teach, and I said, 'I know you can teach. I've done it. You're going to be great.'" But it was far from easy. "The toughest job I ever had was trying to turn myself into a reasonably decent teacher," Dukakis says. "Teaching ain't easy, as one discovers, especially when teaching graduate students, most of whom are experienced government managers."

The two tasks facing Dukakis in January 1979—one academic, the other therapeutic—started out as distinct from each other, but soon began to merge. Dukakis taught a course concerning the role of chief political executives, drawing on cases already prepared for other courses and on his own experience. In addition to his classroom work, Dukakis was assigned the task of developing a program in intergovernmental studies.

At the same time, he had to deal with defeat. "He was reflective about it, but he didn't pick at the wound very much," Champion says. According to Jackson, "The greatest fear [of those opposing his appointment] was that he would just come over and pontificate that what he did was right." Instead, according to Champion, he sought to learn from his teaching. "The great advantage of the Kennedy School was that he could be reflective in a context—he could look at what other states were doing and at academic theory." "It's very much of a real world," Dukakis said at the time. "There's nothing ivory towerish about what's going on over here."

It was not all pleasant, however. Lawrence S. DiCara, a Boston lawyer and former city councilor who worked with Dukakis at the Kennedy School, recalls that when Dukakis first arrived, he was often stared at as a kind of curiosity. And there was whispering, which he could not have failed to notice. Dukakis and DiCara, who had been defeated in the Democratic primary for state treasurer, shared the pain of having lost recently. "It's really like a death in the family," he says. "It was that way with Michael. It's tough to confront someone after something like that. After 'How are you doing?' what do you say? People would try to avoid him . . . There is a fear factor in stepping out on the street the next day after a loss. He had had this three-and-a-half-month wake at the State House. Imagine if you've been humiliated. *Humiliated!* And you want to go back out there." Even with a loving family, which Dukakis had, there is, DiCara believes, "a mental sense of loneliness."

Though the voters' rejection of Dukakis might have inflicted many people with a fundamental self-doubt, none was visible in the way he handled his courses. Case studies that were purposely written to pose ambiguous situations with alternative approaches were taught by Dukakis as if there *was* a correct answer. "That's close," Dukakis would tell a student suggesting another possibility. "You've almost got it." Champion says this is a trait of teachers who have been managers. "We don't teach the cases the way they were intended to be taught," he says. "We're not saying it's the right answer; we're saying it's *our* answer."

Graham Allison has another view: that teaching the cases helped Dukakis learn something important about himself. "In the first term or two, he didn't get very good ratings in his teaching. He was in the bottom third in his course evaluations, some of which contained revealing comments. Many of them were favorable and noted with appreciation Dukakis's characteristic thoroughness in preparing his classes. He was variously described as an "excellent," "outstanding," and "first-rate" teacher. Said one: "Especially valuable were his personal experiences as chief exec in Massachusetts—there is no substitute for hands-on experience."

But a theme that ran throughout the evaluations was that Dukakis was a poor listener, not receptive to views differing from his own. Another said, "A consistent criticism of Dukakis's teaching style is that he pushed a 'right' solution to case problems and did not encourage or entertain much dissent." One student commented that "I occasionally felt that no other contradictory views would be strongly considered," while another stated that Dukakis "sometimes doesn't listen to people's comments and questions as carefully as he should."

Dukakis visited Allison at one point and said, " 'Maybe this is not going to work out.' " Allison says he pointed out to Dukakis that teaching was the life work of most of the other faculty members. "Imagine if you came in here and were in the top third right away, how would all these others feel?" As it developed, says Allison, "the fact that he didn't succeed immediately was a good thing for him. It taught him to listen. He got progressively better, understanding that it wasn't enough just to tell the answer. You need to consider the issues with some curiosity of mind. Sometimes you even change your mind. I think this was a very big thing for him."

Agreeing with that view from a unique perspective is John P. DeVillars, who took Dukakis's course in 1980–81 and later became his chief of operations, a job just below that of chief secretary, at the State House. When Dukakis first began teaching, DeVillars says, "there was not a lot of ambiguity in the last ten minutes of each class." By the end of the year, however, he "had a far more open mind as to the merits of alternative approaches." A constant theme, he says, was Dukakis's newfound determination "to open up the governmental process, to broaden out the participation in policymaking to include legislators, business, labor, and the rest."

Dukakis taught a course in the management of state and local government, which became very popular, then overcrowded. When Schelling talked to him about it, he quickly agreed to split it into two sections. Schelling was impressed. "There was no salary break involved," Schelling says. "He was simply doubling his workload. There aren't many academics who voluntarily increase their work." Ira Jackson says Dukakis turned out to be "a great citizen of the Kennedy School, available for every task, accessible to any student—and he also knew his place."

Dukakis was not politically inactive during his time at the Kennedy School, although he was careful about his involvement. Regular rumors out of Washington throughout much of 1979 had Dukakis being considered as a candidate for the Carter cabinet, specifically as secretary of the new Department of Energy. In May, he accepted a part-time appointment to the National Commission on Employment Policy, a nine-member body established to advise the president and Congress on employment and job training issues.

But in July, Dukakis squashed reports that he was in line to replace Secretary of Energy James Schlesinger. Still, it was clear that he was well thought of by the White House, that the president had a particular fondness for him. In the 1980 presidential campaign, however, Dukakis, though he admired the president and Vice-President Mondale, hedged against the day when he himself might again run for office in Massachusetts and endorsed Senator Kennedy's challenge to Carter. Carter is said to have been hurt by Dukakis's choice. Mondale says now, "It was more or less expected that Michael would have to go with Kennedy, but he didn't do much about it; that was noted, too."

Generally, Dukakis sidestepped any open involvement in state politics. He steadfastly avoided criticizing King publicly, even long after many political observers had declared the governor a bumbling incompetent. He watched, with a degree of pain, as King discarded some of his most cherished initiatives. "A lot of things he had done were being dismantled," Kitty says.

As time wore on, King demonstrated a remarkable lack of skill. Some of his early appointments proved to be hugely embarrassing. One man King named to his cabinet was found to have falsified his résumé. He was dismissed. Another man whom King appointed a commissioner resigned after allegations were made that he had previously misused union funds. Still another appointee, King's insurance commissioner, resigned after it was revealed he had ties to a man convicted of insurance fraud.

One of the most damaging revelations about King came in November 1979, barely eleven months after he'd taken office, and concerned the meals, first-class travel, dry cleaning, and other expenses he charged to the state. The juiciest aspect of the reports concerned King's lobster salad, which he occasionally ate for lunch in his office. The lobster story, originally published by the *Globe,* was based on expense records released as a result of a Freedom of Information request and made King appear to be a lavish spender of the taxpayers' money. It dogged King for the rest of his term and set him in sharp contrast to Dukakis and his more frugal tastes. The story was interesting for its negative effect on King, but what makes it far more noteworthy is that the original source of the story was Dukakis's office in exile.

Even as he worked at the Kennedy School, Dukakis had a small office in Boston and a staff member, Andy Sutcliffe, to take care of his modest political business. Sutcliffe, now an advertising executive in Seattle, says that one of his main objectives during this period was to alert reporters to stories that might embarrass King. After learning of King's expenses from a Dukakis administration holdover who had access to state records, Sutcliffe went to the *Globe*'s top State House reporter, Walter V. Robinson, who obtained records by filing a Freedom of Information request. As promised, the records showed, among other things, that King had spent $1291 in state money for cleaning his clothes and those of the state troopers who guarded him; $17,000-plus for travel; $1209 for lobster and crab salad sandwiches for lunch with his aides; and $7000 for restaurant meals with his aides and troopers.

Dukakis has since decried what he terms negative campaigning, most notably in the 1987 flap over his staff's videotape of Senator Joseph R. Biden, Jr. Back in 1979, he was apparently pleased with Sutcliffe's efforts. Sutcliffe says Dukakis was well aware of his activities on the lobster story. "He thought it was an incredibly arrogant use of public funds," Sutcliffe recalls, adding that it was his impression that Dukakis "thought it was kind of neat that we had the story, and couldn't wait to see it in print."

Dukakis's celebrated memory fails him on this matter. "I don't remember this lobster story," he says. "I mean, I remember the *story,*" but he says he remembers nothing about his office having anything to do with getting it into the press. "I remember a story in the paper about it and I remember reporters asking for records, as you often do. I mean, people stroll in and say, 'Give me all the records' . . . That must happen twice a year around here."

Reminded that his staff man, Sutcliffe, was the key player in getting the story to the public, Dukakis says, "Well, I don't remember that. I mean, it may have happened. I may have known at the time. It's a long time ago."

King's popularity plummeted after the lobster incident and he became something of a laughingstock. During his early days in office, King was not just a bumbler who seemed unable to do anything right, he also began to alienate the party in whose primary he'd been nominated. While Dukakis had been one of Carter's favorite governors, Reagan declared King his favorite Democratic governor. An indication of King's right-leaning style came during a speech he gave in March 1979, when in his inimitable meat-and-potatoes fashion, he bluntly told a group of automobile dealers: "I believe in automobiles and highways and nuclear power."

Under Dukakis, the governor's Commission on the Status of Women fought the chief executive each year over his recommendations for the state's human services budget. The commission would review the budget and send a letter to Dukakis criticizing it. A give-and-take would ensue. The first year of King's administration the same scenario was set in motion, but when the group sent a letter criticizing King's decision to eliminate cost-of-living increases for welfare families, the governor responded by firing the entire commission.

King had portrayed himself as a "can do" manager, but even his ability to manage, which had been demonstrated when he ran the Massachusetts Port Authority, abandoned him in the governor's office. Not only couldn't he get the trains to run on time, at one point he couldn't get them to run at all. As a result of a financial crisis at the MBTA, the whole Boston rapid transit network, the entire system, shut down for twenty-six and a half hours in the heart of the Christmas shopping season, on December 6, 1980.

Barely a month before, Massachusetts voters had shouted a loud "no confidence" in their public officials by passing Proposition 2½. On its face, the referendum put into law much of what King had been talking about in the 1978 campaign—cutting taxes, especially property taxes. But King was unable to make Proposition 2½ work to his advantage either while it was being debated or after it was passed.

The public frustrations that burst open with Proposition 2½ were part of a national phenomenon. Not only had Proposition 13 passed in California two years earlier, but similar movements sprang up in other states, and Ronald Reagan won the White House partly on his commitment to cut taxes. Reagan even triumphed in the Democratic stronghold of Massachusetts in 1980, carried to victory by voters who were simultaneously approving Proposition 2½. The problems specific to Massachusetts had been building for years. The state's traditionally high tax burden was increased significantly by the tax increases enacted under Dukakis in 1975. But the state's reputation as "Taxachusetts" was based primarily on the exorbitant property taxes levied by the cities and towns. Because of strictures in the state constitution, municipalities in Massachusetts had only three significant sources of revenue, apart from whatever federal grants were available from year to year. The three were an automobile excise tax, which produced relatively flat amounts; state aid, called "local aid" in Massachusetts, which depended on the mood of the governor and legislature in a given year; and—the only one local officials could control—the property tax. By the late 1970s, Massachusetts by some measures had the second highest property taxes in the nation (behind Alaska). Dukakis's remark that Massachusetts voters would never approve a version of Proposition 13 was based in part on his own determination to cut property taxes. But he was not immediately successful. In 1978, Dukakis and the legislature sent a windfall of local aid to Boston, with express instructions that it be applied to the property tax. Dukakis's former running mate, Boston's Mayor Kevin White, ignored the instructions, and spent every dollar. Dukakis's efforts were ineffectual as the city's tax rate remained unchanged.

King, running on his tax-cutting platform, took Dukakis's job a few months later and began to grapple with budgetary realities. Using the surplus he had inherited and a determination to slash local expenditures and some state programs, King could claim after one year to have produced about half of the $500 million in property tax cuts he had pledged in the campaign. In

1980, however, King provided virtually no increase in local aid. Rather than rolling property taxes back by another $400 million, as he had pledged, King thereby precipitated the largest one-year increase in the state's history. And the bills went out just a few weeks before Proposition 2½ was on the ballot. In addition, state legislators made it clear they would not support radical proposals: when Proposition 2½ came before the House as a bill in May, it was defeated by 146 to 5.

The voters, though, couldn't wait. When Proposition 2½ came before them on November 4, they approved it by 59 to 41 percent.

In some respects, the new law was more sweeping than its California predecessor. When it took effect in 1981, cities and towns would be barred from setting property tax rates higher than 2½ percent of full valuation. Those communities already higher, like Boston and most of the state's thirty-eight other cities, were required to reduce their rates by 15 percent per year until they were within the limit. In addition, auto excise rates were cut from $66 to $25 per $1000 of valuation. Fiscal autonomy for local school committees and binding arbitration on police and fire union contracts—then prevalent in most communities—were abolished. And renters were allowed a deduction on the state income tax.

To even its most ardent supporters, however, Proposition 2½ and the strong vote that passed it had less to do with taxes than with confidence in government. Barbara Anderson, the executive director of Citizens for Limited Taxation, the lead group in the effort, said, "People didn't vote for 2½ because of the money, they voted for it because of the attitude." She said voters "were fed up with the arrogance. That was bothering people a lot more than the tax burden."

Thomas R. Kiley, a poll-taker and partner in the Boston firm of Marttila & Kiley, said his surveys indicated that "Proposition 2½ was about politics as much as it was about taxes . . . It really was a revolutionary event in the state's politics. It had a major effect. There's a lot less arrogance and a lot more respect for little-"d" democracy among leaders of the state since that event. And there's more accountability." Kiley thinks Dukakis, in particular, learned some lessons from its passage, and Ralph White-head, Jr., a professor at the University of Massachusetts, thinks other Democrats did, too. "It has forced the Democrats to adopt a new strategy for addressing public problems," Whitehead said, "and the strategy is using your head rather than reaching instinctively for your wallet."

Proposition 2½ has continued to be controversial since it took effect. Some analysts say it had a critical role in stimulating the state economy, while others, including Ferguson and Ladd, say the impact was marginal on an economy that was already vigorous. Without question, however, Proposition 2½ helped cut the overall tax burden from well above the national average to well below.

As a committed tax-cutter, at least rhetorically, King would have been a logical leader of the 1980 tax revolt, but he failed to capitalize on it. While Dukakis openly opposed Proposition 2½, King did not take a public position, though he said afterward he had voted for it. His tight-fisted local aid policy had helped push taxes up in 1980, and he made matters worse the following year by failing to recommend the increased state aid for the cities and towns that even the most committed supporters of Proposition 2½ said was needed to implement it effectively. As it had in 1975, the legislature took control of the issue, appropriating some four times what King had recommended.

King's administration had liberals in particular thinking warmly of his predecessor. As it turned out, King accomplished what Dukakis could not: he made Dukakis look good.

On November 6, 1979, Dukakis's father died. Panos Dukakis was eighty-three years old and had failed markedly during the final six months of his extraordinary life.

"My dad had been an iron man until he was eighty-one or eighty-two," Dukakis says. "He'd have one sick day a year. He'd come home in the afternoon feeling lousy and go to sleep . . . Every year he'd have one of these days—and he'd sleep through the night and the following morning he'd be up and out of the house at seven, going to the hospital to see his patients." As he aged, though, "he began slowing down a bit. His driving became erratic, and I remember getting a call from a pharmacist who was a little worried about him. He had called him on a prescription and he was concerned he didn't quite remember everything. So he retired at eighty-two, and from that point on he began having these headaches, which, as it turned out, were small strokes. And each one left him a little more disabled and very dependent on my mother, to the point where, in the last six or eight months of his life at least, she couldn't leave him for five minutes without him calling her. When that happens and it goes on for many months . . . As you watch somebody who has just been getting weaker and weaker and older and older going downhill, there's a kind of relief you have for him or for her. He just wasn't the same person . . . He had lived such a wonderful life, practiced medicine for fifty-two years. But it was just a long, slow process. It was sad to watch, in a way. We were all very supportive and were as helpful as we possibly could be."

The Kennedy School, meanwhile, was having a calming influence on Dukakis. Now the sound of lessons learned could be heard in what he said. In February 1980, nearly a year and a half after he'd been beaten, Dukakis said during an interview that he was "more relaxed. I think I'm more reflective . . . I think I'm more sensitive. For example, I think one of the complaints and one of the serious concerns that people had with me and my administration in my first year or two was that we were making all kinds of cuts, particularly in human services programs, which I'm afraid had to be made under the circumstances because the state was in such a terrible financial difficulty . . . I hated to make them and I was bleeding a lot internally, but I think you have to be able to communicate that sensitivity and that concern a lot better than I did during my first year or two. I don't mean as a matter of public relations, I mean simply as a human being who's being called upon to make some decisions which are really abhorrent to them philosophically and which circumstances compel them to make. I think, were I to do it over again, I'd be a lot more aware of the necessity for expressing that kind of concern and sensitivity more than I did."

It was questionable, though, whether Dukakis was a changed man in a fundamental sense. He would, during the next three years, lose some of the cocksureness that grated on people, and he would learn to listen and to consult others before acting.

After a while, his innate optimism was fully restored. His ambition never flagged. He was driven to be the very best at whatever he was doing, and if he was to teach, then by God, he wanted to be the very best teacher at Harvard University!

On the question of whether he had changed as a result of his loss to King, it was his mother who put it best: "He didn't change as far as I could see. It's just that he learned."

John Sasso stood on the platform at South Station in Boston four days after Dukakis lost to King and was amazed to see the defeated governor walking toward him. Sasso was the manager of the tax classification campaign that year, a referendum intended to amend the state constitution to allow communities to tax commercial property at a higher rate than residential property. The issue would be put to a vote in November, and, to kick off the post-primary campaign, Sasso had organized a whistle-stop train trip. Mayors of cities throughout the state were the driving force behind the effort, and the train was packed with them as well as union officials, elderly activists, and others. Sasso had long before invited Dukakis to join the group—assuming, of course, that the governor would be in the flush of a primary victory. Now Sasso assumed Dukakis, whom he had never met, would not make the trip, but when he saw the governor walking along the platform toward the train he was struck by Dukakis's resilience. In Sasso's mind, it took some guts for Dukakis to come out after such a humiliating loss. Sasso liked that. He wondered briefly about Dukakis's future, but he suspected the truth, that "the man on that platform at South Station didn't know whether he would ever be in public life again."

Dukakis saw something there as well. He saw the energy that many politicians and activists were putting into Sasso's referendum drive, and he knew that these were supporters who should have been working in his campaign had he not let them slip away.

Sasso didn't see Dukakis again until nearly two years later, at the 1980 Democratic National Convention in New York. Sasso was thirty-three at the time and had worked as a field organizer for Ted Kennedy in seven different primary states that year.

During a break in the proceedings, Sasso spotted Dukakis and went over to say hello. He immediately told Dukakis that under King, Massachusetts was "going cuckoo." He asked whether Dukakis was thinking of running. Dukakis said he didn't know. He said he was enjoying the Kennedy School greatly, that he'd had a very good two years there. Nonetheless, he said that when they were both back in Boston that fall he would like to sit down with Sasso and talk politics.

After the convention, with Carter renominated, Sasso returned to his job as manager of Congressman Gerry Studds's district office. In September, Dukakis called Sasso and invited him to lunch at the Kennedy School cafeteria.

"I'm seriously considering running again," Sasso recalls Dukakis saying over lunch. Dukakis said he intended to make a decision within a couple of months. It was clear he had a lot to think about. Dukakis quizzed Sasso closely about the tax classification campaign. He was fascinated by the details, and he listened intently as Sasso explained how the campaign—which was ultimately successful—had been put together. Dukakis said he thought it had been a terrific coalition—the mayors' association, the AFL-CIO, senior citizens, human services groups, the archdiocese of Boston, and advocates for women, minorities, teachers, and environmentalists.

Toward the end of their conversation, Dukakis asked whether Sasso would help if he were to run again. Sasso said he would. He said he thought people regretted what had happened in 1978. About a month later, Dukakis invited Sasso and his wife, Francine, to Perry Street. It was a chance for the Sassos and Kitty to meet.

During the same time period Sasso was offered the job of running Kennedy's re-election campaign in 1982. He felt a sense of loyalty to the senator, but thought that Kennedy would win with ease and that the campaign wouldn't be the least bit challenging. Sasso said no, hoping to be offered the job with Dukakis.

Soon after Thanksgiving, Dukakis called Sasso and asked him to come to the tiny office near the State House where he kept his political files. When Sasso arrived, he saw what was left of the former governor's political organization—"a few card files and a crummy old list of contributors from '78." Dukakis was there with Paul Brountas. They chatted for a while, and Dukakis told Sasso that he intended to send out a newsletter to his list of supporters telling them he was planning to run again for governor. He asked if Sasso would run the campaign. Sasso said he would like to think about it and discuss it with his wife. Fine, Dukakis said, but he wanted an answer soon. Within the week Sasso was at Dukakis's Kennedy School office saying he would do it.

Dukakis was pleased. He and Sasso sat down and had their longest conversation to date. Dukakis talked about how poorly King was performing. He questioned the administration's integrity, wondered about the quality of King's people, and said he believed King was badly mismanaging the MBTA.

He said that they had to "put the Democratic coalition together and raise as much money as Ed King." He asked Sasso detailed questions about how they would find staff, a pollster, a media consultant, and whether they would use computers. It was plain that Dukakis knew that if he was to take the governor's office back from King, he would have to run a campaign using the most sophisticated techniques available.

But the most critical thing he said that day—a conviction without which he would almost surely not be in public life today— concerned not campaign techniques but himself. He told Sasso that he had to be a first-rate candidate, and that meant a different approach from '78. He said that he had to "find a way to say to people 'I hear ya. I know what you were saying in '78. It was my fault. I've learned from that and it's gonna be different this time. I made a mistake.' "

Instead of being seen as condescending and arrogant, Dukakis would be a sensitive listener. Rather than apolitical and sanctimonious, he would become an inside player, a loyal political friend.

"We talked for a couple of hours," Sasso says. "He was upbeat. There was a real sense of determination."

Dukakis was eager for Sasso to start right away, although Sasso didn't see any need to begin full-time until the following summer. They compromised and Sasso started on April 1, but before that he spent many evenings and weekends meeting with people, often at Dukakis's home. Dukakis's first request was that Sasso draft a budget. By Christmas, Sasso gave him a detailed spending plan for the next two years, totaling $2.5 million.

"That's a lot of money," Dukakis said, "but I think we can raise it."

The union of Dukakis and Sasso marked the beginning of Dukakis's new political career. His determination to shed his past righteousness was half of what he needed to succeed politically. In John Sasso, he found the other half.

From the time Dukakis sent out the newsletter announcing his intention to run until shortly before the 1982 gubernatorial primary—a period of more than eighteen months—he was blessed with remarkably good fortune: Sasso signed on; King seemed to bungle everything he touched; and a cloud of corruption settled over the state. On top of it all, Dukakis improved his political style. Events beyond his control, principally the fiscal crisis, had damaged him politically eight years earlier, but now it seemed the political gods would do their best to make it up to him. His greatest bit of fortune was King's performance as governor. If King had done even passably well, been even moderately popular with the voters, the chances are that Dukakis would never have challenged him and would be today a quiet lecturer at the Kennedy School.

As Dukakis moved back into the world of real politics, his first task was to try and shape the field of candidates competing for the nomination. He and Sasso believed that he simply could not beat King in anything but a one-on-one campaign; three or more candidates would scatter the anti-King vote and ensure the incumbent's renomination. In spite of widespread fears of that scenario, a number of other politicians were interested in making the race. The two most serious possibilities were Frank Bellotti, the attorney general, and Tom O'Neill, who was still lieutenant governor, rather uncomfortably, under King. Both Bellotti and O'Neill were friends of Dukakis's—perhaps not intimates, but political friends at least. A good measure of Dukakis's ambition was his statement long before the race started that he would have no problem running against a friend. He'd been through it in 1970, he pointed out, when he beat Beryl Cohen for the Democratic nomination for lieutenant governor. And he'd competed with another friend, former Congressman Michael J. Harrington, when both men were interested in running either for governor or attorney general, in 1974.

The most serious threat to Dukakis was Bellotti, a seasoned, popular attorney general who had the advantages of a fat political bank account and the capacity to raise a great deal more money quickly. But Bellotti was cautious. He had challenged an incumbent Democratic governor once before—Endicott Peabody in 1964—and although he won the nomination he was so bloodied from the primary fight that he lost to the Republican John Volpe in the general election. Many of Bellotti's closest supporters wanted him to run against King, but the man himself wasn't so sure. For one thing, he loved being attorney general. For another, he had no interest in running against Dukakis, whom he liked and respected. Dukakis early on visited Bellotti to find out whether he planned to run for governor or re-election. Bellotti wasn't coy. He said that as long as Dukakis was running for governor, he, Bellotti, would not. A relieved Dukakis went to work on O'Neill, hoping he, too, would choose not to run.

But all of the talk by Dukakis and his emissaries only made O'Neill more determined to make the race. He was unshakable. He believed he could win, believed he *would* win, and he refused to yield simply so that Dukakis could have a clean shot at King. Dukakis had had his chance and he had blown it, O'Neill's people argued. Now it was their man's turn; he had earned it.

That O'Neill would eventually get out was certainly in Sasso's mind early on. The question was not whether, but when. He was sure O'Neill would not get past the Democratic nominating convention. The Dukakis organization would see to that.

To try to minimize O'Neill's effect on the campaign, Dukakis's advertising man, Dan Payne, devised a theme for the primary, calling it "The Rematch," a slogan the Dukakis people used over and over again. When it was originally proposed, Dukakis immediately liked it, but others in the campaign weren't so sure. Some people felt that the slogan might open old wounds, but

Dukakis overruled any objections. The notion was to treat O'Neill as an afterthought. The Dukakis camp tried to portray the campaign as something akin to a title fight between two bitter foes. Implicit in the message was that there was no room for a third fighter in the ring.

O'Neill's decision to run was about the only bad break Dukakis got as the 1982 race approached. The polls looked particularly promising. A January 1980 poll conducted for the CBS-TV affiliate in Boston, Channel 7, showed that more than half (56 percent) of those surveyed in the greater Boston area believed Dukakis had done a better job as governor than King. A February poll conducted for the *Globe* found that Democrats and Independents statewide preferred Dukakis over King by three to one. When voters were asked which of the two men they would prefer if a Democratic primary were held that day, Dukakis led by an incredible forty points (60 percent to 20 percent). The extent of King's trouble within his own party was reflected in numbers showing the incumbent more popular among Republicans than Democrats, the very voters he would need to win renomination. Another *Globe* survey conducted in October 1980, two years before the primary, showed Dukakis to have a remarkable level of popularity. The poll indicated that more than four of every five persons surveyed who had an opinion of Dukakis held him in high esteem. King, in contrast, was viewed unfavorably by seven of nine voters surveyed who had an opinion of him. While 74 percent of those surveyed said they liked Dukakis, nearly the same number, 71 percent, said they didn't like King.

There were other, smaller signs of encouragement for Dukakis. In June 1980, at a fund-raiser intended to collect money to keep his political office open, he received $45,000, double what he'd taken in the previous year. More than that, though, was a difference in atmosphere. The previous year's fund-raiser, Andy Sutcliffe said at the time, was a bow to the past. "This time, however," he said, "a lot of people were there for the future, not the past."

And soon after the October *Globe* poll was published, Dukakis appeared at a dedication ceremony for a Harvard Community Health Plan center in Kenmore Square. Speaking briefly, Dukakis allowed that he hoped to be back in the governor's office one day. His words were greeted with a stomping ovation. A group of his supporters showed what was on their minds when they formed a softball team. They called themselves the Exiles, and on every player's jersey was the number 82. Particularly heartening to Dukakis was the response he received from the December 1980 newsletter he mailed to supporters announcing his intention to run again. In return, he received notes and phone calls pledging support and far more money than he had expected.

Meanwhile, throughout 1980 a well-publicized investigation by a special state commission documented wrongdoing in the award of architectural and construction contracts on state and county buildings. John William Ward, a tough-minded scholar and former president of Amherst College, chaired the commission, which had been established in 1978 by Dukakis and the legislative leaders to look into political corruption in Massachusetts. Its final report found that, for many years, Massachusetts had been "for sale," that contracts had been awarded because of payoffs or favoritism during the administrations of Governors Peabody, Volpe, and Sargent. Further, it said that design contracts awarded during King's tenure as head of the Massachusetts Port Authority appeared to have been subject to "favoritism and influence."

This was Dukakis's kind of issue, recalling his 1966 charges that campaign contributors to Volpe had been "paid off handsomely" with design contracts.

The most dramatic moment of testimony came in May 1980, when William V. Masiello, who by his own admission had paid numerous bribes to politicians to get state contracts, said the system had been rotten until Dukakis was elected governor. Masiello, the commission's star witness, testified that the "open hand" of public officials who took cash payoffs closed when Dukakis took office in 1975.

"I hate to give him an endorsement, because if any one man destroyed me, it was Governor Dukakis," Masiello said. "When he came in there were no open hands. And the game was over. And you had four good years, and what did Dukakis get for it?

He got kicked out . . . the people of Massachusetts deserve what they get."

The audience burst into applause.

As 1981 approached, "The Rematch" was on. The Dukakis fund-raising operation, led by Robert A. Farmer, got off to a very fast start. From the beginning, Farmer proved an adept money man. He was a successful businessman who had, in his first political fund-raising effort, collected a great deal of money for John Anderson's presidential campaign. Sasso and Dukakis had held meetings with some of the country's leading media people. And in an important step, both real and symbolic, Dukakis made peace with Barney Frank.

By early 1981, Dukakis was building a solid organization. It proved its strength in April, when the Democratic party held an issues convention in Springfield. Dukakis rallied his supporters in an effort to win a platform that reflected his beliefs more than King's. But more important than the issues themselves was the contest between King and Dukakis. When Dukakis won nearly every important vote at the convention—including a fight over King's proposal to reduce the significance of the convention in the 1982 state election—it proved a huge embarrassment to the Democratic governor and motivated Dukakis's workers.

At the same time, Dukakis was also attacking King. In a newsletter to supporters shortly before the issues convention, he wrote that "the failures of the present state administration are so serious and widespread, I feel a responsibility as a citizen, a former governor, and a candidate for governor to speak out." He said that he had been campaigning across the state and found great dissatisfaction with King. "Time and again," he wrote, "they characterize the King administration with words such as 'bungling,' 'inept,' 'lousy appointments,' 'out of touch with the average guy.' They almost always mention 'the mess at the MBTA.'" Dukakis stated that he had long "declined to comment publicly on the failures of the King Administration," but that "the time for grace periods is over.

"This, then," he wrote, "is the beginning . . ."

7. Rematch

---

*"You . . . have given me something that
one rarely gets in American politics—
and that is a second chance."*

I T *was* the beginning of one of the most successful periods in Michael Dukakis's political career. Just as the 1978 campaign had been a reflection of his disdainful blindness to how the people of his state felt toward him, his 1982 campaign was a reflection of his fervent determination to avenge his earlier humiliation. At the heart of Dukakis's success in 1982 was a well-plotted strategy that he laid out with Sasso and a handful of other advisers. It was an approach marked by caution, for Sasso was convinced that Dukakis's lead was large enough so that if he worked hard and avoided serious mistakes he would win. This new caution, read by critics as timidity or lack of political courage and by supporters as a determination to set achievable goals, grew throughout 1982 and became a central theme of Dukakis's progress toward the national scene. His caution during his second term along with his desire to build coalitions stood in sharp contrast to his singularly prideful and self-contained style during his first term.

The strategy was straightforward. First, Dukakis would try to make the election a referendum on *his* issues, competence and integrity, and to use those issues to keep King on the defensive. Second, he would work to recruit a vast grass-roots organization that would not only help win the nominating convention, but also—in a new campaign technique—serve as the core of his fund-raising operation. And third, the campaign's sine qua non was to be a new approach from the candidate himself. He was chastened. He would be a humbler man, who had learned to listen. The self-reliant boy who had said *"monos mou"* would now be the man whose watchword was "coalition."

On January 11, 1982, when he formally announced his candidacy, Dukakis said that if he was elected governor, Massachusetts's government would be founded on "integrity, competence, compassion, and effectiveness." Throughout his career, Dukakis's hallmark has been his reputation for unquestioned integrity, and that reputation was the most critical element of his campaign. So crucial was this quality that without it, he surely would have been defeated in 1982. That he was coldly unforgiving of public corruption stood in stark contrast to the breaking scandals within the King administration. It stood in relief, as well, to King's own attitude toward corruption. King was not perceived by voters as personally dishonest, but rather as not vigilant in preventing corruption.

A key example of Dukakis's determination to stay on the attack was his effort to tie corruption to the tax issue in order to counter King's criticism of Dukakis for signing a 7½ percent income tax surtax during his first term. King called it "the Dukakis surtax," and rare was the day that he did not remind voters of it. In response, Dukakis tried to convince the voters that corruption in government, like taxes, cost them money. One Dukakis radio commercial claimed the state had a serious tax problem that King "never talks about. The corruption tax . . . Corruption is the worst kind of tax because you pay and pay and get nothing in return. You won't find the corruption tax on your tax form, but you pay it every year. The Ward Commission says corrupt politicians have taken billions from Massachusetts taxpayers."

Dukakis was aided in this approach by bizarre scandals in the heat of the campaign as well as by the findings of the Ward Commission, which criticized King's lack of cooperation with their investigation. The commission claimed that King had slowed its work and in the final report stated that by early February of 1979, it "had heard nothing from the governor concerning its funding since almost a month before, other than a public statement by King that in his view the request was not an emergency and therefore didn't belong in a deficiency budget."

Dukakis promised voters both a new substantive direction for the state and a stylistic change as well. He alluded to the "painful lessons" he'd learned, and signaled his new style by peppering his announcement speech with personal anecdotes intended to present himself as warmer and less aloof.

Throughout the campaign, a relaxed, unflappable Michael Dukakis talked repeatedly of having made mistakes in 1978; he said over and over again that he had learned the hard way how to become a good listener. Rather than lecture voters in a humorless, rigid style, Dukakis chatted informally, spicing his talks with humor, much of it aimed at himself. "I thought he was terrific," said Hilda Friedland, of the Jamaica Plain section of Boston, after listening to his pitch one night during April 1982. "I never thought he had that much charisma. I could have listened to him all night."

"I am a lot more sensitive to the political side of things," he said during an interview at the time. "The defeat had a lot to do with it. Defeat wonderfully concentrates the mind."

In staking out his campaign turf, Dukakis was mindful of his opponent's strengths, summarized in King's theme, which was repeated throughout the campaign: On the issues you, the voters, care most about, Michael Dukakis disagrees with you and Ed King agrees with you. King's major advantages were on the issues of taxes and crime. Voters saw Dukakis as a man who had raised taxes, King as a man who had cut them. They perceived King as tough on crime, Dukakis as weak. Dukakis knew that King would win the votes of people whose sole or primary interest was crime or taxes, but he was unwilling to concede both issues. "Is there anyone," Dukakis asked in a speech, "who thinks . . . that all the political hot air on crime coming out of the governor's office these days is making us more secure in our daily lives?" Throughout the campaign, Dukakis ridiculed King's rhetoric, repeatedly claiming that violent crime had escalated 30 percent during King's tenure.

Dukakis's frequent talk about crime was important, his handlers believed, not to beat King on the substance of the issue, but to avoid getting outmuscled on the issue. Against a tough-talking former professional football player, Dukakis needed to talk tough, act tough, and *be* tough if he was to avoid being portrayed as a wimp. One TV ad showed Dukakis talking from the door of a police cruiser. Significantly, his first major policy proposal during the campaign was on crime, and its centerpiece was the politically appealing proposal of increasing the number of police officers in the state by seven hundred and fifty.

Dukakis followed a similar approach on taxes. He skillfully embraced Proposition 2½, defining it not as a tax issue but as a management challenge. During his first term, he had scoffed at the notion that Massachusetts voters would ever catch Proposition 13 anti-tax fever, and he had explicitly opposed Proposition 2½. Now that it had been passed, with 59 percent of the vote in a 1980 referendum, Dukakis would try to convince voters that whether one had supported or opposed the measure was irrelevant; the question now was who had the administrative ability to implement it. He sought to head off any comments about his raising taxes by stating during his announcement speech that "the most important single thing we have to do is make Proposition 2½ work." He outmaneuvered King on the issue by pledging a more generous increase in state financial aid to the cities and towns than King had offered.

Dukakis's campaign was simply and intelligently conceived, but it was far from perfectly executed. Its press operation lacked speed and imagination, and its primary campaign advertising was uninspired. Nonetheless, it was founded on a sound basic belief—that a safe, conservative campaign would win. What it lacked in communication skill it made up in superior field organization, fund-raising, and luck. The fact that his opponent was weak and unpopular was crucial, and Dukakis stayed on the attack for nearly the entire campaign.

When the year began, Dukakis's political abilities were a question mark. Could he put together the sort of first-rate effort that would be required to beat King, improving on the considerable skills he had demonstrated in 1974, or would he run the same sort of lackluster operation he had in 1978? The first test came at some six hundred Democratic caucuses, held to select delegates to the Democratic endorsing convention in May. It was in its lengthy and painstaking preparations for the caucuses that Dukakis's campaign produced a significant political innovation. Traditionally, fund-raising and field organization are separate and distinct within political campaigns. Dukakis aimed to blend the two, using the field organization as an important source of fund-raising, and it worked superbly. The theory, proposed by John Marttila, a Boston political consultant who advised Dukakis as a volunteer, was that people willing to give money would have a vested interest in working hard for the campaign. And the emotional nature of the Dukakis-King rematch provided whatever added incentive was needed to mobilize an army of Dukakis workers. In his original memo, Marttila suggested a 1981 goal of recruiting ten thousand contributors, people who would also serve as the organization's backbone. The campaign met its goal and by midsummer of 1982 had doubled it, to twenty thousand donors. Although King was popular in the business community and was considered to have unlimited fund-raising potential, Dukakis attracted more money in 1981, $879,203 to $711,330.

The Dukakis organization not only raised money, it also delivered convention delegates in spectacular fashion. Sasso had been putting the organization together for a solid year, aiming all the while toward the statewide February caucuses. This was Dukakis's first major test, and he passed in high style, winning the caucuses in a landslide: he garnered twice as many delegates as King and O'Neill *combined*. More than 68 percent of the 3270 delegates were pledged to Dukakis (2230). King won 32 percent (1034), O'Neill less than 1 percent (6 delegates).

"I think it's a pretty powerful statement about this administration when you have [68] percent of people voting against the sitting Democratic governor," Dukakis said the following day. "It says something about people's feelings about the kind of state government they have been getting."

Dukakis strategists, still convinced that they had to face King one-on-one, were quietly just as happy at O'Neill's poor showing as they were at Dukakis's margin over King.

The Dukakis organization could help its man in many ways,

but not during a debate. There, he was alone. Dukakis, King, and O'Neill had agreed to appear together in a live televised debate a month before the Democratic convention. Anticipation of the event created palpable tension within the campaign. There were already more than four years of bad blood between King and Dukakis, each of whom was openly contemptuous of the other and what he stood for. Although O'Neill's poor performance at the caucuses left him far short of the number of delegates he would have needed to get his name on the primary ballot, he too raised the campaign temperature. Under the party rules engineered by Dukakis, any candidate failing to get 15 percent of the vote on at least one convention ballot was barred from entering the primary. But the televised debate gave O'Neill one last opportunity to take his case to the public and, possibly, get into the contest. His goal was to present himself as a fresh alternative to his two better-known competitors. King went into the debate aiming to convey a very simple message: voters wanting a tax cut should choose him. Dukakis's message was also simple: the state was under a cloud of corruption, and King had done nothing to disperse it.

Sasso recalls that as the debate approached, his candidate grew increasingly intense. Dukakis had watched a tape of his debate with King four years earlier, and saw that he had been far too passive. Dukakis is by nature not confrontational, but his dogged determination can overcome that; he can take a very tough approach if he decides it is necessary. This time Dukakis would be the aggressor and put King on the defensive. But even Sasso was surprised by the level of intensity Dukakis displayed. Moments before the debate, as the three contenders stood behind their podiums going through a microphone check, O'Neill and King, in turn, began the customary count to ten. When it was Dukakis's turn, rather than counting, he looked grim and said, "Crime went up 30 percent in the last three years."

From the outset, Dukakis and King were at each other's throat. This really was the beginning of "The Rematch." On wit, intellect, and debating skill, Dukakis dominated. King had always been considered a political tough guy, but on this night Dukakis was the aggressor, charging that the man King had appointed as his secretary of transportation "is not behind his desk, but behind bars." Dukakis was referring to Barry M. Locke, who had been convicted of conspiracy to commit bribery and larceny and became the highest-ranking state official ever imprisoned. Dukakis charged King with "stonewalling" the Ward Commission proposals and asserted that "the central issue of this campaign is honesty in government."

King attempted to counter Dukakis on the corruption issue, charging that while Dukakis was governor, a scandal in the state's vocational education programs resulted in the conviction of nineteen persons. The most dramatic moment of the debate—and of the campaign—came next. Clearly furious, Dukakis turned toward King, pivoting away from the camera. He jabbed his finger at King as he sternly warned: "I hope this is the last time we hear about the so-called voke-ed scandal. I wish you'd get the facts. That guy was appointed in the previous administration by the board of education. Frank Bellotti and I found out he was stealing and we put him in jail."

Dukakis was pleased with his performance. But far better than the general view that he had decisively beaten King was the news two weeks later that O'Neill was withdrawing from the race. His decision was dictated in some measure by his inability to raise enough campaign money (he was $120,000 in debt at the time) and by his poor showing in the polls. Most important, though, O'Neill did not have enough delegates to win the 15 percent of the convention required to get his name on the primary ballot. His departure spared Dukakis's having to fight over the 15 percent and turned the convention into a coronation.

On May 22, Dukakis won the endorsement over King by the nearly two-to-one ratio the February caucuses had presaged. This victory by a challenger to a sitting governor was overwhelming. "We put together a force that is too large, too diverse, and too strong to be stopped—today, in September, or in November," Dukakis said as the delegates roared their approval. And his attack on King did not let up, even in the flush of the convention victory. He told the delegates that "we must make state government an honest agent of the public trust, a state government that isn't an embarrassment, a state government that we can be proud of once again."

The four months until the primary would be nothing but unadulterated, toe-to-toe combat between two bitter adversaries. "The Rematch" continued.

The campaign was going so well that Dukakis felt compelled to warn his supporters against overconfidence. Expressions of such concern from a politician leading in the polls by twenty, thirty— even an absurd forty-eight points in one survey—would ordinarily be dismissed as posturing. But Dukakis's history made his concern believable. He told reporters immediately after winning the convention that he was "forever wary after what happened in 1978."

And with good reason. For in spite of Dukakis's dominance over King in every survey during the first half of 1982, there were clear indications that this would be no runaway; that somehow, before it was over, King would make a race of it. "From our earliest polls we saw that King would come back, but we knew he would have trouble getting to 50 percent because of his high negative" poll rating, Sasso recalls. "And we knew King would win if it was a three-person field. We knew King was going to get close. He had too much going for him on a whole range of issues people cared about—he was tough on crime, he cut taxes." Sasso believed King would reach, at a minimum, 40 percent, but he never thought King could get the 50.1 percent he would need to win a two-way race. Dukakis and Sasso always believed King would charge at the end, although they had a difficult time convincing the news media and even a few of their own supporters. It seems remarkable in view of 1978, but the danger of overconfidence did exist.

King knew he had an enormous amount of ground to make up and, in June, he sought to undermine Dukakis's basic strategy by trying to portray the so-called new Dukakis as a sham, accusing him of being the same arrogant man he'd always been. King sought as well to portray Dukakis as a wimp by needling him about his wife.

"Mr. Glib, the man who seemingly knows everything," is how King characterized Dukakis during a speech to labor union supporters. Calling Dukakis "arrogant," he said "that glibness and arrogance have to be dealt with." He also ridiculed Dukakis's practice of going home each night at six for dinner with his family. "He had to take the five o'clock [subway] train home from Park Street every day. And you know what happened when he did not get home on time," King said, rolling his eyes. The union officials—overwhelmingly male—roared with laughter.

King also took to branding Dukakis as "the worst governor in the history of the commonwealth" on tax and economic issues. He attacked Dukakis on crime as well, and as the summer wore on he spoke of Dukakis as "the newfound crime fighter." He said Dukakis talked a good game about his anti-crime plans should he win election, but "you have to ask him the question, 'What did you do anti-crime when you were in office?' The answer is nothing, absolutely nothing." King criticized Dukakis for vetoing bills that would have made the death penalty legal in Massachusetts, raised the drinking age, and established mandatory sentences for drug pushers.

As King was attacking, both in his campaign speeches and, more important, in his blizzard of radio and television commercials, Dukakis's campaign was making mistakes. The first came in late June, when a television commercial was shown in which, in a man-in-the-street format, a young man said to Dukakis, "You've got to make it. You've got to make it. We've got to get rid of that son of a bitch." The word *bitch* was bleeped out of the spot, but it was nonetheless clear what the man had said. Dukakis said the spot was aired by mistake, and his campaign officials pledged not to use it again.

The second error came to light in mid-July and concerned the creation by a Dukakis supporter of a tape recording using parts of a King radio commercial in which King's wife, Jody, talked about how her husband had helped her overcome polio. King's staff learned about the tape from a *Globe* reporter, and King sharply criticized the tape as referring to his wife "in a very derogatory and tasteless manner." He said in a letter to Dukakis that he had been informed that the tape "parodies my relationship with my wife and demeans my wife's struggle with polio." The Dukakis campaign volunteer apologized for making what came to be known as the "sex tape," and Sasso, who had played it for two reporters, offered to resign, but Dukakis said no. King, however, continued to talk about the matter and even made a radio commercial about it.

The incident embarrassed Dukakis and gave King an issue on which he had clearly been wronged and which allowed him to press the attack against Dukakis. Neither of the two errors was crippling, but each one cut against Dukakis's reputation for absolute integrity and uprightness, making him appear haughty and spiteful, and chipped into his lead.

The truth, though, was that Ed King was snakebitten in 1982. Certainly much of what occurred that year was his fault, but other events, even those for which he was indirectly responsible, were bad luck of a remarkable sort. As August approached, King's chief strategist, Edward J. Reilly, began to believe that their worst days were behind them; a King poll showed him trailing by only eight points. Whatever the margin, the trend was clear—King was closing in, and Reilly believed their communications plans for the final forty-five days would be good enough to win the race. But as soon as it seemed King was about to sprint forward, he would find himself shoved back on the defensive, usually by events beyond his control or Dukakis's.

For King, it was bad enough that Barry Locke, one of his closest advisers and a man he had appointed to his cabinet, had been sentenced on February 17 to serve seven to ten years in prison. Locke's arrival at state prison on March 19 attracted an enormous amount of publicity. Dukakis said little, preferring to let the news reports work in his favor. King might well have hoped that the Locke case was the last damaging incidence of corruption.

But on June 24, a Revenue Department employee from Lawrence named Stanley J. Barczak was arrested by state police "in the act of bribery," according to state investigators. Barczak, sixty-two years old, was a low-level employee whose job was to chase down delinquent taxpayers—owners of small businesses, for the most part—and try to collect the money owed. Barczak was arrested at the Parker House Hotel in Boston while accepting a bribe from a businessman who owed the state taxes. No sooner had Barczak been put in a police car and driven the few blocks to the state office building housing the attorney general's office than he began telling the troopers about other cases of bribery committed by himself and other officials in the department. It was clear from the start that Barczak wanted to please the prosecutors, and his arrest triggered an investigation into alleged corruption within the tax agency. A grand jury began looking into the possibility that Revenue Department employees had settled cases with delinquent taxpayers in return for payoffs. Soon after the arrest, King was again embarrassed when it was revealed that Barczak, hired under the King administration as a tax examiner, had served time in prison in 1953 after having been convicted of tax fraud in Pennsylvania.

It got worse for King when it was learned that Barczak, who had worked as a volunteer in King's 1978 campaign, was carrying King campaign bumper stickers at the time of his arrest. What's more, he had been hired by John J. Coady, a friend of King's who had been promoted to the position of deputy commissioner of the department. Coady was a thirty-one-year veteran of the department and his new job placed him in charge of all district tax-collecting offices, one of the most sensitive positions in the department. King and Coady had been friends since they had gone to Boston College High School, where they both played on the baseball team. King was shaken when he was told on July 21 by the first assistant attorney general, Thomas R. Kiley, that his friend Coady was a subject of the grand jury investigation.

Nine days later, John Coady, fifty-five years old, went up into the attic of his North Andover home. He scrawled a brief note to his wife on a piece of graph paper, and smoked a number of cigarettes. Then he put a rope over a rafter and hanged himself. Late that afternoon, one of Coady's sons discovered the body. A medical examiner estimated that Coady had died at about one or two P.M. When the news of Coady's death broke, King seemed all but finished. But Ed King would not go down easily.

While King's barrage on television continued—he eventually spent $2 million on media alone—Dukakis responded with a half-million-dollar television campaign of his own. It was designed to keep voters focused on the issues that constituted Dukakis's political strengths, and thus to keep Dukakis in the lead for the final six weeks of the campaign. One of his commercials, a five-minute presentation, sought to portray the post-1978 Dukakis as a man of compassion, competence, and humility. It showed Dukakis speaking with a group of young children in a classroom. Asked by one of them if he was hurt by his loss in 1978, he said it had been a "very painful experience. Yet at the same time, out of defeat, sometimes you learn some things and you're a better person . . . I was mostly disappointed in myself because I really felt that I had blown that election. I had really lost it."

Another, rather dramatic advertisement, which made no mention of the campaign, was about crime touching his family. Dukakis stood alone against a white background wearing a dark suit. He spoke intensely about a seventy-eight-year-old doctor who had been bound, gagged, and robbed in his office in the middle of the afternoon. He spoke as well of a young man struck by a hit-and-run driver and left in the street to die. In a poignant moment, Dukakis revealed that he was speaking about his own father, his own brother: "I know what it feels like when crime touches my family. I want to be sure it does not touch yours."

In another commercial, Dukakis put sentiment aside. It began airing on August 19 and had him denouncing "corruption and cronyism" in King's administration. The next day Dukakis outlined the specifics of his plan against corruption. He also referred directly to the Revenue Department scandal, asking, "Why was Mr. Barczak hired in the first place? Why was a man convicted of tax fraud in another state hired as a tax examiner in our state? What kind of judgment allows the most sensitive agency in state government to be used as a dumping ground for political cronies?"

In spite of Dukakis's efforts and King's appointees' misfortunes, the gap continued to narrow. And it might have narrowed even more had King shown up for a debate scheduled just two weeks before the primary. But King backed out at the last minute, thus giving up an opportunity to go after Dukakis on live television before a huge audience. King's handlers made the move because they feared Dukakis would win. They recalled the April debate, in which Reilly said King had "performed very poorly." Reilly believed King could win without the debate, and he was unwilling to risk placing his candidate in a "very uncontrolled, highly visible one hour of television."

By late August some polls indicated that Dukakis led by twenty or so points, but others showed a closer race—and one indicated it was much closer. Six days before the primary came news of a poll that electrified the state. On September 8, James Hosker, who polled for the state treasurer, Robert Crane, completed a survey that showed King and Dukakis running dead even. Sasso immediately challenged the numbers, agreeing that the race was "close but not that close." He maintained that the Dukakis in-house polls showed his man with a twelve-to-fifteen-point lead.

But the story was Hosker's reading that the race was essentially tied, that Dukakis's huge lead had been wiped out. To the Dukakis people it all seemed rather eerie and more than a little foreboding. Some Dukakis partisans felt a sense of déjà vu as they recalled the polls' predicting throughout 1978 that Dukakis would win and the sickening reality of primary night. Could it be that the horror was to be repeated?

Ironically, it soon became clear that the Hosker poll so frightened Dukakis's vast organization that any possibility of their being complacent was eliminated. On primary day, Dukakis's people all but stormed polling places throughout the state, and Michael Dukakis had, at long last, sweet revenge, defeating Edward King by 631,911 to 549,335. The key was the massive turnout. An exit poll for the NBC affiliate in Boston, Channel 4, showed that one in five persons who said they voted for Dukakis in 1982 said they had not voted at all in the 1978 primary.

As Dukakis stood before his supporters at the Park Plaza Hotel in Boston on September 14, the crowd in a state of near pandemonium with people crying and hugging, he said, "You . . . have given me something that one rarely gets in American politics—and that is a second chance."

Dukakis went on to win the general election in a landslide against John W. Sears, an intelligent man with the misfortune of carrying the standard of the most pathetic state Republican party in the nation. Dukakis was criticized by Republicans for waging a somnolent campaign, in which his strategy was to do and say as little as possible. But after the fierceness of the primary fight, the voters had little stomach for more political violence that fall. On Tuesday, November 2, Dukakis defeated Sears by nearly two to one.

Some politicians were not impressed with Dukakis's comeback. Their view was that he had beaten an unpopular, vulnerable incumbent and made the race a lot closer than it should have been. The criticism was that Dukakis's campaign had been lifeless, far too safe. And there was a bit of truth to that notion; indeed, the risk of playing things too conservatively was acknowledged in the Dukakis strategy. "From the very beginning we felt we had the upper hand," says Sasso, conceding that the campaign had "a little too much of a tendency to hang on."

Still, it was a winning strategy. A central reason for Dukakis's victory was that the Democratic primary voters regarded integrity and competence—Dukakis's issues—as more important than a candidate's position on taxes and crime—King's issues.

Dukakis's field organization played a major role, for it not only raised and contributed much of the $3.4 million that Dukakis collected, it also helped swell the primary day turnout by more than 300,000 voters over the 1978 count. King actually received 107,000 votes more in 1982 than he had in 1978, but Dukakis boosted his vote by 266,000—an increase of an astounding 75 percent. More than 30,000 persons either gave money to Dukakis or actively worked for his election. So large was the Dukakis field organization that one poll-taker found that 60 percent of Dukakis's primary voters had been contacted by his people during the previous forty-eight hours. That translates to the organization's reaching more than 350,000 voters in two days.

Rather than discuss the reasons he had lost, King continued to talk about differences on issues between himself and Dukakis. "We disagree on many issues," King said a few days after the 1982 primary. "That disagreement was one of the reasons I became involved in elective politics in the first place." King listed abortion as one of the more important issues upon which he differed with Dukakis. "I have been particularly troubled," he said, that Dukakis lacked "the strong personal commitment to the pro-life movement which I have. I regard that as a prerequisite for my personal involvement in any campaign." In spite of their differences, however, King said he would vote for Dukakis, though he would not work for his election.

Reilly, King's man, believes that ultimately Dukakis won the election because of King's weaknesses. "Ed King's own negatives beat Ed King, not Dukakis's positives: the résumé problems, lobster problems, Barry Locke, Coady's suicide, being Ronald Reagan's favorite Democratic governor, and Proposition 2½ chaos."

The corruption issue hurt King badly. The Revenue Department scandal that had been prompted by Barczak's arrest was bad enough. Coady's suicide exacerbated the situation.

All of these factors played a part in Dukakis's victory, but the single most important element was the new approach adopted by the candidate himself. The aloof, arrogant man of 1978, who depended on himself for so much and who was unaware of his own blind spots, had become seasoned, more down-to-earth, and now reached out for help through consensus and coalition. Thus was Michael Dukakis resurrected.

8. Redemption

*"Intellectually, he's learned a good lesson.
Whether he's changed internally,
I don't know."*

THE RESURRECTION OF Michael Dukakis in 1982 began a period of sustained political success that lasted for years. It was a time rich with change and activity in his life: a time when he took firm and unquestioned control of the state government and the Democratic party in Massachusetts; a time of unparalleled economic prosperity in the state; a time when he spread the stories of two successful Massachusetts programs across the nation, and, in so doing, became a player on the national political stage.

Most significant, the new term marked the beginning of the government of a new Dukakis, a man who would operate with a far more accommodating, practical style. He had learned that politics truly was the art of the possible and that was how he would practice it. This government by consensus was facilitated by John Sasso, who was becoming the closest working partner ever in Dukakis's political life.

During Dukakis's first term—commonly known in Massachusetts as "Duke I," the second term as "Duke II"—cabinet meetings were open to the press and public; as a result, they became showcases and little was accomplished. At the outset of "Duke II," the governor sent a signal that he meant to do the state's business, not bow to goo-goo liberalism. Cabinet meetings were private.

In Dukakis's second term, says Kevin Harrington, the former Senate president, the governor "had totally, totally changed. The governorship of Michael Dukakis from 1983 to 1986 was a success in large measure because he did the exact opposite of what he'd done in the first term." Harrington's characterization goes too far, but it sketches the outlines of a new Dukakis, or at least a new Dukakis *style*. As though symbolic of what was to come, the terms began in dramatically different fashion. Whereas Dukakis started his first term with a meat cleaver aimed at social service budgets, he began the second term with an urgent cry for help on behalf of the homeless.

During the first month of his new term, Dukakis described himself as "older and wiser," and others agreed. His first year back was a particularly productive one. He pushed through laws limiting condominium conversions and requiring companies to notify employees working with toxic chemicals—the "right to know" bill. He also approved increased welfare benefits and won passage of a plant-closing law, which provided for retraining of laid-off workers. He increased state aid to cities and towns, and he managed to get his budgets through the legislature with many fewer changes than had been customary. The year also ended with Dukakis's popularity soaring: in the governor's own polls, seven of every ten Massachusetts voters surveyed said they believed he was doing a good job.

"He's had an incredible year, absolutely totally different from his first term," said Charles Flaherty, the House majority leader at the time.

Insiders saw a markedly more cautious, deliberate, and politically savvy governor than they had known in "Duke I." This showed most clearly in his attitudes toward patronage, the legislature, and the business community.

The man who had characterized patronage as "a cancer" on state government that "must be destroyed" installed one of his most trusted aides, Nicholas T. Mitropoulos, as head of his personnel operation for "Duke II." During the first year, the vast majority of Dukakis's appointments went through this office, where campaign workers were given first consideration. So dramatic was the turnaround that Harrington said in August 1983 that "Dukakis has raised patronage to a fine art." Frank Sargent said, "Some of the things he criticized me for he's doing—and *better* than I did, like patronage."

The most obvious sign that he had abandoned his earlier objections to patronage came just four months into his term, when it was announced that the celebrated lottery system for distributing state summer jobs—used during the first term to avoid patronage—had been abandoned. At the same time, Mitropoulos said that the summer jobs program would be run out of his office and that political considerations would indeed be important. "Legislators will be used as key referrals and sponsors," he said at the time, but he added that political connections would be only one factor. He would also consider affirmative action and candidates' qualifications, saying that "we need lifeguards who can pass all their tests."

Dukakis rationalized his changed view by claiming that, in retrospect, it had been "manipulated politically." That was a rather different characterization from the one he offered in 1977, that the lottery "exceeded our hopes, eliminating political favoritism and allowing all young people an equal chance to be hired. In fact, it has become a model for other states to copy."

Dukakis was criticized, by Republicans mainly, for playing the age-old Beacon Hill patronage game, working within the system he had self-righteously condemned as a young reformer. But there were defenders of the practice as well. Judy Meredith, a lobbyist for social service groups, said the operation was "a very efficient system" that "put together a lot of extraordinarily talented people [from] the campaign, many of them professional bureaucrats."

Sasso says a significant step was Dukakis's appointment of Louis Nickinello, a former House member and close friend of the House leadership's. Nickinello had experience on transportation issues, having been House chairman of the legislature's transportation committee. Nonetheless, the appointment took many lawmakers by surprise, inasmuch as Dukakis had fired Nickinello, a King supporter, from the position of executive director of Massport soon after taking office. But in an effort to close the schism between the Dukakis and King wings of the Democratic party, Dukakis appointed Nickinello to a key position at the state Department of Public Works.

"It meant an enormous amount to [House Speaker Thomas] McGee and [Majority Leader George] Keverian that we appointed Nickinello," says Sasso. "The expectations for Michael were so low that just a few strategically placed appointments sent the signals that this guy wants a partnership here."

When the chairman of the House Committee on Ways and Means, Representative Michael C. Creedon, was informed of Dukakis's new personnel policy, he said, "That is the new Mike Dukakis. I like it. I like it better every day."

This change was seen as dramatic by other politicians, but Dukakis doesn't share that view. "I think what has changed for me is my sense of what makes for a good public servant, public official . . . I look for people who are honest, able, and intelligent and have good political skills. One of the things I learned in my first administration is, people can be very intelligent, very thoughtful, very honest, and so on, but if they don't have political skills in the best sense of the word, if they can't work with the legislature, if they can't work with the press, if they can't work with constituencies, then they aren't going to be very effective."

Marty Linsky, Dukakis's former Brookline colleague, says that in his first term, legislators were prepared to jump through hoops for the new governor, but Dukakis "wouldn't even hold up the hoops."

The second term was different, and the groundwork for better dealings with the House in particular started even before the election. One important gesture came during the primary, when Dukakis offered to hold a fund-raising party for Speaker McGee's political committee. During the first term, McGee couldn't stand to be in the same room with Dukakis, but the speaker, surprised by Dukakis's gesture and pleased at the prospect of additional funds to distribute to House candidates of his choosing, was delighted. As it turned out, Dukakis's finance people put together a successful party at the Parker House that raised about $25,000 for McGee's committee. A King supporter,

McGee said that night that he would support whoever won the primary. It was a signal from McGee to Democratic regulars that his feelings toward Dukakis had thawed.

Dukakis also made sure that he ate a bit of humble pie within sight of the lawmakers. He did just that during a meeting of delegates to the National Conference of State Legislatures in Boston in March 1983. "The failure to bring the legislature into the process of policy-making, in my opinion, is the most serious problem of chief executives, including this one," said Dukakis. His first term, he added, had been characterized by "arrogance and cockiness" toward the legislature. They were mistakes, he vowed, he would not make again.

One index of Dukakis's performance was that during his first term, he vetoed thirty-five bills and was overridden by the legislature twenty-three times. During his second term he vetoed just one bill and was overridden.

Another mark of the new Dukakis was his improved communication with the business community. During his first month back in office, he went to a chamber of commerce executive club luncheon in Boston and delivered a conciliatory speech that impressed his audience. Most reassuring was the absence of the go-it-alone, superior rhetoric he'd once used. After the speech, Kenneth R. Rossano, a senior official at the Bank of Boston, told a reporter that "much of the business community was not involved" with Dukakis in his first term, whereas "this time, he sees that he really needs true coalitions involving major players." Rossano added, "I think this is one of the lessons he's learned in exile."

Not everybody in business was so supportive at first. In January 1984, Edson D. de Castro, a King supporter and the president of Data General Corporation, one of the state's largest high tech firms, told his company's annual meeting that in the year since Dukakis had taken over, "Massachusetts state government has become much less supportive of economic growth. There is no clear voice within the state administration representing the economic health of the state or the industries that create economic growth." De Castro and some of his colleagues were apprehensive about Dukakis's plant-closing and "right to know" proposals.

Dukakis helped himself with the business community while at the same time broadening his world view when he visited Japan and China in the winter of 1985. During his two-week trip, Dukakis sought greater access to Asian markets for Massachusetts's high technology companies.

By the end of 1986, the midpoint of his second term, Dukakis had even managed to bring de Castro around, prompting the latter's remark: "I guess I'd have to say I'm encouraged. Nineteen eighty-five was a year in which things were moving in the right direction."

To some environmentalists, they were moving too far. The symbolic battleground was Prowse Farm, a fifty-five-acre former horse farm at the foot of Great Blue Hill, just south of Boston. The property abutted Route 128 and had been purchased by the Codex Corporation, a high tech subsidiary of Motorola, for its world headquarters. In his first term, Dukakis wanted to take the site for parkland and fought to secure that right in court. While the suit was pending, the court warned Codex that any construction at the site would be at the company's risk. Nevertheless, Codex poured a foundation and began raising steel—unimpeded by the King administration. In May 1984, however, the state's highest court ruled in favor of Dukakis.

Dukakis wrestled with his victory for a few days and then basically walked away from it. He let Codex complete its massive headquarters. This was the new, pro-business Duke II. He was influenced by the prospect of a future challenger—perhaps Ed King again—running against him with a TV ad showing the hardhats dismantling the building girder by girder. But environmentalists said this rationale only made the decision worse, since it was giving in to a bully. The Friends of Prowse Farm, the group organized to fight Codex, accused Dukakis of "selling out to big business."

By the time his second term was finished, Dukakis had a mixed reputation with environmentalists. Some never forgave him for Prowse Farm or for what they saw as other examples of his caving in to development, including the controversial International Place in downtown Boston. But others credited him with diligence in protecting the coastline, inland wetlands, and other open space, and innovation in protecting Massachusetts's dwindling farmland through the state's purchase of development rights.

The theoretical nucleus of Dukakis's second term—and, indeed, of his approach to politics to this day—is a belief that he can best achieve results by building coalitions. Said the governor in his 1984 State of the State address: "What for me has been so extraordinary about this year is that we have achieved . . . successes not in endless pitched battle both inside and outside this State House but thoughtfully and cooperatively, at the conference table and in the community, in an atmosphere that could scarcely have been imagined eight years ago."

This new style of governance worked well, enabling Dukakis to get many of his major policy initiatives from the legislature. He brought together landlords and tenants, bitter adversaries for years, and negotiated the compromise condo conversion bill. The Senate approved the measure with not a single dissenting vote.

While this new approach was generally successful, it also brought criticism from some who claimed that strong leadership and coalitions are often incompatible. Critics said the new Dukakis almost never took a bold leadership position on issues—at least in his first term, it was easy to tell where he stood. Dukakis and his supporters responded by pointing to the record. Leadership, they said, should be measured by achievement, not by the number of speeches a person makes.

"If I were on the outside, I'd be one of those people who said Dukakis has lost his rudder trying to be all things to all people," said John DeVillars, Dukakis's chief of operations. "Consensus-style politics doesn't generate headlines, but if it works successfully, it can generate results."

Along with Dukakis's caution came a new appetite, never before revealed, for the nitty-gritty of State House politics. The give-and-take he so disdained during his first term he seemed to relish in the second term. "In the first term he often had contempt for the political process and politics, and that's changed," James Segel, head of the Massachusetts Municipal Association and a former state representative, said at the time. Speaker Keverian said that he was "much easier to work with," adding, "I admire many of the solutions he has been able to achieve by his new method of consensus politics."

Exhibit A of Dukakis's new style was the "right to know" bill. In his first term the governor would probably have filed the bill, offered an argument on its merits, and said, in essence, shame on anyone who opposes it. This time he engaged in four months of intensive bargaining with people representing business, labor, the legislature, and the environment before even proposing the measure. The bill sailed through the House and Senate.

While 1983 was a very good year for Dukakis, 1984 was not. The governor won approval of a massive cleanup effort in Boston Harbor, but only under the gun of a federal court, and he lost on a number of initiatives, including a proposal to consolidate the rebuilding of the state's infrastructure. MassBank, as it was called, was to be funded by new business taxes and, during an election year, lawmakers had no interest in hiking taxes. Mass-Bank, like Dukakis's proposals on gay rights and public-pension reform, went nowhere in the legislature.

But 1985 was his most productive year as governor. Dukakis won the enactment of stiff administrative penalties for Massachusetts "acid rain" polluters. He pushed through a major housing bond issue to help the poor, one of the elements of a housing initiative that his adversary of old, Barney Frank, says may be the best of any state in the country. After months of tugging and negotiating with business and labor, Dukakis fashioned a workers' compensation bill. He helped shepherd a piece of landmark legislation that gave the City of Boston important new sources of revenue. And he signed the repeal of the 7½ percent income tax surtax—the one he had raised in 1975 to help bail the state out of its fiscal crisis.

Perhaps the toughest test of Dukakis's ability to win legislative battles came over a death penalty bill. The proposal, which he ardently opposed, sought to legalize capital punishment for persons convicted of committing certain types of first-degree murders, such as the killing of a police officer. No one had been executed in Massachusetts since 1947, and Dukakis had no interest in ever permitting such killings.

The polls consistently showed that through the years, a solid majority of Massachusetts voters favored a death penalty law. And the lawmakers were determined to give them such a law, one that would pass muster with the state supreme court, which had invalidated two previous statutes. The legislators believed they had struck the right balance with a bill that went to the Senate in the fall of 1985. They hoped to pass the bill quickly and then go back to the House and Senate and find enough votes to override Dukakis's veto.

Dukakis wanted very much not to have to veto the bill. If it was stopped before it reached his desk, he would be able to run for re-election without facing constant harping that he had vetoed capital punishment. Dukakis went to work to head the bill off in the Senate, although his prospects seemed dim, for the Senate had never before turned down a death penalty proposal. But Dukakis now had a decent rapport with the Senate leadership and with many of its forty members, and his arm-twisting and cajoling paid off. On October 2, the Senate defeated the death penalty, 20–18.

One of the critical differences—some would say *the* difference—between Dukakis's terms was the presence in "Duke II" of John Sasso as chief secretary.

Sasso was raised in East Paterson, New Jersey, where his father worked as an electrical engineer and served many terms on the school board. He worked in his father's campaigns—his first taste of politics—and when he went to Boston University he worked as a foot soldier in the antiwar movement. After graduating in 1970 with a degree in political science, Sasso managed rental property for a Brookline real estate development firm and became involved with condominium development on Cape Cod, an area represented in Washington by Congressman Gerry Studds. Sasso was attracted by Studds's antiwar stance, and in 1972 he worked as a volunteer for Studds. Sasso volunteered again at the beginning of the 1974 campaign, and his work was so good he was soon indispensable. "Before very long, it became clear to the campaign manager that this was not the average volunteer," says Studds, who then hired Sasso as his field coordinator. His performance was superb, in Studds's view, and he hired Sasso to manage his district office in New Bedford. Soon, Sasso "knew everyone who was anyone politically in that city," says Studds. "He was fearless . . . He had a great deal of self-confidence. There was no setting or person he would not confront—on the waterfront or in the mayor's office, in a corporate suite or a labor hall—it didn't matter. He had a very strong presence."

Sasso became Studds's chief political operative in the district. After managing Studds's 1976 re-election campaign, he took a leave of absence in 1978 to work for the Massachusetts Mayors Association, running the referendum campaign that first brought him into contact with Dukakis. That campaign was also a success, and by 1980 word of Sasso's abilities had reached Washington. He joined Ted Kennedy's 1980 campaign for the presidency, where he began by heading the field organization in Iowa. Subsequently, he was the state director in Maine, Michigan, and New Jersey. In this campaign, Sasso learned presidential politics from the perspective of a field worker. Four years later, when he took a leave of absence from the Dukakis administration, he learned national politics from the other view—as national manager for Geraldine Ferraro, the vice-presidential nominee, working out of Washington, D.C.

National politics broadened Sasso, but his most notable achievement was managing Dukakis's 1982 comeback campaign, and it established his reputation as an intelligent, methodical strategist who understands communications, organization, and personnel selection.

Sasso's control over the 1982 campaign was substantial, but how much influence he would have in the administration was unclear at the outset. In fact, the governor was not sure that he even wanted Sasso as his chief secretary until he had successfully managed the transition.

At the beginning of the second term, says Thomas Glynn, Dukakis's deputy commissioner of public welfare and a member of Sasso's intimate circle, "John's relationship with Michael and his influence was not what it was at the end. After the election in

'82, Michael's view was that John was the expert in elections and Michael was an expert in government, and running the government was about government." Furthermore, he says, "John had never worked in the State House before."

Nonetheless, Dukakis had enough confidence in Sasso to appoint him his chief secretary. In that position, Sasso demonstrated his true mastery of the political process. At first, it appeared that the man closest to the corner office was Frank T. Keefe, whom Dukakis named secretary of administration and finance, a position referred to as "deputy governor." Keefe was a gifted and able administrator, and Dukakis's confidence in him carried over from the first term, when Keefe ran the Office of State Planning. But Sasso soon emerged on top. He was an exacting taskmaster who never made a move without considering its effect, politically, on Michael Dukakis. Sasso won the respect of legislative leaders, who found him a tough but fair negotiator whose word was reliable. When Sasso bargained, they knew he carried the authority—more than any other administration official—to speak for the governor.

So warm was the rapport that it touched even the formidable Kitty, who called Sasso "one of the most special human beings I have ever met." John Dukakis said that "I always feel with him that he is looking after Mike Dukakis's interest the way we do," becoming so valuable that Sasso had to fight to be allowed to run Ferraro's campaign in 1984.

Sasso became widely respected by national politicians as well as those in Massachusetts. One of his greatest admirers is Governor Mario Cuomo of New York. Even the man Dukakis defeated in 1974, Frank Sargent, who has had some dealings with Sasso on an environmental issue, praises him. "Sasso *made* Dukakis," says Sargent. "He's the most talented cuss I've ever seen in my life . . . a very classy guy."

Former Representative Thomas J. Vallely once called Sasso "the best political insider I've ever met." James Johnson, who managed Walter Mondale's 1984 presidential campaign, says that of all the new people he encountered during that process, the "most outstanding" was Sasso. "He's got enormous good judgment," Johnson said. "He's totally calm under pressure. He's disciplined in a way that's really unusual, and he's a very nice person, to boot. It's all the right combination." Mondale himself said that managing Ferraro's campaign was "in many ways the toughest job" that year. "He had the job of coordinating the campaigns between myself and Ferraro, and setting up staff for her overnight, and launching a national campaign almost within twenty-four hours—and did it."

Dukakis says of Sasso and himself that "we not only work well together, we get along well together . . . He's really superb. He's got a very rare ability . . . I told him once it was genetic—whatever he had it couldn't be learned."

Until Sasso left Dukakis's presidential campaign in October 1987, he seemed indispensable to Dukakis. Jack Corrigan, who has worked closely with both men since 1981, says they get along so well "because their differences are complementary and their similarities mesh well. Both are extremely well organized, systematic, intelligent." As to their complementary differences, he says, "Mike Dukakis gets up in the morning and thinks about good government, and John Sasso gets up in the morning and thinks about politics."

Tom Glynn notes that Sasso and Dukakis "are both detail-oriented, they are both cautious, they are both progressive in their values. They are probably the two best planners in politics. [Sasso] figured out how to get Michael to change his mind. Michael likes to debate, and he's very hard to beat in a debate. But John never debated with Michael. John always understood that the way to help Michael make a decision was to give him more information.

"A strength John has that Michael doesn't is that John is a very good operations manager. John could go to work for General Motors running one of their plants and they would make more money. He's very good at setting goals, recruiting people, holding people accountable."

Corrigan says, "Sasso understood Dukakis. He knows how he thinks. Sasso could predict a lot of what Dukakis's reactions to things would be."

There were others in addition to Keefe and Sasso who played important roles in Dukakis's second term. Two of the other three key players, in fact, had held important jobs during Dukakis's first term. Frederick Salvucci served as secretary of transportation in both terms. Salvucci and Dukakis had been ideological soulmates ever since the mid-1960s, when they worked together to prevent highway expansion. During Dukakis's second term, Salvucci achieved an impressive feat by getting federal approval and dollars to undertake the largest transportation project in the state's history—the depression of Boston's Central Artery and the construction of a new tunnel under Boston Harbor. Evelyn Murphy had been secretary of environmental affairs in Dukakis's first term and had won the governor's respect for her persistence and keen intellect. In the second administration she was given the more challenging position of secretary of economic development, a position from which she eventually ran for and won the job of lieutenant governor. The other notable member of Dukakis's administration had not been with him in the first term—Lieutenant Governor John F. Kerry, a decorated veteran of the Vietnam War whose rhetorical and political skills made him a valued member of the administration. In 1986 Kerry was elected to the U.S. Senate.

Several others played important roles as members of Sasso's select kitchen cabinet that met in his office every Thursday night to discuss political strategy. Ira Jackson, a member of the group, described the sessions as being "a poker game without cards." The other regulars were Tom Glynn, Dan Payne, and Ralph Whitehead.

When the second term began, Sasso was intent on the governor's setting a very limited agenda and ardently working to get it through the legislature. One of the central elements on that list involved work and welfare, a topic Dukakis had been thinking about for many years. During his exile, he spent a good deal of time talking about how to get poor people off welfare and into jobs that would provide them with both dignity and a chance for a financially secure career. It was among the most confounding of all social problems, and more than once during his public life Dukakis had said that "the issue of work and welfare has been often called the Middle East of domestic policy. Everybody talks about it; nobody does anything about it."

Dukakis wanted to change that. During his time at the Kennedy School, he held a series of informal discussions, both at the school and around his kitchen table, on this topic. He was searching for ideas, casting as wide a net as he could, in the hopes of coming up with an approach that might work. It was clear that if he ever did make it back to the governor's office, he would try to do something about the problem.

As Dukakis was talking with academics and administrators who'd worked for him in government, Ed King was implementing the sort of traditional workfare program Dukakis had tried to institute earlier. But King's Work Training Program had a very short life. When Charles Atkins, Dukakis's welfare commissioner, visited the program's Worcester office, he found six welfare mothers sitting around a table with six telephones and six copies of the Yellow Pages. They began at the beginning and dialed businesses, asking for work. They received little counseling, training, or education. The program flopped, and Dukakis disbanded it about a month after returning to office.

The question remained, however: Was there a way to get welfare recipients, principally mothers, off the rolls and into meaningful private jobs? Manuel Carballo, Dukakis's secretary of human services, who died tragically in January 1984 of pneumococcal meningitis at the age of forty-two, was working with a coalition of human service advocacy groups on the subject. One day he handed their leaders the federal guidelines for welfare work programs and told them that if they could come up with something that abided by the rules, he would try it.

The welfare advocates came back to Carballo in May 1983 with a proposal. Carballo turned it over to Atkins, who developed a detailed management plan. By September, Atkins was ready to present it to Dukakis. The governor liked it, but he was cautious. He peppered Atkins and Glynn, who would both run the program, with questions. What about day care? How would they find employers? Glynn recalls that Dukakis was neither skeptical nor enthusiastic. He was pleased that something so important was ready to go within the first nine months of his administration.

The new program would have none of the pejorative aura attached to the term workfare. In fact, it was named Employment and Training Choices—ET, for short—conjuring up images of the lovable character in Steven Spielberg's movie.

Soon afterward, Atkins and Glynn presented the plan at a cabinet meeting. Since six agencies would be involved, it was essential to win the support of the entire cabinet. At that meeting Dukakis decided to go ahead with the program, but not to announce it publicly until it had been up and running for a while. Glynn's sense was that Dukakis didn't want to raise expectations for ET; he knew how difficult it would be to put together a program like this and make it work.

ET began quietly on October 1, 1983. The idea was to create a program that would get welfare recipients permanently off public assistance and into entry-level private-sector jobs that would launch them on productive careers. ET was different from anything tried in the past. First, it was voluntary, the only voluntary welfare work program in the United States. Welfare recipients had to register for the program, but no person who didn't want to get involved would ever be required to do so. Run jointly by the Massachusetts Welfare Department and the Division of Employment Security, ET offered men and women on welfare (about 90 percent were women) professional assessment and counseling services. The notion was that some people needed training, while others were capable of going to work immediately if given some help in finding a job. Still others needed basic education. A critical element of the program was that participants continued to get their welfare checks while receiving career counseling, training, education, and job placement services. Nearly as important was that the state also paid for day care—a huge expense—and transportation.

The most remarkable feature of ET was that it worked. By June 1984, just nine months after it began, 6100 welfare recipients had graduated from ET and found jobs—1000 more people than had been put to work during a similar period by King's workfare plan. Dukakis was thrilled with this initial success. In June 1984, when he officially announced the existence of the program, Dukakis said that ET "is proving that when welfare recipients are given a genuine opportunity to work, they'll pick wages over welfare every time."

In the process of moving welfare recipients into the job market, ET also succeeded in reducing the state's welfare budget. In June 1984, state officials projected that if ET job placement continued apace over five years, it would save the taxpayers $100 million.

Dukakis's decision to hold off on the announcement of ET until it had produced results turned out to have been very wise, for once the press realized that a social welfare program had actually succeeded, it couldn't get enough of the story. "We were announcing something that *worked*," says Glynn. "ET is a social program that works."

By October 1985, after two years of ET, an increasingly delighted Dukakis announced that Massachusetts's welfare caseload had declined by nearly 10 percent, the largest decrease among the twelve major industrial states. "The difference is unquestionably ET," Dukakis said at the time. By then, the program had placed 20,000 welfare recipients in private-sector jobs, and 70 percent of them were off welfare. Administration officials estimated at the time that without ET, the welfare caseload would have climbed to more than 93,200. Instead, it dropped below 88,000. However much credit he took for the program's success, Dukakis knew very well that it was not due to his managerial inspiration or abilities, at least not entirely. Without a booming economy, he noted, ET's success would surely have been less spectacular.

It was not long before word of the program reached other provinces, including the nation's capital. Anything that put a dent in one of the most intractable social problems of the century, and ET seemed to do so, was eagerly sought after by government officials throughout the land.

In early 1987, Senator Kennedy proposed an incentive plan to get other states to adopt an ET program. So appealing was the idea that in April of that year the U.S. Senate, in an unusual 99–0 vote, approved Kennedy's proposal.

While ET was widely trumpeted as a great success story, it also attracted a band of detractors. Critics complained that the program only worked for the most highly motivated welfare recipients and that it provided little opportunity for the hard-core unemployed. But the most frequent criticism was that it placed people in jobs that simply didn't pay them enough to be self-sufficient. It was charged that some graduates of the program were actually worse off financially than they had been on welfare.

But, on balance, ET has been very successful. In its first four years, it placed 38,000 welfare recipients in full- and part-time jobs with average wages of $6.50 an hour, or $13,000 a year. Since ET began, the state's welfare caseload has declined 5 percent, even as welfare benefits increased 47 percent, and eligibility levels were raised. After deducting the cost of running ET, the state saved more than $100 million in reduced benefits. Without ET, officials estimate the caseload would have increased about 10 percent.

The Massachusetts Taxpayers' Foundation, an independent group funded by the business community, released a study in August 1987 that found ET to be an effective way for the state to save money on welfare costs while reducing welfare dependency.

Some liberals defended the program as well. Robert Kuttner, economics correspondent for the *New Republic* and a man not always friendly to Dukakis's policies, wrote in the *Globe* in September 1985: "ET is Dukakis at his best. It combines a liberal premise—most poor people want to better themselves—with a conservative premise that most people ought to be working rather than living on the dole. It adds a good-government premise, that an efficient, well-managed program is good for both recipients and taxpayers. Workfare tries to get people off welfare into a job, any job; ET tries to improve their condition. Workfare exacts society's pound of flesh from the poor; ET provides ladders out of poverty. More than a program, ET is an attitude."

Michael Dukakis declared in August 1987 that "the thing that I am proudest of, of all the things that I've been part of as governor, has been ET, because it represents in such a very special way what this state is all about, what our country is or should be all about."

The other major substantive success of Dukakis's second term involved taxes. When he returned to the State House in January

1983, Dukakis may well have experienced a bit of déjà vu, for he quickly found that the state faced an estimated $300 million deficit. It was a serious matter, though not nearly the crisis of the early days of his first term. Dukakis approached the problem calmly, having had some experience in cutting a deficit. He wanted to solve the problem as quickly as possible, but he didn't want to take the predictable route of cutting spending or raising taxes.

One of Dukakis's first acts as governor had been to hire his friend and fellow Brookline native Ira Jackson away from the Kennedy School to be commissioner of the Department of Revenue, the tax collection agency. Under King, a prosecutor had said that there was "widespread corruption" in the department. In fact, very little legal action came of the investigation, but the agency was in disarray and remained under a cloud of suspicion.

By far its most serious problem when Dukakis took over, however, was that tax evasion was widespread. Large amounts of taxes simply weren't being paid; thousands of people didn't file returns, and were never caught. Dukakis appointed a commission to recommend how to improve the department's performance. Meanwhile, the department staff under Jackson came up with its own ideas. The best proposals by both the commission and the staff formed a bill that Dukakis told the legislature was one of his top priorities. It was called REAP, Revenue Enhancement and Protection Program, and it moved through the legislature with minimal difficulty and was signed into law on July 1. REAP gave the tax department the authority to revoke the licenses of more than a million businesses and professionals should they fail to pay taxes. It also made tax evasion a felony rather than a misdemeanor, and gave the tax department the power to publicize the names of delinquents owing more than $5000 in back taxes, and to establish an amnesty program.

Tax amnesty, which proved to be hugely successful, was not in the bill as originally proposed by Dukakis. It was suggested by Representative Robert Ambler of Weymouth, who raised the idea during a meeting in the governor's office with Dukakis and Jackson. But Dukakis wanted no part of it, Ambler recalls.

Ambler argued that there were a lot of taxpayers, small business people in particular, who had suffered during the early 1980s and who had failed to pay taxes because they were unable to do so, not because they were criminals. He believed an amnesty program would bring a flood of honest people forward. But Dukakis was vehemently opposed. "He rejected it out of hand," Ambler says. Dukakis doesn't remember the meeting well. He says he "certainly might have raised questions about" the amnesty proposal. But Jackson immediately liked the idea, he recalls, and was able to convince Dukakis of its merits. Under the plan, delinquent taxpayers were granted immunity from criminal prosecution and penalties were waived, although taxes and interest payments had to be made. After it proved itself, Ambler says, Dukakis "wanted to take all the credit in the world" for the idea.

When the REAP package was enacted, it provided the Revenue Department with the computers and additional staff needed to beef up enforcement. Wasting no time in putting its provisions to work, Jackson caused a tremendous stir when he published names of tax delinquents, embarrassing more than a few prominent citizens. He also went after restaurants with a vengeance. Some restaurant owners, who collected sales taxes from customers and withholding taxes from employees but never paid the state, were among the worst tax cheats, and theirs were the properties most commonly shut down. During fiscal year 1985 alone, the Revenue Department seized 158 pieces of property, including businesses, boats, construction equipment, and airplanes, which yielded more than $7 million in unpaid back taxes. In addition, much more was brought in by the voluntary compliance generated by publicity from the seizures. Jackson understood publicity's role: one Fourth of July weekend, he searched boatyards for delinquent yachts himself.

But the most spectacularly successful aspect of REAP was, ironically, the only major part of the program that the governor had initially opposed—tax amnesty. During the amnesty period, from October 17, 1983, until January 17, 1984, the department expected to take in anywhere between $5 million and $20 million. By the time it was through, however, tax amnesty, which cost just over $1 million, had brought in an incredible $86 million in money the state never dreamed of receiving. In all, 52,000 individuals and corporations came forward and paid their due.

"Whether out of fear, guilt, or gratitude," Jackson said at the time, "they came in droves, from every walk of life, with cashier's checks in hands." One key benefit for the state was that, having come forward, these 52,000 put themselves back on the tax rolls, and the state's computers made sure they kept paying annually thereafter.

As with ET, news of REAP's success spread to Washington, D.C. In February 1985, the executive committee of the National Governors' Association endorsed a tax program modeled on REAP. "We've had great success with a beefed-up, stepped-up policy of public tax enforcement," Dukakis said at the governors' meeting. He estimated that a national REAP effort could yield at least $20 billion. "It's essential this be a key element in any federal deficit reduction strategy ... We're not talking about the underground economy ... we're talking about legitimately earned income on which taxes have not been paid," he said.

One reason for the success of REAP was the astonishing growth in the state's economy. During a speech Dukakis gave in January 1983 to the Boston Chamber of Commerce Executive Club at the Copley Plaza Hotel, the governor sensed that the economic revival that had already begun in the state was to continue, and he was right. "We have gone through that difficult period when traditional manufacturing businesses went into decline," he said. "We went through it and came out the other side with a knowledge-based industry. At a time when the rest of the country is having a hard time finding its way, we have what it takes to put it all together."

By the middle of Dukakis's term, thirteen years after he had first been elected governor, the economy had experienced a turnaround so remarkable that it was the envy of the nation. Between 1975 and 1986, unemployment in Massachusetts fell from a peak of 12.3 percent, the highest of the industrial states, to 3.8 percent, the lowest of *any* state. In 1975, Massachusetts had a budget deficit of more than $500 million. In 1985, there was a $400 million *surplus*. The state's tax burden had gone from being 9 percent above the national average in 1978 to 8 percent *below* in 1984.

Much of the prosperity was owed to a thunderous boom in high technology. The production of textiles and shoes gave way to the manufacture of computers and missiles, creating tens of thousands of new jobs. De Castro's Data General, for example, which employed 800 people in 1973, had a workforce of 5500 ten years later. The state Division of Employment Security estimated that in 1975, high tech manufacturing alone employed 167,000 people. By late 1987, the number stood at 248,400. During the eight years from 1967 to 1975, the number of jobs in the state increased by just 4 percent. But during the eight years from 1975 to 1983 jobs in the state increased 16 percent. And in 1984 alone, jobs increased an additional 5 percent, a significant figure considering that the population remained constant.

Dukakis, increasingly ready to take the credit for the good times, began to be studied by analysts like the Kennedy School's Ronald Ferguson and Helen Ladd. They found that "most of the initiatives of the first Dukakis administration were too late to be given credit for the initial turnaround. Moreover, the state's stringent property tax limitation measure, Proposition 2½, often cited for its favorable impact on the state's tax and business climate, passed in 1980, well after the state's unemployment rate started dropping . . . This suggests that policies initiated during the 1975–85 period probably contributed little to the initial turnaround of the economy."

Ferguson and Ladd left Dukakis with a right to claim that "the strong performance of the economy after 1979 . . . leaves open the possibility that policy initiatives may have helped sustain the growth once it began." But this finding too they qualified: "A plausible competing hypothesis is that rising defense-related activity along with other exogenous forces that sustained rising incomes in Massachusetts in the early 1980's account for the state's outstanding performance . . ."

A study released late in 1987 by the Economic Policy Institute, a liberal Washington think tank, reached conclusions similar to Ferguson and Ladd's. The study praised Dukakis for working to improve the business climate and create jobs, but it claimed that the governor played only a limited role in the revival. The study attributed the growth to the expansion of the high technology industry, the concentration of prominent universities, and ballooning military spending.

Even as Dukakis was criticizing President Reagan for increased defense spending, Pentagon dollars were contributing to the prosperity of Massachusetts. Dukakis's own budget proposal recognized as much in March 1983. "As the federal government implements its planned defense preparedness program, the economic impact on Massachusetts will be highly stimulative," it stated. "This economic stimulus . . . will create an additional 50,000 jobs in the commonwealth. Thus, as one looks at the decade of the 1980s, it appears likely that defense-related industries in Massachusetts will experience considerable growth."

The state was far better suited to profit from Reagan's increased defense spending than it had been to gain from expenditures during the Vietnam era. While Pentagon dollars during the late 1960s went for soldiers and ammunition, Reagan's build-up spent billions on research and the development of highly sophisticated new weapons systems, most of which are electronically guided. Throughout the early and middle 1980s defense dollars flowed to companies such as Raytheon, where the Sparrow and Sidewinder missiles are built; to the General Electric Company, which builds aircraft engines; to the Avco Corporation in Wilmington, for work on the MX missile; and of course to MIT, for research on radar and communications and high tech weaponry.

Dukakis rarely mentioned defense spending in his discussions of the state's economic resurgence. In his 1985 State of the State address he said that Massachusetts was on the threshold of being able to promise "a future which, for the first time in our history, for the first time in the history of any state, creates a society of opportunity for all, in every community, for every citizen of Massachusetts."

He claimed that the state government had helped to foster a model environment for the private sector. The state's economy was in "overdrive," he said, having created 140,000 new jobs in the past year, 40,000 businesses in the past two years. The state, he said, has passed through the economic darkness of the 1970s and emerged into the light of a "momentous, remarkable, unprecedented decade of progress" that could continue to the year 2000 and beyond.

The fear among some people was that Massachusetts had grown too dependent on high technology. But David Birch, a regional economic specialist at MIT, thought such fears were groundless. He said in early 1985 that "high tech isn't that important a part of Massachusetts's economy, anyway. If high tech wiggles, we really don't get hurt very much the way we used to." In his view, the state's growing diversification was yielding economic health. Birch said that Massachusetts's new industries ranged "from medicine to computer software to insurance, education, database services, financial services, money market funds, parcel delivery services, health maintenance organizations. These are all computer-based, but it's a much more diversified mix."

Ferguson and Ladd were unswerving in their belief that it was not Michael Dukakis—or any other politician—who was responsible in large measure, or even *moderate* measure, for the economic miracle in Massachusetts. They wrote that "neither the scope nor the timing of recent policy initiatives in Massachusetts supports the view that they were an important catalyst in the remarkable economic turnaround of the past decade; the turnaround in the unemployment rate reflects slow labor force growth and the capacity of the state's private sector to respond to growing worldwide demand for certain goods and services. At the same time, state initiatives helped to attract growth to some depressed central cities and slow growing regions, and may have helped at the margin to sustain the state's revival once it began."

Dukakis may not have been the engine of the state's economic success, but it constitutes much of his national political underpinnings. Without such a glorious story to tell, Dukakis would certainly not be a candidate for national office.

He does not shy away from taking at least some credit, and has not been reticent about describing the situation as "the most extraordinary economic turnaround of any state, maybe, in the history of the United States." He has acknowledged that a variety of factors have contributed to the state's success, but he adds that "I have to conclude that a good deal of this has to relate to what we are doing here, and I think that's something to be proud of."

Perhaps the closest he has come to taking primary credit for having made the miracle happen was when he said in August 1987 that "the first question I'm asked wherever I go is, 'Can you do it for us here?' And my answer is, 'Yes, we can.'"

Sasso believes that the views of economists on the question of how much credit Dukakis should get for the prosperity are essentially irrelevant. "The question," says Sasso, "is not whether Dukakis created every one of these jobs himself—of course he didn't. There were factors outside his control. The standard is, 'Did he do everything as chief executive of Massachusetts to promote economic opportunity, and to make sure it got to people who did not traditionally share it?' The answer is yes. Because that's the question for the next president—'Will he do everything *possible*?' not 'Can he do the *im*possible?'"

Prosperity also allowed Dukakis to paint a picture of a new goal for Massachusetts—a state with virtually no poverty or serious deprivation—and to suggest that it was an achievable goal. As he had before, Dukakis approached the effort with self-confidence bordering on presumption. His most determined effort to describe a political vision was contained in his 1985 State of the State speech. "The Massachusetts success story," he said, has led to "the threshold of an era which can surpass anything we have ever experienced in this or any other state—a future which—for the first time in our history—for the first time in the history of *any* state—*creates a society of opportunity for all*—in *every* community—for *every* citizen of Massachusetts. These are not idle words or vague dreams. They are real and achievable goals . . .

"For I firmly believe that over the rest of the century we *can* build a Massachusetts where anyone who dreams a dream of a full and rich future can live that dream. We *are* the land of opportunity . . . But in Massachusetts there must and will be *opportunity for all.*

"Not an elusive Utopian dream, but an opportunity . . . *that is within our grasp.*"

The state's unprecedented prosperity added immeasurably to Dukakis's political strength. Entering his re-election year, he seemed unbeatable from the outset. For one thing, his control of the Democratic caucuses and convention eliminated all primary opposition for the first time in thirty-six years. As it turned out, the 1986 gubernatorial election was a farcical affair marked by astonishing ineptitude on the part of the Republicans. Early on, the potential threats to Dukakis—former Governor King, who had become a Republican and Raymond Shamie, who had twice been the Republican nominee for the U.S. Senate—announced they would not run. This left the GOP searching for a candidate to take on a governor whose popularity soared at a time that the state was projecting a half-billion-dollar surplus and boasting the lowest unemployment rate in the nation.

The first Republican challenger was a thirty-two-year-old lawyer from Lawrence named Gregory Hyatt. Hyatt had been a leader in the Proposition 2½ campaign, but he had never before run for public office. His candidacy didn't last long. In April, officials at Associated Builders and Contractors, an organization for which Hyatt had previously worked, accused him of bizarre behavior and lack of production. The group's executive vice-president, Stephen P. Tocco, said that Hyatt did little work and spent a good deal of time sitting in his office staring into space. Tocco said his staff told him that Hyatt had talked on the telephone when there was no one on the other end of the line and that a young woman working at the organization walked into Hyatt's office twice in two weeks and found him naked.

With Hyatt wounded, the GOP convention turned to one of the party's loudest voices in the legislature, Royall Switzler of Wellesley. Switzler was a right-winger who was a sharp and persistent critic of the Democrats in the legislature and who was strongly disliked by House members for his abrasive, often dilatory, tactics during floor debates. No sooner had Switzler won the endorsement of the convention, however, than he admitted he had lied about his military service on his campaign literature. He had not, as he had claimed, been a combat officer in the Vietnam War but was an enlisted man who never fought there. Switzler dropped out of the race. At this point, the GOP was the laughingstock of the state, and it was questionable whether it would be able to field a candidate at all. Into the breach stepped George Kariotis, a successful businessman who had been a member of King's cabinet but who had not the slightest electoral political experience. Kariotis raised little money and was an ineffectual campaigner. He never had the slightest chance of beating Dukakis.

Dukakis, however, hardly laughed his way through the campaign. In 1982 he had run hard *against* King and, while he had been victorious, the win may have had as much to do with the voters' desire to get rid of King as to bring back Dukakis. To put to rest, finally, the ghosts of his 1978 loss, Dukakis had to win re-election in 1986.

This view was shared even by Dukakis's most persistent critic, Barbara Anderson, the woman who had led the fight for Proposition 2½. Anderson never liked Dukakis, yet she says she found his administration easy to deal with in the second term. "All you had to do was threaten trouble and he'd give you what you wanted," she says. "If you just threatened trouble to upset the next campaign, he would basically back down. He didn't seem to stand for anything except avoiding losing again. That seemed to be the entire theme of his entire four years. This is politics, where you win some and you lose some, and he can't seem to deal with losing."

Approaching the campaign, Frank Keefe said he believed that Dukakis "will not see himself as successful until he gets a stamp of approval on his performance in office." Philip W. Johnston, Dukakis's secretary of human services, said that victory would mean "vindication" for Dukakis. And Ralph Whitehead said that election day 1986 was "the most important date in his life. He won't close the psychic loop until he wins in '86."

"I have just one ambition," Dukakis said during an interview in 1985, "and that is to see if I can at least put two terms together successively." The 1986 campaign, he said, "means making sure that what happened to me in 1978 doesn't happen again."

On November 4 he swept to victory, crushing Kariotis, 1,157,786 to 525,364. With 69 percent of the vote, Dukakis won by the largest margin of victory of any Massachusetts governor in more than a century. It was, finally, his redemption.

The vote was an affirmation of "Duke II," yet exactly what was being approved wasn't clear. Between his first and second terms Michael Dukakis had changed. But was it simply a matter of something learned—a lesson that had been taught by bitter defeat and that Dukakis had grasped through his characteristic force of will? Or had he changed more fundamentally? Was he a different person?

Clearly, his approach to politics had changed. His style had changed. He had even altered some of his positions on issues, seeming, in the process, to have become if not more conservative, then more moderate. Symbolically, perhaps the most revealing shift came on the issue of the drinking age. During his first term, Dukakis so adamantly opposed increasing the drinking age that he vetoed a bill that would have raised it from eighteen to nineteen. In his second term, he became an unrelenting opponent of drunk driving and supported boosting the drinking age to twenty-one.

The most interesting question, though, was not whether Dukakis's style had changed but whether *he* had changed, whether the essential Michael Dukakis was different. From the perspective of people like Thomas McGee, the former House speaker, Dukakis had "learned a lot being out." McGee says Dukakis was far more arrogant in his first term, but that when he returned to office, "basically it was a change in him as a person . . . He grew while he was out and was . . . much more humble, much more affable, and much more easy to deal with. He would listen . . . The second term when you went in to discuss something with him he was much more affable and friendly when you came in the door, much more outgoing, a better guy."

While Dukakis says he's a better listener than before, there is still a self-assurance that can be strikingly similar to his first-term arrogance. Asked what has been tough in his second term, Dukakis had difficulty coming up with an answer. "It's not cockiness," he said. "You have some confidence—you have a sense of what information you need."

Sasso's view was that Dukakis was "someone who has his basic values and beliefs, which are strong and have not changed over the years. But like the smart person that he is and the good politician that he is, he has learned from his experiences in office, in losing, at the Kennedy School, and going through a tough campaign."

Dukakis said in 1985 that he dealt with matters "somewhat more calmly, more thoughtfully. If there's one thing that's different about me in a personal sense, it's that I stop and I think a little more, and I spend some time. I'm not sure I always listen as much as I should."

He had also learned how to communicate with voters better, he believed. One of the major lessons of President Reagan's victory, said Dukakis, was that "who you are, how you communicate, how they perceive you, is very important. I certainly take that side of my life a lot more seriously than seven years ago. In the first term, I don't think I communicated very effectively."

"He was a young, vigorous reformer," says Paul Brountas. "He was a true reformer, and I think an ideologue" in his first term. "He probably thinks he still is." In fact, Brountas talked with Dukakis about this once, and Dukakis said, "I'm still just as much of an idealist." But in Brountas's view, he has become "much more pragmatic."

Some critics charged that by seeking consensus on nearly every issue Dukakis had lost his backbone. And it was obvious that after the loss in 1978, Dukakis had little stomach for political street-fighting. He'd gotten punched in the face—hard—and hadn't liked it one bit. Mark Shields, a columnist for the *Washington Post* who has watched Dukakis closely through the years, said in 1985 that most political candidates run for office for fairly noble reasons. But, he said, once a politician loses a race, "then not losing becomes the most important thing in many of their lives."

It certainly seemed true with Dukakis. Said Shields: "Before his one upset defeat in the 1978 gubernatorial primary, self-doubt and Michael Dukakis had never spent much time together."

Michael Widmer, Dukakis's communications secretary during the first term, believed it. "I think he desperately, very strongly wanted to have a successful term in which he was re-elected. He didn't want to lose again, more than he even wanted to win." During "Duke II," says Widmer, "much of the driving force in many respects was to make sure he didn't commit the great mistake, that he wasn't too far out on a limb . . . He was more cautious, and that had its virtue in the total accomplishments of the administration, but it had its price in the sense that he did not take the kind of forthright stands that he took and use the power of his office as forthrightly as he did in the first term." He had lost, says Widmer, "some of the courage and steadfastness of conviction."

Dukakis's top appointees were angered by objections to the governor's new style. "Some people," says Finance Secretary Keefe bitterly, "think leadership is offending everyone around you and raising taxes, big."

But in other respects Dukakis hadn't changed at all. His father-in-law, Harry Dickson, who has known him well since the early 1960s, says, "I've seen no change in Mike."

Frank Bellotti, who has known Dukakis for more than twenty years and admires him particularly for his integrity, agrees with Dickson: "I don't think he's really changed very much . . . He probably thinks more about communication with groups that would have an opposite position than he would have, but that's a pragmatic change, not a change in kind. Inside the guy, I think he has the same fairly rigid values."

The essential man remained true to character. When he was deciding whether to run for president—the most important political decision of his life—Kitty was not sure what he intended until he told her. Even Sasso didn't know. Though he had changed in some ways, he remained, inside, the little boy who so stubbornly wanted to do things by himself. He has gone through his adult life without ever telling some of his closest friends about what was surely one of the great traumas of his life—that his older brother, to whom he had been so close and who came, clearly, to resent his success, had tried to take his own life. It suggested an extraordinary determination to internalize emotional pain.

"Intellectually," says Fran Meaney, "he's learned a good lesson. Whether he's changed internally, I don't know."

9. Marathon

————

"Dukakis has blossomed into a national figure . . .
the hottest governor of all."

MICHAEL DUKAKIS CALMLY picked up the morning mail on Saturday, March 14, 1987, closed the front door of his home in Brookline, turned to his wife, and said, "It looks like I'm going to do it."

Kitty Dukakis calls her husband "the least complicated man in America." Yet she was not at all sure whether he would seek the presidency—what was going on inside the brain of the man to whom she'd been married for twenty-three years—until that crisp winter morning when he delivered the news. Two days later, everyone knew. The decision was made public in a well-orchestrated announcement at the State House and was designed to rally diverse Massachusetts Democrats into a solid base of support.

Dukakis had been moving toward that decision quite openly. Two weeks before, Kitty said, "He's not there yet, but he's getting closer." The announcement itself was not a great surprise to most of those who know him well.

But six months before that, few would have guessed. Many friends had heard him disparage Washington, had seen him concentrate on state issues and decline dozens of opportunities to cultivate a national reputation. As Dukakis conducted his semipublic exploration of a candidacy during the first ten weeks of 1987, he said over and over that he had never really thought about it before. And his wife and closest friends insist that, if he had, he never discussed the subject with them; that he would, in fact, wave it away if they brought it up. Nick Zervas remembers probing Dukakis about running for president or vice-president and getting a peremptory response: "I wouldn't go down there. I hate Washington."

Fran Meaney also remembers spurned attempts at presidential discussions years ago: "If I'd raise it, he'd kind of brush it aside." But Meaney saw Dukakis as a presidential candidate for a long time. "To me, it was always just a matter of when," he says. From early in Dukakis's career, "I saw him as a real possibility of making it all the way." Given Dukakis's skills and ambition and his focus on executive elective office, Meaney says there could be only two jobs that would interest Dukakis: governor and president. Once the voters had given his performance as governor their seal of approval in 1986, Meaney felt, it was virtually inevitable that Dukakis would run for president, given an opening. "Michael is a very ambitious and tremendously confident person," he says.

In many ways the decision, once made, was logical and natural. Many of the themes in Dukakis's life pointed toward a presidential campaign. Yet when Dukakis was pondering the candidacy, as at many other times, those close to him were left to guess. It is of course possible that Dukakis secretly harbored presidential ambitions for years but thought about them only by himself. John Sasso, for instance, claims that "I never had a discussion with Dukakis about the possibility of [his] running for president until a few days after the election in 1986. Never."

Still, it is clear that long before 1987 he was doing things that would eventually benefit his national candidacy. There is a parallel here with 1979. At a time when Dukakis seems to have been genuinely uncertain whether he would try to recapture the governor's office, he and his supporters were taking actions that would pave the way for a candidacy.

The few minor parts that Dukakis played on the national stage in his first term were a warmup. He became a leader in the National Governors' Association and headed the committee that drafted the Democratic platform in 1976. Out of office from 1979 through 1982, he still took two steps that ended up affecting his national campaign enormously: he hired Sasso, who already had campaign experience nationally as well as in Massachusetts, and he cultivated the politicians, government workers, and academics from all over the country who circulated through the Kennedy School.

Back in office in 1983 and 1984, he was determined to become a national voice for the Democratic party and to take an influential part in the coming presidential campaign. When the Democrats were preparing a response to Reagan's election-year State of the Union address in January 1984, Senate Minority Leader Robert Byrd and House Speaker Tip O'Neill chose Dukakis to moderate the program, speaking to a national television audience. He mentioned unemployment and education, but his emphasis was on foreign policy. He referred to the marine from Quincy, Massachusetts, who had died in the Beirut suicide bombing. "A foreign policy which angers our friends and confuses our enemies is no substitute for sound diplomacy," he said.

In mid-1983, Dukakis invited John Glenn, Gary Hart, Ernest Hollings, and other presidential candidates to his State House office for extensive interviews. On October 28, with some fanfare, he endorsed Walter Mondale, calling him "the best hope we have."

Dukakis had grown to know Mondale when he was vice-president, and the relationship became a warm one. Dukakis and other prominent Massachusetts Democrats supporting Mondale were embarrassed by the state's primary voters on March 13, when they gave Mondale a drubbing, barely 26 percent of the vote to Hart's 39 percent. But Dukakis had cemented the relationship two weeks earlier, when New Hampshire voters stunned Mondale with his worst setback of the campaign. In the late afternoon of Tuesday, February 28, as Mondale was on his way to the Granite State to eat the crow that the exit polls said had been prepared for him, Dukakis introduced him at two Boston fund-raisers with glowing personal affection. And the next morning, just after dawn, there were Dukakis and Mondale, shaking hands at a Boston subway stop, showing the nation that one governor remained enthusiastic about the wounded candidate. Mondale never forgot it.

For six weeks in mid-1984, Dukakis was involved in a flurry of activity that could easily be seen as promoting his chances for national office sooner or later. He spoke out on foreign policy. He was the no-fault candidate on Mondale's short list for the vice-presidential nomination. And, when that role went to Geraldine Ferraro, he allowed his top aide, Sasso, to run her national campaign. Yet in each case, national ambition seemed far from uppermost in Dukakis's mind.

The foreign policy statement, for instance, was limited to a few offhand remarks on Central America, expanded in a single interview with a columnist. Dukakis said the United States has a strong interest in the region, including Nicaragua, and cannot walk away from it, but should not try to enforce its will militarily. "We've got to recognize that revolution is inevitable, and that it can either be peaceful and constructive or violent and destructive," he said. As a permanent member of the party Platform Committee, which was led by Ferraro, Dukakis pushed for firm language on Central America at the convention. But he made no other effort to disseminate his views nationally. His motive in speaking out seemed clearly to be the strong interest in Latin American affairs he had retained since college rather than national political ambition.

A similar situation applied when Dukakis became the anchor on Mondale's vice-presidential list in late June and early July. Other potential candidates were higher on the list because they would bring more pizzazz to the ticket. Two were women, Ferraro and Dianne Feinstein, the mayor of San Francisco, for Mondale was eager to find an acceptable female running mate. The third was the party's most charismatic Hispanic, San Antonio's Mayor Henry Cisneros. But Mondale viewed Dukakis as a solid alternative. He says he called Dukakis and told him that, if none of the others panned out, he might "have to go with someone I'm absolutely sure of. If that's the case, I'd like to go with you." When Mondale picked Ferraro on July 12, however, Dukakis was relieved. He had gone through the personal and financial disclosures Mondale had needed, and he would have taken the role dutifully if offered. Politically, some advisers liked the idea. If the team won, Dukakis would become a national figure as vice-president. In the more likely event that it lost, Dukakis would still be governor, having gained enormous exposure around the country with little risk to his standing in the state. But Dukakis seemed genuinely uninterested in pursuing such ephemeral gains, especially before his work as governor had received the voters' confirmation—the redemption he was pointing toward in his 1986 campaign. When Sasso called to say that Mondale had made a decision, Dukakis responded, "Come on, John, tell me it's not me."

As soon as the choice was made, ironically, Sasso was recommended as a likely national campaign manager for Ferraro, whom he had never met. One connection was Susan Estrich, a politically zealous young Harvard Law School professor who knew Dukakis and Sasso well and who had just finished working closely with Ferraro for six months as executive director of the Platform Committee. "It just struck me as a perfect match," she says. She talked to Mondale's top aides, campaign manager Jim Johnson and counsel John Reilly, who knew Sasso well and were already thinking of him. They asked him to talk with Ferraro at the convention in San Francisco. The meetings were positive but inconclusive; no job offer was made. "I mentioned it to Dukakis," Sasso recalls, "and he said, 'Absolutely not under any circumstances.' I said, 'Fine.' " But a week later Ferraro, in Boston, asked Sasso to fly back to Washington with her. They talked, and she offered him the job.

Estrich was among those who felt this was an incredible opportunity for Sasso—and, by extension, for Dukakis—because, as she puts it, Sasso could "be at the top of a national campaign without having to leave home for two years." Yet Dukakis was still reluctant. A long agenda of unfinished business was on his desk, and Sasso was close to indispensable as Dukakis's right hand and chief State House facilitator. Finally, after pleas from Mondale and others, Dukakis relented. Ferraro announced Sasso's appointment on July 27. But the resistance Dukakis had put up sent out a clear message: that on his list of priorities, running the state came not only first, but second and third as well.

At the convention, meanwhile, on the evening following Mario Cuomo's stirring keynote address, Dukakis introduced the platform in a speech that was sprinkled with Massachusetts success stories. A few rhetorical flourishes also decorated the performance, including his assertion that Democrats "are committed to justice and decency and opportunity, for in them are the blood and sweat of our parents and the future of our children." But it was clear from his assignment that the party leaders were looking to Dukakis more for substance than for oratory, and they weren't disappointed.

Dukakis turned down requests to speak outside Massachusetts for the ticket in the fall, but he worked to deliver his home state—unsuccessfully, as it turned out. He also represented Mondale in a public television debate against William A. Rusher, the publisher of the *National Review,* in which Dukakis was repeatedly put on the defensive. All the same, he campaigned vigorously for Mondale, and he gave the impression late in October that he had actually convinced himself that Mondale might win. The country's voters, of course, had a far different idea.

One Democrat who emerged from the campaign with what he thought was an education, at least, was Sasso. The problem for Democrats, he felt, was that they had no credibility on handling the nation's economy, which was the overriding issue. "At the national level, people distrust us [Democrats]," he said. "People think we have hearts, but no hands."

Sasso insists that his work on the Ferraro campaign was not designed as a warmup for Dukakis, but it seemed to serve that purpose. Sasso found that governors were among the most talented Democrats in the country, men like Bob Graham of Florida, Jim Blanchard of Michigan—and Dukakis. "I'm not thinking Dukakis when I take the job, but I'm beginning to think more and more Dukakis as I travel the country," Sasso recalls. "I say, Jesus, Dukakis would be perfect for this, on the basis of judgment, on the basis of temperament, on the basis of experience."

But, says Sasso, "I didn't act on it." Some weeks after the election, he says, he described his views to Dukakis in a long talk that never once focused on a possible Dukakis candidacy. "He listened, he was very interested," says Sasso, "but he never said anything about himself. He didn't have to."

Still, the lesson about the central importance of the economy found its way into Dukakis's message. The title of his State of the State speech in January 1985 was "Opportunity for All," a predominantly economic theme that was pushed throughout 1985 with an elaborate communications strategy. "We promoted it to the hilt," Sasso says. "We laid a foundation: this guy has made things work."

A key vehicle in the communications strategy was a project called "Massachusetts: Discovering the Future." From late 1985 into 1986, Dukakis took business, labor, and academic leaders, along with public officials and reporters, on tours of a number of innovative businesses in different parts of the state. The trips were designed to show off the Dukakis programs that had stimulated some of the success stories. But they had the effect of stimulating Dukakis as well.

At the same time, Dukakis moved swiftly to influence the reorganization of the shattered national party. He had learned a lesson in 1978 about the peril of ignoring the organized party's potential to help a campaign. In 1982, he demonstrated that the lesson had sunk in. Now, just weeks after the national party's debacle at the polls, he assumed a major role in guiding its rebirth. To begin with, he moved quickly to support the candidacy of Paul G. Kirk, Jr., for national chairman. Kirk had been the party's treasurer, so he knew something about fund-raising. More important, he was the son of a Massachusetts judge and had been an aide to Ted Kennedy, so he knew something about politics. Dukakis flew to Kansas City in December to lobby for Kirk at a meeting of state party chairmen, and he wrote letters to all thirty-four Democratic governors. In the final days of January 1985, he loaned Sasso to the effort. When Kirk won the job on February 1, Dukakis was among the victors over several other key Democrats, including Cuomo, who had done all they could to stop Kirk.

Kirk soon rewarded Dukakis by naming him to head a group drafting the crucial economic development language for the

Democratic Policy Commission, a vehicle Kirk established to give the party cohesion and substance. And in February 1986, when Kirk launched a series of publicity events designed to spread the word about innovative programs being operated successfully by Democrats around the country, Dukakis was first, showcasing the ET program to a well-attended press conference in Washington, then traveling on to South Carolina for a second pitch.

Increasingly, politicians and commentators looked to Dukakis as a potential candidate, but he was in the enviable position of seeming, at least, to be focusing on policy rather than politics. A congressman from California, Don Edwards, told a Boston press conference in October 1985 that Democrats "want the White House in 1988 . . . and we might want your governor to be that person." But Dukakis, while smiling broadly, made clear his goal: "I have yet to demonstrate I can be elected to successive terms."

Then, on December 19, 1985, Kennedy announced he would not be a candidate for president in 1988. Until that moment, he had stood squarely in Dukakis's path. Despite the smattering of national attention Dukakis was receiving, he and Kennedy were two Massachusetts liberals with different styles but many of the same allies; there was no chance both could run. So now Dukakis's door was opened to the political reporters and campaign professionals who make up the lists of "potential" and supposedly "viable" candidates years before the next election. One after another, the mentioners took a look.

In February 1986, David Broder wrote a long, page 1 story for the *Washington Post* that credited Dukakis as being the father of "the New Deal-Making politics."

Later that month, *Business Week* highlighted Dukakis's "demonstrable success" in Massachusetts and quoted a Boston pollster, Irwin Harrison, as saying Dukakis was "testing the waters" for a presidential candidacy. The observation was especially interesting coming from Harrison, a frequent adviser to Dukakis who subsequently went to work for the campaign.

A crucial story came in the March 24 *Newsweek*, in which the nation's governors rated Dukakis their "most effective" colleague. Of the forty-three governors surveyed, each of whom could make three choices, Dukakis was mentioned by 35 percent. Tennessee's Lamar Alexander, a Republican, was second with 30 percent. *Newsweek* said that Dukakis in his second term "has tapped the innovative and activist potential of state government."

"Move over, Mario," headlined the *New Republic*'s evaluation in April. "Dukakis has blossomed into a national figure renowned for a welfare program that puts the hopelessly unemployed in solid jobs and a tax-enforcement effort that produces unforeseen revenues." Governors, said the magazine's Fred Barnes, are "hot now, and Dukakis is the hottest governor of all."

In May, *Time* contrasted the economic fortunes of Massachusetts, which it described as "back in the vanguard," and Texas, which was hurting from a collapse of oil prices. In his second term, *Time* said, Dukakis "became a born-again business booster" who presides over a "go-go state that is leading the transition to what economists see as the country's future—a high-tech, service-oriented economy."

A *National Review* cover story in July asked of conservative tax-cutters in Massachusetts: "Can They Dump the Duke?" Though it labeled Dukakis's claims to prowess as an economic manager "a fraud and a farce," the story's answer to its own question seemed to be: probably not.

And, just two days later, George F. Will, the nation's most influential conservative columnist, wrote that "Massachusetts's prosperity is . . . obscene." He added, "Now, in a fresh affront to conservative sensibilities, Massachusetts's boom coincides with the tenure of a highly popular Democratic governor."

In the *Wall Street Journal* of September 30, David Shribman said that Dukakis had "won a national reputation" for his ET and REAP programs and for his efforts to rebuild old industrial centers, efforts that political analysts believe "point the way toward a new Democratic view of partnership between business and government."

James J. Kilpatrick, a columnist who seems to cherish his role as the nation's conservative curmudgeon, declared that "the Duke is on a roll" in October. "He has performed amazingly well," wrote Kilpatrick. "Dukakis naturally claims credit for much of the prosperity, and on the record he's entitled."

Favorable columns came as well from Mary McGrory and James Reston. And positive editorials appeared in a number of newspapers, including the *Atlanta Journal and Constitution,* the *Los Angeles Times,* and the *San Francisco Examiner.*

Much of this coverage was substantive, referring to Massachusetts's overall economic health, programs like ET and REAP, and Dukakis's initiatives to work with business and to discourage drug and alcohol use in schools. But most of the stories at least mentioned the possibility of a national candidacy. A few suggested that Dukakis was running for vice-president, and several called him a long shot for the White House. On November 6, right after Dukakis's re-election, the *Wall Street Journal*'s Albert R. Hunt labeled him "a serious dark-horse presidential possibility for 1988."

This run of predominantly favorable comment was capped—made official, in a way—on December 31. The *Union Leader* of Manchester, New Hampshire, the far right bête noire of the nation's newspapers, editorialized about Dukakis's acceptance of an invitation to address the state's biggest Democratic dinner the following March: "Big Mike Dukakis, the mushy-headed ultra-liberal governor of Taxachusetts . . . Come on, little Duke. Come get the rudest awakening of your naive and irresponsible public life. No state in the Union better deserves the opportunity to introduce you to political reality."

Much of this national exposure was encouraged by Dukakis and his staff. Occasionally, there was even a wink at a possible candidacy during 1986. In May, for instance, Dukakis took the podium to accept the state Democratic convention's renomination for governor. Reminding the delegates that he had placed the portrait of fiery Sam Adams over his desk, Dukakis said, "He came from a family of great political leaders that achieved great things—first here in Massachusetts and then in the highest office in the land, *the presidency of the United States.* Often these days I look at that portrait for inspiration, and sometimes I can almost hear old Sam Adams's voice. And I can hear him saying to me, 'Dukakis, if you win this election in November and if you play your cards right, maybe someday—just *someday* . . . they'll name a beer after you.'"

Dukakis is often mocked for his wooden attempts at humor, but this line was delivered well and got a big laugh from the receptive audience. The rest of the speech, however, dealt with Massachusetts issues. Similarly, Dukakis's performance nationally was for the most part determinedly substantive. Because of his participation in Kirk's Democratic Policy Commission, in the National Governors' Association and in the Democratic Governors' Association, Dukakis traveled widely and became increasingly familiar with aspects of national policy.

In his work for the Policy Commission, for instance, Dukakis conducted hearings around the country and produced a report emphasizing ways to improve U.S. competitiveness in the world economy. This put him at odds with the Democratic Leadership Conference, a new group composed mostly of southern and western Democrats who had set themselves up as a regional counterpoint to Kirk's operation. This group, under the urging in part of Congressman Richard A. Gephardt of Missouri and Charles Robb, the former governor of Virginia, had produced a report placing a stronger emphasis on sanctions against trading partners such as Japan that restricted American goods. A year later, Dukakis and Gephardt would debate the issue with spirit and contention in Iowa, but in 1986 the tone was congenial. Robb and Gephardt both traveled to Boston in March for a public hearing.

For the National Governors' Association, Dukakis was co-chair in 1986 and 1987 of the Task Force on Jobs, Growth and Competitiveness, a group that pursued these goals in hearings around the country, including in Iowa, the site of the first presidential caucus. Dukakis was also a leading advocate of welfare reform, and in February 1987 he was one of three governors to present the NGA welfare proposal to the key senator on the issue, Daniel Patrick Moynihan of New York.

Dukakis, meanwhile, was working actively within the more partisan Democratic Governors' Association and was elected the group's chairman in August 1986.

Though all of this activity helped generate stories in the national press, an effort was made to keep the coverage focused on issues, especially Dukakis's record at home and the booming Massachusetts economy. In fact, though Dukakis was traveling widely, he frequently penciled out proposed meetings with groups that he considered purely political, especially potential contributors. Bob Farmer, his chief fund-raiser, implored Dukakis to talk to these people, but he usually refused.

His staff actively promoted him with the national press, but even here the emphasis was on Massachusetts. Sasso, for instance, sent videotapes of Dukakis's 1985 State of the State speech to a number of reporters who inquired about Dukakis— and to some who didn't. In Sasso's view, the resulting national exposure harmonized with the immediate state goal—re-election by a big margin in November 1986. One benefit, says Sasso, is that local reporters tend to lose a bit of their normal cynicism when they see positive assessments from national opinion-makers. "When you get press nationally, it has some effect with the local press," Sasso says.

So while Dukakis accumulated a stack of national clippings in 1986, it was accomplished in such a way that it did not hurt his re-election campaign. Asked late in October if he would pledge to serve out a third term, Dukakis declared that he had learned "never to say never," but that his attention was focused wholly on the state.

As far as those closest to him were concerned, this was accurate. And it was true not only for Sasso and the rest of his staff, but for his family as well. "His consuming passion was to make sure that he was in a position to be re-elected," said his son, John. "I don't think he allowed himself the luxury of thinking beyond November 1986. I think it was upsetting to him that people were talking to him about it before then." Kitty agreed. "People started talking about it before the election, but he didn't at all," she said. "He was totally focused on his re-election campaign."

When Dukakis did win by a near record margin on November 4, he began to come to grips with a national candidacy, but even then the process was slow. About a week after the election, Sasso asked Dukakis, "Do you really want to look at this thing?" Dukakis seemed unsure. Sasso went to Florida on vacation, leaving behind a memo outlining his view of the potential.

"Knowing him as I do, I felt he could go either way," Sasso says. "I thought he could walk away from it for personal reasons." And Sasso was also not sure that Dukakis really wanted to be president or that he wanted to go through the grind it would take to mount a campaign. Sasso remembered accompanying Dukakis on a trip to South Carolina, for instance, that included a couple of legs on bumpy small planes, which make Dukakis nervous. "You went through three months of this?" he said to Sasso, referring to the Ferraro campaign. "You've got to be nuts."

After Thanksgiving, Dukakis told Sasso he had read the memo, but that he wanted to focus on state issues and the start of his new administration until closer to Christmas. In mid-December, Sasso gave him one of his few nudges. "A judgment's got to be made here, Mike," he recalls saying. Dukakis asked for advice on how to approach a decision: what questions needed to be asked, and how he could find the answers. Shortly after Christmas, he said he wanted to look at a candidacy.

Then, to an extraordinary and sometimes comical degree, the decision-making process began to unfold, much of it in public.

At the end of his third inaugural address, delivered on January 8, 1987, to a packed House chamber and statewide television audience, Dukakis paused, then continued with remarks not in the prepared text. "I've got some awesome decisions to make in the next few months," he said. "And they are decisions that I intend to make only after much thought and much reflection. Whatever decision I make, I want you to know that being the governor of Massachusetts has been the richest, the most fulfilling, and the most enjoyable experience anyone in public life could ask for."

"*Has been,*" he said. Past tense. Swarms of reporters and legislators fastened on the two words as a clear signal that the decision had been made, that he was off and running. George Keverian, the House speaker, said, "The feeling I had was, he was telling everyone he was going to run." No, no, said Dukakis. It was all a mistake. No signal was intended. The decision-making process was just beginning.

A month later, Dukakis took his embryonic campaign to Iowa. Since 1976, Iowans, who cast the first votes that count in the

nomination process, have grown to expect considerable attention from presidential candidates. But they weren't ready for
what Dukakis brought to Iowa a year and four days early. While
Hart, Gephardt, and Arizona's former Governor Bruce Babbitt
were already frequent visitors, they usually traveled with one or
two aides and possibly one or two reporters, but often none.
When Dukakis and his wife landed in Des Moines on February
4, their plane disgorged three full television crews, a score of
reporters, and two aides—more than thirty people in all. Here
he was, not even a candidate yet, and he was traveling like a
nominee. Several Iowa reporters filed stories focusing more on
Dukakis's press contingent than on the man himself. The numbers should have come as no surprise. First, Greater Boston is
the nation's sixth largest media market, with competitive newspaper, television, and radio outlets. Second, Dukakis had doubled the impact by choosing Iowa for his first exploratory trip.
The interest in Massachusetts was enormous. But the entourage
made a mockery of the kind of person-to-person campaigning
for which Iowa is famous. Dukakis, sporting new hiking boots
and a ski parka, trudged to a tractor retailer, a livestock auction
house, and a cattle breeding farm, but every brief discussion was
overwhelmed by a crush of reporters and boom microphones.
Though he followed many of the traditions of campaigning in
Iowa, Dukakis would only go so far. He milked no cow; he petted no pig.

Apart from the awkwardness of his entourage, Dukakis had
only one real setback on his first trip. It began even before he
arrived. In the airplane, he talked with reporters about the farm
crisis. Dukakis believes most of the economically depressed regions of the country have been hurt by relying too much on one
or two industries, just as Massachusetts depended too much on
textiles and shoes in the early part of this century and defense
contracts in the 1960s. He wondered aloud if farm states like
Iowa relied too much on bulk crops like feed corn and soybeans,
crops that are vulnerable to weather and the viscissitudes of
foreign trade. In Massachusetts, he noted, declining agriculture
was turned around by new approaches, including diversification
into specialty crops like Belgian endive. A few hours later, he
told the same thing to a group of farmers at the livestock auction

house in Limoni, Iowa. The farmers were not impressed. Here was the governor of a high tech state seeming to tell Iowa how to farm: grow something no one can pronounce. Didn't he understand? Massachusetts is a tiny state with lots of people; its minute agricultural economy is suited to labor-intensive crops like endive. But Iowa has rich farmland stretching for hundreds of thousands of acres and its population is dropping faster than that of any state. It is best suited to bulk crops. Dukakis had tried to be careful. He had spoken favorably of agricultural diversification, but had never specifically recommended that Iowans grow endive. Still, there were several moments on the trip which reminded veteran Massachusetts reporters of some of the low moments in his first term—when he had seemed to know the answer before he knew the question.

But these problems were relatively minor. For the most part, Dukakis listened, asked questions, and learned. His discovery of Gus Thorakos and Tom Boosalis at Gus and Tom's Pizza in Osceola started a Greek connection that became a key asset of the campaign. His description of the booming Massachusetts economy excited considerable interest, easing fears that the story was too parochial and would not travel well. Even the entourage, comic as it was, demonstrated to Iowans that someone took Dukakis seriously, and it gave Dukakis and his staff a three-day exercise in big-time campaign logistics. Most encouraging was the obvious willingness of Iowans to give Dukakis a chance. Jim Hendrock, a farmer in Osceola, assured him that "we are not one-issue voters." And Jack Hatch, a state representative from Des Moines, was impressed with a brief pitch from Dukakis. "We respond well to people who believe in themselves, who have substance," Hatch said.

On the plane coming back, Dukakis grilled Sasso on the politics: Who's already committed? Where are the teachers? What would it take to organize the state? When would it have to start?

In the following five weeks, Dukakis went on other political trips—to North Carolina, Washington, D.C., New Hampshire, and to Baton Rouge, Louisiana, where one goal was to see if his stand against an oil import fee was necessarily fatal in the oil patch. The answer: possibly not.

All the while, Dukakis's staffers were under strict orders not to begin a campaign before there was one. No one could be hired, no political calls could be made, or it would seem that the decision had been made. This limited the most trusted aides to a few surreptitious calls to their closest friends, asking them to refrain from joining another campaign until Dukakis had decided.

While part of the exploration was public, Dukakis also held dozens of private discussions with academics, political activists, governors, senators, and former candidates, including Mondale and Glenn and one former president, Jimmy Carter.

As he described it openly, Dukakis was looking for answers to four questions: Was it right for the family? Could he carry out his duties as governor and run a national campaign at the same time? What was the political landscape like—did he have a chance to win or would it be tilting at windmills? And what of the job? What did it require, and what skills and goals would he bring to it?

It was, as Sasso put it, "a characteristically thoughtful process." As it began, the barriers seemed formidable, and Dukakis seemed skeptical, but, predictably, he went at it full throttle. "We tried in a ten-week period to cram as much in as possible," Sasso said. "Everywhere we went it kept coming up green lights."

Many of these Dukakis helped turn green; others were simply lucky. Not least among the latter was Mario Cuomo's announcement on February 19 that he would not run and his encouragement of a Dukakis candidacy.

A milestone was the March 6 speech to nearly eight hundred active Democrats in Bedford, New Hampshire. It was here that Dukakis developed the immigrant theme, introducing his mother from the audience, and touched on a broad range of national issues. Dukakis was clearly testing a campaign speech when he concluded: "Let the journey begin . . . let the future begin here." The response varied from an audience that included many activists already committed to other candidates, but it was generally enthusiastic.

Nearly everyone who was there, including Nick Zervas, was convinced by the performance that he would run, but they still didn't know for sure. To this day, George Papalimberis thinks he was the first person to be told. Papalimberis, Dukakis's barber, had been pushing for a presidential bid since Dukakis had returned to office in 1982. But he told Dukakis that, if he did go national he should have his hair cut shorter in front. On the morning of the New Hampshire speech, Papalimberis recalls, he gave Dukakis another nudge about the presidency and repeated his advice. Dukakis said, "If you think it would be better, go ahead," Papalimberis says.

Dukakis had said he would make his decision by mid-March. Sasso thought he was warming to the idea, but the strongest evidence did not come until March 10, when Dukakis told Sasso he wanted to speak to his wife, Francine. That night, gathered around the Dukakises' kitchen table, the two couples talked for three or four hours about what a campaign might be like. "Your lives are going to be disrupted as much as mine," Dukakis told Francine Sasso. "If my kids were your kids' age [six and eleven], I wouldn't be doing this." It was, perhaps, an example of the human empathy that clearly resides somewhere in Dukakis, though it is sometimes hard to detect. And it may also have been an example of Dukakis's learned approach to politics—seeking the support of all the most important constituencies before starting out. Francine signed on.

The next night, after a successful speech in Washington, on his way to Baton Rouge, Dukakis asked Sasso how an announcement should be made. Sasso said that depended on what it was. If he wasn't running, the logistics would be easy. If he was, some thought should go into it. Dukakis asked Sasso to break away from the trip and think.

When Dukakis called Sasso to Perry Street the following Saturday, shortly after talking to Kitty, Sasso was ready for the decision, though he wasn't certain until he heard it.

Like most candidates, Dukakis went for a two-stage affair—an immediate disclosure so that the news wouldn't dribble out ineffectively, followed by a formal declaration of candidacy. On Saturday, Dukakis and Sasso decided to make the disclosure on Monday and to try to pull the legislature in if possible. Sasso thought it was crucial to protect the story, so Dukakis did not even call his children until midday on Monday, although Kitty had quietly passed the word to them the night before. John Dukakis, the former actor, says he had little trouble sounding surprised when he got the call from his father on Monday.

The interval produced some laughs, especially since this all happened to be taking place on the weekend of Boston's St. Patrick's Day political spectacular, a corned beef and green beer breakfast in South Boston run by William Bulger, the state Senate president.

Bulger and Keverian were not told of the decision until Monday morning, when Sasso asked if they could pull together a joint session that afternoon. Despite the short lead time, the event was a smash. With crisp articulation, Dukakis talked first to a jammed press conference and then to the legislators, addressing the major questions he had faced.

He indicated that he had weighed the personal sacrifice. "As a husband, a father, and a son," he said, his time with his family "is very, very precious indeed."

Then he faced head-on the question of whether he could be a governor and a candidate simultaneously. "I don't like the idea that public servants are somehow disqualified from seeking the presidency," he said. "I don't want an America where only full-time professional candidates are eligible. If that's what the system is becoming, then now may be a very good time to start changing the system." He then dealt with his inevitable absences from the state in a novel way: by asking "the citizens of our commonwealth to campaign with me." This seemed a flight of rhetoric at the time, but in fact it was pursued, with thousands of Massachusetts voters and activists being encouraged to contact friends, relatives, and people in similar work situations in other states on behalf of Dukakis. In addition, the announcement itself was designed to give the legislators a sense of participation, encouraging them to work for a smooth and productive session. It was an effective response to a potential problem. No one raised the contrast with 1974, when Dukakis said he would talk about that campaign with Governor Sargent, "but not at the State House and not on the public's time."

In his remarks, Dukakis compared the presidential race to the marathons of Greece and of his youth, and he was blunt: "The odds against winning are very, very long," he said, adding one *very* to his prepared text. But, he said, "I have the energy to run this marathon."

Most important, Dukakis began to sound some campaign themes, to talk about the job and the personal qualities that are important to it. "I have . . . the strength to run this country, the experience to manage our government, and the values to lead our people," he declared, saying he invited "tests of character and competence."

The formal announcement six weeks later drew on the same themes. The day, April 29, was notable in two respects—apart from the late snowfall that blanketed New England in the morning. One was that Dukakis chartered a jet and pushed hard so that he could add a southern stop—Atlanta—to the usual announcement day itinerary of home base, Iowa, and New Hampshire. The southern primaries on Super Tuesday would have an enormous impact, and Dukakis was determined to make a visible effort in the South from the first day.

The other notable aspect was that Dukakis organizers worked strenuously to pack the announcement ceremonies with hordes of people, including family, politicians, celebrities, labor leaders, workers, people who had benefited from state programs—hundreds and thousands of people with whom Dukakis could connect. It was at once an indication of support and a plea for help. And it was a clear statement that here was one task Dukakis knew he could not accomplish by himself. The contrast was obvious, in particular, to Gary Hart, who took his family to a park in Colorado and made his formal announcement alone, standing on a rock.

Dukakis started life as a presidential candidate with several assets. Most apparent was his ability to mount a serious campaign. Sasso's skills were widely thought to be as great as those of any political handler in the country. Bob Farmer, who had coordinated fund-raising for Dukakis in 1982 and 1986, worked in the interim setting records for John Glenn's presidential campaign. He was eager to go to work again. A healthy number of other first-rate veterans with significant experience in national campaigns was either on the state payroll or nearby. The networks of governors, academics and students from the Kennedy School, and Greek Americans guaranteed that Dukakis could start with contacts, advice, and money. Mentioned less frequently, but most important of all, was Dukakis's own political skill. From the days of going door-to-door for Sumner Kaplan, through the convention fights in 1966 and 1970, and on to the modern, computerized campaigns for governor, Dukakis had proven his relentless determination as a battler, whether in a precinct coffee klatsch or a televised debate. As an example, at first it seemed reasonable to dismiss his potential to compete in Iowa because he was so utterly unfamiliar with the state, and its voters with him. But his strength was his experience with what it takes to win caucus politics.

These assets proved themselves swiftly, as Dukakis soon jumped ahead of his Democratic competitors in fund-raising, matched or exceeded them organizationally in most areas, and even became a leading contender in Iowa.

In addition, the cautious style Dukakis had displayed since the beginning of his second term was augmented by Sasso's attention to detail and natural inclination to worry; the result was a campaign that many insiders felt was likely to make few mistakes. "He's the closest you're going to come to a gaffe-proof candidate," his media adviser, Dan Payne, said in August 1987.

Dukakis's campaign themes developed piecemeal and a bit shakily at times. For instance, many of his earliest appearances included a bland pitch for arms control, often introduced by the statement that, while he had never met Mikhail Gorbachev, he had been told that "Mikhail" in Russian was pronounced almost the same as "Michael" in Greek. Apparently, the observation failed to enlighten or amuse a single one of the dozens of people who heard it, for it was eventually dropped.

But the major themes were competence and integrity, and they scored immediately. Just six days after his formal announcement, the Iran-contra hearings began in Washington, once again raising doubts about Reagan's laissez-faire management style and about whether some of his top assistants might have broken the law. The image Dukakis was projecting, as a hands-on manager who was guided by clear and lofty values, contrasted sharply.

At the same time, the stories of Gary Hart's womanizing, and his reaction to them, were exploding his candidacy, and on May 8 he was gone. Luck had found Dukakis once again. After less than two weeks as an official candidate, his most formidable opponent had vanished, and under circumstances that made him look good. All those years of riding the subway and browbeating his office to get him home for dinner with his family now worked for Dukakis politically.

Suddenly, he was catapulted into the campaign spotlight, far sooner than even his most ardent supporters had ever thought possible. The *Los Angeles Times* printed a national poll on May 10 that placed Dukakis at the head of the Democratic pack. Though his support was pegged at only 12 percent, it was still a remarkable showing for a newcomer to the campaign, especially one who was still largely unknown to the country. Nine days later, Dukakis went on his first western swing. When he woke in Seattle to find more than five hundred people waiting for him at 7:00 A.M., it was clear that his candidacy had caught fire.

Within weeks, Dukakis scooped up many of Hart's key supporters, set fund-raising records, and appeared on the cover of *New York* magazine, the *New Republic,* and *National Journal.* Major stories appeared in other national publications, including *Vanity Fair* and the *Nation.* Early in July, Kitty made a dramatic announcement, revealing that the use of diet pills that began with her first marriage had continued for twenty-six years, ending only in 1982, when she checked in to a treatment center in Minnesota for a month. Dukakis also made a disclosure—that he had covered up for his wife's absence in 1982 with the false story that she had hepatitis. Given the same circumstances, Dukakis said, he would do it again. Neither revelation seemed to hurt; if anything, they made him seem more human. Within days, *Newsweek* proclaimed him the front-runner. Dukakis's favorite mention came from *Playgirl,* which named him one of the ten sexiest men in America. It noticed "what a snappy dresser he is" and "how seductive those bushy eyebrows are." When it was remarked that Dukakis had no reputation as a playboy, Nancie Martin, *Playgirl*'s editor, responded that, these days in particular, monogamy is sexy. For weeks afterward, Dukakis mentioned the honor at every campaign stop. He told audiences that his pride was reduced only slightly when he heard that George Bush had made the list in 1986 and when his daughter Kara, responding to the news, laughed uncontrollably for three minutes.

In late September, just when it seemed to be running smoothly and with growing momentum, the campaign had a blowout. Sasso admitted that he had secretly distributed videotapes to news organizations which showed that another Democratic candidate, Senator Joseph R. Biden, Jr., of Delaware, had lifted a large portion of a speech from Neil Kinnock, a British Labour candidate, and on at least one occasion had not attributed it. Within hours, Sasso left the campaign.

To some people close to Dukakis, it seemed to be the toughest moment in all his political life, rivaling the 1978 defeat. Indeed, there were some similarities, for Dukakis contributed to both problems through his attitude of moral superiority, almost smugness. In 1987, he said his campaign was too clean to do anything such as distribute tapes. In fact, there was nothing immoral about the tapes themselves, but Dukakis made it seem that way.

He said in 1987 that he opposed negative campaigning, and he made a distinction between tough debate on issues carried out in public and material distributed privately, even if it was accurate. This distinction, of course, flew in the face of Dukakis's own conduct in 1979, when he cheered his political office as it planted negative stories about Ed King.

Even so, Dukakis's rhetoric and the theme of integrity combined to make the case of the Biden tapes more urgent. However, Sasso had himself to blame as well. When the brouhaha subsided, most commentators concluded that the distribution of the tapes was not in itself wrong—campaigns regularly alert reporters to deficiencies in opposing camps; Sasso was simply more resourceful in sending the material out on videotape instead of in a printed text. But when *Time* magazine checked a report that the Dukakis campaign had been the source of the tapes, Paul Tully, the political director and a top assistant of Sasso's, knew the truth, and he denied it. When Dukakis asked Sasso about the *Time* story, Sasso said he would look into it—he was not lying, exactly, but he did not tell Dukakis the full story at that point. Dukakis then told a press conference he would be "astonished" and "very, very angry" if anyone in his campaign was responsible. The next day, Sasso went to Dukakis and confessed. The following morning, Dukakis called another State House press conference to make the disclosure. He said he had put Sasso on temporary leave, but had declined to accept his resignation. Four hours later, however, Sasso told his own press conference that he was leaving.

The final decision was Dukakis's, according to at least one version. Sasso, besieged by press inquiries, had called his press conference for 3:00 P.M. at a downtown hotel, near the campaign headquarters. But when John DeVillars, Dukakis's chief of operations at the State House, talked at about two-forty to Tom Glynn, at the campaign headquarters, it was not clear what Sasso intended to say about himself or about anyone else in the campaign who had played a part in distributing the tapes. DeVillars went to the governor's office, where he found Dukakis and Kitty still devastated from the day's events. "Michael and Kitty were in there, not exactly crying, but I had never seen either one of them looking so drawn or wrenched," says DeVillars. He reported what he knew. Dukakis's first response was: " 'This has all got to come out, and come out today,' " DeVillars recalls. "Then he said, with tears welling in his eyes, in a halting voice, 'John's gotta go.' " His secretary, Jean Hines, was asked to place the call. Glynn says he believes Sasso reached the same conclusion independently.

Assessments of Dukakis's performance in this instance varied widely. Some analysts said he betrayed indecision in trying to weather the storm for four hours; others said he showed commendable loyalty by trying to hang on to Sasso for that long. Still others blasted him for letting Sasso go at all. Says his former rival Frank Sargent: "Sasso *made* Dukakis II . . . To throw your best friend and the guy who made you over the side is inexcusable."

Sasso had a unique relationship with Dukakis, one based on respect. As a result, Sasso more than any other person could tell

Dukakis when he was wrong, and Dukakis would listen. The absence of that voice is likely to be Dukakis's greatest loss, more important even than the loss of Sasso's skills as campaign manager and more important than the immediate damage. And there *was* immediate damage. A candidacy that had been based in large part on competence and integrity now came into question on both counts. Dukakis apologized to Biden, personally and publicly, then flew to Iowa to express his regrets there. The campaign was at a standstill.

Even in this disaster, however, Dukakis was blessed with a bit of luck in the timing. The blowout occurred when he was already far down the road, but not yet in heavy traffic. In six months of active campaigning, Dukakis had built a strong base of support organizationally and financially. The Biden tape episode stopped his momentum in its tracks, but the base gave him a cushion to fall back on. And there were still more than four months left before the first balloting in Iowa—plenty of time to regain speed.

While competence and integrity needed to be proven again, the substantive backbone of the campaign remained intact: the Massachusetts success story. Occasionally, other campaigns questioned how much credit Dukakis could rightfully take for the state's economic vitality or how applicable state policies were to national problems, but these doubts were rarely raised by the candidates themselves, since they only helped Dukakis focus on his state's prosperity, which was undeniable. To a degree that surprised even many in his own campaign, people all over the country listened to the Massachusetts story and gave Dukakis credit, either for specific programs that might be translated into national policy or, more generally, for proven skills.

In addition, Dukakis still had the immigrant story. This theme was enormously successful with Greek Americans, who contributed lavishly to his campaign treasury and who made up a key organizational network as well. They ranged from entrepreneurs who organized five- and six-figure fund-raisers in the Greek communities in New York, New Jersey, Michigan, California, and elsewhere to people like Gus Thorakos, the Osceola, Iowa, pizza man Dukakis met on his first day as a prospective candidate.

Dukakis also attempted, with some success, to broaden the immigrant story and make it connect with Americans in general, and with first- and second-generation immigrants in particular.

From the first, Dukakis said he intended to run a fifty-state campaign, and as the year progressed he tried to shed the stereotype of a Northeast liberal and make an appeal to various regions and ideologies. Some supporters, for instance, saw him as a candidate bridging the Hart and Mondale factions of the Democratic party. Part of the pitch was seen as neoliberal, almost Republican: he campaigned as a tough and innovative manager who was able to deliver services and still cut taxes. But another part was distinctly Democratic: a fervent commitment to public service and belief in government as an engine of good, with a goal of opportunity for everyone.

Overlaying these themes was Dukakis's persistent optimism. As Nick Patsouras, his chief fund-raiser in California, put it: "The other candidates are talking about doom and gloom. Dukakis is the Democratic Reagan because he is preaching optimism and makes people feel good."

10. Self

"He doesn't shrug his shoulders very often."

MICHAEL DUKAKIS DEFIES easy labels. He is a liberal, but he took a "meat cleaver" to welfare in his first term and resisted legislative efforts to raise it in his second. He is a progressive, but he cut taxes, saying that the state must show some concern for the people who pay the bills. He is a reformer, but he has taken over the smoke-filled rooms, both in state government and party politics.

The job of placing Dukakis in a historical context is also difficult, although there are threads—some sturdier than others—extending back and connecting him with most of this century's leading Democrats.

His approach has much in common with that of Walter Mondale, the epitome of the regular Democrat, a soulmate whom he supported for president in 1984. But at the same time he has marketed ET and REAP as innovations that would qualify for Gary Hart's claim to "new ideas"—highly targeted programs that try to limit, rather than increase, the scope of government.

Dukakis is frequently compared with Jimmy Carter. It's much more than the gubernatorial approach or their simple lifestyles—carrying their own suitcases and the like. Both are masters of retail, small-group politics. Both claim expertise with the detailed mechanisms of government. Both have a moralistic tone. And both can communicate an impregnable self-assurance.

As a presidential candidate, Dukakis often refers to himself as "a full-employment Democrat," a phrase reminiscent of Hubert Humphrey and Harry Truman.

Dukakis says John Kennedy was his political inspiration, and he talks of Franklin Roosevelt as the ideological bedrock for all Democrats today. "Philosophically," he says of Roosevelt, "that's where I came from." And in his zeal for reform can be heard an echo from the Progressive movement.

Even people familiar with the sweep of twentieth-century Democratic politics see different facets in Dukakis. James Mac-Gregor Burns, the historian and active Democrat who has known Dukakis since the two were active in COD, says that in his most recent tenure as governor, "Dukakis very much reflects this pragmatic generation" that wants to solve problems and achieve results. "Does he believe in some value that transcends himself? I just don't know," Burns says. The historian Arthur M. Schlesinger, Jr., makes the comparison with Carter, but says Dukakis seems to have more sense of direction, a better idea of where he is going.

These varying views of Dukakis are at odds with his oft-repeated statement that "what you see is what you get." At a minimum, they mean that Dukakis is not the least complicated man in America, as his wife claims—not as a politician, anyway.

Is he new? He has campaigned on "the Massachusetts miracle," but does his success with a high tech economy mean he could lead the nation to the threshold of the twenty-first century? Might he give the country a sense of rejuvenation and new direction after Ronald Reagan, much as Kennedy did after Dwight Eisenhower?

Certainly, Dukakis has worked to develop an approach to government that fits the times—and the approach more often than not is to use government as a facilitator rather than as the ultimate problem solver. Whereas government itself has often been seen by liberal Democrats as the answer to major problems, Dukakis frequently takes the position that the best government is one that helps steer the private sector to providing solutions for public problems. This approach, in which government is a "deal-maker," as David Broder put it, could be an effective way to make liberal government operate in an era of somewhat limited resources.

To Mondale, Dukakis has the potential to create "intergenerational unity," bringing young voters into the same camp with older Democrats, who grew up during the New Deal. "There is the traditional base, plus modern, competitive, high tech issues," Mondale says.

Dukakis's energy and determination can be infectious. His personality, combined with the economic success of Massachusetts, communicates his eagerness to tackle tough problems, an impatience to find solutions. To this extent, Dukakis embodies some of the vigor that was a key part of Kennedy's appeal. There is little chance, however, that Dukakis will duplicate Kennedy's rhetorical call to action, his grasping of the generational torch and his sounding of reveille for the New Frontier.

But there are clear signs of the promise Dukakis offers. The combination to look for in a prospective president is "between energy on the one hand and pleasure in doing the work on the other hand," says James David Barber, a presidential scholar at Duke University. "A candidate who puts out a whole lot of energy yet conveys a certain bitterness, darkness, a downside—watch out for those guys. They've turned out to be rigid tragic figures in the White House—Nixon, Johnson, Hoover, Wilson."

If governing makes Dukakis as happy as it appears to, "if he really does have fun doing government work . . . that is encouraging," says Barber, who adds, "The combination of high energy and enjoyment are . . . indicative of adaptability, a capacity to move into strange, weird situations like being president of the United States and to make it happen, to go with it rather than to get hung up on some aspect that gets you done in."

Dukakis describes himself as being similar to a number of others in his "generation" of Democratic governors, state leaders who "are all progressives philosophically, but [who] also as chief executives know that you've got to run the store and you've got to pay your bills." He once called himself "a liberal who can count."

Part of this pragmatic liberalism is his emphasis on jobs. "I really am a *full employment* Democrat," he says. "I think that's one of the principal goals of economic policy—to provide good jobs at good wages for every adult citizen in this country. That's something I believe in very, very strongly. And that goes back to FDR, to the Full Employment Act of 1946, to Humphrey-Hawkins . . . When I say, as I often do, that full employment is the most important human services program we have in this country, I believe that very strongly." In contrast to the spirit and substance of those pieces of legislation, Dukakis's view of full employment is that it flows not from public works programs on the order of Roosevelt's Works Project Administration, but from the private economy.

To Dukakis, jobs are part of opportunity, the passkey to progress. "If the Democratic party loses its claim on the American electorate as the party of economic opportunity, then we're done," he warned in 1984. "Ever since Franklin Roosevelt, that's been our strength."

Two historians and presidential scholars, Richard E. Neustadt and Henry Steele Commager, see a reformist fire burning in Dukakis. Neustadt came to know Dukakis well at the Kennedy School, and he traces Dukakis's political antecedents back beyond Roosevelt to the Progressive movement. Commager, who wrote Dukakis's favorite book, *The American Mind,* is reminded of the Progressives as well, though not as strongly. Dukakis is "a kind of good, New Deal Progressive," he says.

The "Progressive" label, used by Neustadt, Commager, and Dukakis himself, is apt in several ways. For in the reform efforts that have propelled him through his thirty-year political career, there are distinct echoes from the Progressive era that dominated American politics during the earliest days of this century. In some respects—particularly in his lifelong drive for political reform—Dukakis is a descendant of Progressives like Theodore Roosevelt, Woodrow Wilson, Hiram Johnson, and Robert M. La Follette—all determined reformers and all governors.

The Progressives, at their most influential between 1900 and 1914, went to war against political bosses who controlled the votes of the hundreds of thousands of new immigrants packed into city slums. The Progressives were driven by a good government, reform ethic. They were unrelentingly optimistic in their

outlook and conveyed a sense of moral superiority, which sometimes tended toward the condescending and self-righteous. As
progressivism took hold, it drew to its banner farmers, middle-
class professionals, and owners of small businesses. They
worked to enact child labor laws, clean up the slums, protect
female workers, bust trusts, and strip political bosses of their
power.

Like Dukakis, the Progressives were not radicals, but reformers. Although they were sometimes angry at the abuses they
fought against, their proposals were not extreme or impractical.
According to Albert C. Ganley, "they recommended reasonable
steps to guarantee each citizen the opportunity to have a dignified life." They were well educated, civilized, and used little if
any of the hyperbolic rhetoric that marked populism. As Arthur
Schlesinger noted, they favored the "enforcement of middle-
class standards of civic decency against greedy wealth and crook-
ed politics."

The apex of the movement came in 1912 when a former
president, Theodore Roosevelt, and the man who was to win
that November, Woodrow Wilson, both ran on platforms reflecting Progressive ideas and goals. Wilson was the Democrat
and Roosevelt ran that year as the Bull Moose challenger to his
onetime protégé President William Howard Taft, then the leader of the established Republicans. A measure of the popularity
of the Progressive ideas was that between them, Roosevelt and
Wilson won nearly 70 percent of the vote.

Elected governor of New Jersey in 1910, Wilson succeeded in
winning enactment of numerous Progressive programs, including workmen's compensation and regulation of both railroads
and public utilities, reforms similar to those won in Wisconsin by
La Follette six years earlier. His approach to state and national
government blended the styles of the scholar he once was with
the preacher he often sounded like.

From such spiritual antecedents came Michael Dukakis, a zealous reformer elected first to the leadership of the Brookline
Democratic Town Committee. His regulatory streak, most visible in his wariness of big business during his first term and in

his emphasis on aggressive regulation of the insurance, banking, and utility industries, was distinctly reminiscent of the approaches taken by TR, Wilson, and others nearly six decades earlier.

First the Progressives, then the New Dealers, articulated what Richard Hofstadter has called "a far greater willingness than had been seen in previous American history to make use of the machinery of government to meet the needs of the people and supplement the workings of the national economy." On the stump, Dukakis is comfortable with that battle cry: "I believe in activist leadership," he said frequently during his presidential campaign. "I don't believe you're elected to stand on the sidelines and watch the world go by."

Of all the Progressive leaders, Wilson is the one whom Dukakis resembles the most. It is not merely the emphasis on reform and regulation but also more personal qualities—confidence in their own intellects, for instance—that invite comparison. Commager says that Wilson "applauded the work of the expert in government but did not use him to any large extent, regarding himself, perhaps, as sufficiently expert for most purposes." Wilson's appeal, Commager said, "was intellectual rather than emotional." Though these remarks could apply equally to Dukakis, there are obvious limits to the comparison. Wilson was a scholarly man who wrote political philosophy and studied history. Dukakis is a smart man who tackles the problems in front of him, evincing little interest in the perspective of history.

The Progressive analogy has frayed a bit in Dukakis's second and third terms. For one thing, the Progressives were generally suspicious of entrepreneurs, whereas Dukakis celebrates them. For another, the reformer's drive in Dukakis—while still evident rhetorically on some issues—is often negotiable if it will help achieve political goals. Some have criticized this change as a failure of leadership and have yearned aloud for the return of "Duke I." For all his faults in those days, such critics have said, one knew where he stood. Dukakis has responded consistently that the true test of leadership is accomplishment—not pretty speeches but a solid record. There is logic to Dukakis's view; in the long run it promises more substance from a public leader.

But it is still a long way from the principled, take-it-or-leave-it morality of the first term.

Despite his celebrated ability with the details of government, Dukakis lacks a sweeping vision, and even when the question is forced on him, he conveys little sense of history, philosophy, or ideological context in what he says and does. It is not that he lacks intelligence, far from it, but that he does not think that way; it is simply not his intellectual style. Thomas Vallely, a former state representative, spent years working with Dukakis, but he initially supported Senator Joe Biden for the presidency in 1987. "The country has to change a lot and I want to affect that change," Vallely said. "Michael's just not in the change business. You have to see the future in order to get there."

Dukakis claims to rank the communication of a vision as the most important function of a political leader, but he is not himself a conceptual thinker or speaker. He still refers to *The American Mind,* which he read as a senior in high school upon its publication in 1950, as the most influential book in his life. But he says, while it opened a new world of thought to him as a teenager, "I can't even tell you now what it was about the book that substantively kind of struck me." Dukakis also disdains anything that smacks of demagoguery. John DeVillars, who writes some of his formal speeches, says his own efforts to include obvious applause lines or rhetorical flourishes are usually penciled out by Dukakis.

Still, it is clear that Dukakis is not simply a technocrat, handling issues with the soul of a robot. He is a manager, a problem solver guided by values and a sharply defined morality that have been instinctive with him since childhood.

To what extent these values are rooted in faith or religious training is difficult to discern. From the age of five to thirteen he regularly attended Sunday school, but as an adult he is "not a regular church attender. I go at holidays." He says that he believes in God. He says he prays, but not much. Asked what role faith plays in his life, he says, "Well, I think a great deal of what I am and what I believe is a reflection of faith, at least as I define it." And how does he define it? "Well, not only belief in a supreme being but in the fundamental goodness of human beings. I don't want that to sound naive. I understand that we all have our strengths and our weaknesses, but a sense that we all have a responsibility to our fellow citizens as people, as fellow human beings . . . That's an important part of your expressed faith in religion."

In Nick Zervas's view, Dukakis's clear moral tone had a lot to do with his political appeal when he was starting out. "He had a very idealistic approach . . . that people found very appealing," Zervas says.

Ira Jackson, who, when he wasn't collecting taxes, also spent some time writing speeches for Dukakis, believes that clearly stated values, along with the record, have helped Dukakis to move audiences across the country as effectively as some of the more emotional orators, though in a different way. "It's not demagoguery, it's rational empowerment," says Jackson. The appeal to listeners is based on their own principles, their own sense of accomplishment, rather than dreams, Jackson says. "I call it rational lift. It makes people not followers, but vested participants. It's not a leap of faith; it's an understanding of fact. It's linear instead of metaphysical. It's disciplined as opposed to poetic."

Dukakis and the values that guide him are very much a product of his strong-willed and highly disciplined parents. Panos and Euterpe Dukakis taught young Michael by example to work hard, to be frugal, to help others. There was a spartan quality to life in the Dukakis household. From his intelligent parents Michael inherited an exceptional mind, and he grew to have nearly total confidence in his analytical ability. No problem was so great that it could not be solved by rational analysis and hard work. Indeed, for all of the Dukakises there was a sense of simplicity about life: the notion that working hard, contributing to the community, raising a family—that is what life *is*.

Sandy Bakalar believes that Dukakis's values and goals have changed little over the years. She remembers one high school summer when Dukakis was a counselor at a camp for under-privileged children in Duxbury, on Boston's South Shore. "He

wanted to do something good, he wanted to help people," Bakalar says. "That's what Michael is really all about. There's a consistency about the whole thing."

One consistency is that, after more than a quarter century in
public life, Dukakis's personal qualities are fairly well established. Indeed, his failings are almost invariably seen as growing out of his strengths—positive qualities carried to extremes.
Persistence can become stubbornness; a sense of purpose, rigid-
ity; self-assurance, cockiness. Depending on the moment or the
observer, he can seem reserved or cold, serious or humorless,
energetic or compulsive, frugal or miserly. His idealism still
occasionally takes on shades of self-righteousness. Dukakis almost never apologizes for mistakes, or even admits them; but
the other side of that coin is that he almost never complains,
either.

Even his brilliant mind can take on negative overtones when
he relies too completely on his own reasoning capacity. This can
lead to blind spots. "One of the things about people who are that
smart and that confident," says Marty Linsky, "is that they can
talk themselves into anything." And Fran Meaney, who still
thinks enough of Dukakis to support him for president, also
pinpoints this failing: "He's the number one master of self-delu-
sion that I've ever met in my life."

Dukakis has heard the voices. And he has learned something
significant since 1978—that he cannot solve every problem by
the force of his intellect alone. "I'm less rational than I used to
be," he said late in 1987, meaning that he was relying less exclusively on his own reasoned analysis and now understood that
affected parties must be taken into account if solutions are to
stick. The choice of words was instructive, for many would say
that his newfound pragmatism is "rational" in that it is politically
sensible. But Dukakis clearly equated pragmatism with being
"less rational"—he was depending less on his own brainpower.

Still, there are times when his inclination toward sophistry
appears undiminished, when he does not see, or refuses to see, a
reality that seems obvious to others.

On the question of patronage, for instance, there are only two
conceivable explanations for his dramatic change: either he lost

the idealism that drove the no-patronage policy of his first term or he was simply subordinating that idealism to pragmatic expediency. Dukakis, however, cannot admit either to lost idealism or to hypocrisy, so he takes the position that there really wasn't that much change in the policy after all. He seems to have convinced himself this is true, though the evidence to the contrary is overwhelming.

He is also unable to see the similarity between John Sasso's providing a videotape of Joe Biden to a reporter and his eagerness in 1979 to have a top aide supply the press with the damaging lobster story about Ed King. In that case, he couldn't wait to see the information in print. After Sasso had done precisely the same thing—provide accurate information to a reporter—Dukakis condemned the action and abruptly cut off the man who had made his presidential campaign possible. Says Robert Kiley, the man Dukakis appointed to run the MBTA: "The Sasso incident reminds all of us that [Dukakis] really hasn't changed that much."

Dukakis's prediction that personal qualities would be central to the presidential campaign raises not one but two questions: What are the personal qualities of the candidates, and how do they relate to the presidency? The second question is important. In Dukakis, for instance, the strong family bonds, the six o'clock dinners at Perry Street, and the apparently wholesome relationships with his wife and children are all appealing, yet they probably have little value as predictors of performance in office. The roster of great presidents is crowded with men who had difficult private lives: some of the best husbands were some of the worst presidents. On the other hand, the coolness with which Dukakis has cut off some of his closest political associates over the years, disquieting as it is in a personal sense, might not be a liability in the White House.

The notion that he is who he is, that there is no hidden "inner man," is at the core of Dukakis's self-image. He sees himself as particularly smart, of course. Even after his loss in 1978, Dukakis recalls that "I don't know that I doubted my own abilities. I'm always a guy that has had a fair degree of confidence."

Throughout his life, Dukakis's intellectual achievements have surpassed those of the overwhelming majority of his peers, and his record is impressive: Eagle Scout, brilliant student, superior athlete, Student Council president, proficient in five languages, precocious politician, and, according to a survey of his peers, the best governor in the country.

Many friends see the straightforward side of Dukakis—the openness and reliability—as an important part of his appeal. "There are not a lot of shadows or illusions," says Graham Allison of the Kennedy School. And his media adviser, Dan Payne, says, "He's very rational, very ordered. There are no three-cushion shots here. He's a straight-ahead thinker . . . He's not wishy-washy . . . He's not an emotional person. He does not go to extremes . . . He does not do cuckoo things; he does not yell at people or blow off or blunder . . . Maybe it means that the prose is very prosaic, but no one is going to force him to push that red button unless there's no other option."

But Zervas sees a more forceful man than Dukakis is often thought to be. "I don't think he's a dove at all," says Zervas. "He wouldn't provoke an incident, but he would be very tough if attacked." Dukakis once said to Zervas, "I'm a very tough guy. If I have to do something, I just do it."

There is some disagreement, even among people who know him well, on the accuracy of Dukakis's assertion that he is precisely as he appears. Paul Tsongas is one who believes it. With Dukakis, he says, "people who spend a lot of time trying to get underneath find out that they're on top."

Beryl Cohen says that Dukakis "won't veer from what we know him as . . . You won't find anyone to whom Michael has told a dirty joke or has seen him wear a bow tie."

But this notion that he is a simple person, that he is extraordinarily consistent, falls far short of explaining the whole man.

Nick Zervas does not view him as simple. "He is very private personally. There is a lot there you don't see," he says. "There are a lot of things he wants to do he'll never tell anybody because it's too dangerous to say . . . There are more dimensions to Mike."

Based on the evidence of his life—one in which achievement

has been interspersed with more emotional strain and personal loss than most people realize—both views are true in their way. The part of Dukakis that is visible is, indeed, unusually straightforward, honest, dependable, predictable.

But there are, clearly, other dimensions. One is that, looking back at the crucial episodes, such as the fiscal crisis of 1975 and the election of 1982, he sees himself as a hero, even a savior. Though he doesn't use such words, he says that in 1975 "somebody had to come along and straighten the mess out, and I was the governor, so that was my job."

This sense of mission ties in with the characteristic seen so often in Dukakis's career, self-confidence that he and he alone is the man for the job. This helps explain how Dukakis could allow deep splits to develop between himself and his closest political associates without any real sign of loss.

Surely one of the hidden parts of Dukakis is the effect on him of his brother's attempted suicide and subsequent chronic mental instability. The image conveyed by Dukakis and his mother is one of young Michael eagerly following his older brother's lead, though it is clear that there was intense competition between the two boys. In many families where a child is emotionally disturbed, a sibling takes on additional responsibilities and ambition, often in an unconscious desire to achieve for two. Michael has plenty of ambition, but it was evident well before Stelian's breakdown. Still, it is hard to imagine that the news of Stelian's attempt to kill himself didn't profoundly shake the seventeen-year-old Michael. The heartbreaking episode when Stelian distributed leaflets urging people to vote against his brother must have wounded Michael, who was then in the infancy of his political career. How could Stelian's being "aggressively hostile" to his brother, as Sapers put it, not have hurt Michael terribly? Yet no scars are evident on Dukakis today, no signs of the suffering his brother surely caused. In fact, his otherwise superior memory fails him on the subject. When asked during an interview about the events surrounding Stelian's attempted suicide and breakdown, Michael says he remembers little. Yet only minutes later, when asked when he came down with mononucleosis, he recalls precise details: it was on Washington's birthday in 1962;

it snowed heavily that day; after shoveling, he felt tired and napped for five hours.

Not long after Stelian died, Dukakis demonstrated the coldness of which he is capable by splitting with Joe Grandmaison, Sumner Kaplan, and Fran Meaney in what seemed to some an extraordinary sequence of abandonments. The distance Dukakis has allowed to develop between himself and so many close comrades is the best indication of his deeply held belief that he needs no one; that he can reach his goals *monos mou*. This distinguishing characteristic, that he is the most singular of men, within him when he entered the world, was developed in childhood. Panos and Euterpe saw it as a positive quality, and as she put it: "We didn't want to discourage it too much. We didn't want to weaken the spirit."

"We've always felt that he's had a very strong sense of himself," she said in an interview in 1974. "It is part of his own strength of character and integrity."

This trait of guarding his thoughts and emotions even from his closest friends sometimes works to his advantage. Paul Brountas remembers a time early in the 1974 campaign for governor when money had dried up and momentum seemed lost, but the candidate's optimism—or at least his apparent optimism—was unquenchable. "Dukakis was incredibly up," Brountas remembers. "When everybody else was down, he was up, and he lifted everybody else up." In reality, he says, "maybe he was down at the time, but he was putting on a damn good face."

There are also times, however, when Dukakis's habit of internalizing his true reactions, and sometimes snuffing them out, can be dangerous. Criticism, for instance, rolls off him with little effect, even when he should be listening, such as during the budget crisis of 1975 and the Ed King challenge of 1978. The self-confidence and certitude that are part of this personality are captured succinctly by his mother: "He doesn't shrug his shoulders very often." The downside, of course, is that sometimes he can be wrong when he is certain, and his faith in his own rationality often makes him very stubborn, even when he is wrong.

No such blindness afflicted him during his rejuvenating campaigns, however. The vindication against King in 1982 and the affirmation he received in 1986 had marvelous effects on Dukakis. They seem to have relaxed him some, calmed him to a point where he appeared more at ease with himself. He even changed his pitch, emphasizing practical results over reformist principles. In his new comfort with himself, Dukakis seemed to discover his ethnicity. It has been of great political benefit, for it has given him his central theme—that as the child of immigrants he thoroughly understands the concept of opportunity that America can offer. But his new fondness for his Greek roots seems genuine, as well. In this and other ways the national campaign has broadened Dukakis.

What is at work now in Dukakis is a battle between the self-contained, independent core that spills over too easily into arrogant pride—hubris, as the Greeks called it—and the broadening lessons of the 1978 defeat and the presidential quest—lessons that could save Dukakis from a flaw that has already been nearly fatal to his career once.

Dukakis is not suddenly humble—far from it. Describing his defeat and return to office, Dukakis portrayed himself in late 1987 in the role of a Greek hero. After the loss in 1978, he says, a state official gave him a book about an ancient Greek statesman named Aristides the Just. He "was a very fine political leader in Athens," says Dukakis, "and he had a reputation for being absolutely honest, and they finally threw him out because his integrity was getting a little much. About six years later things got very, very bad and kind of corrupt, and they went to Aristides, who was in exile, and said, 'We gotta have you back.' " The fact that Dukakis would still tell the story that way raises a question about whether he has reined in his pride at all.

But the point is not to forgo pride. Contained within hubris are the ambition and self-assurance that make great achievement possible. That is the tremendous strength of Greek drama, the reason it has lasted for twenty-four centuries: personal qualities are not purely positive or negative, black or white. It is, in fact, an excess of positive qualities—overreaching in the pursuit of greatness—that is dangerous.

This was clearly the case with Dukakis in 1975, when he faced

the fiscal crisis, and in 1978, when his overestimation of himself
proved fatal. Then he believed he had the right answers on the
basis of his own rational analysis, that he could do the job alone,
that he didn't need help. It was an excess of pride, hubris in its
classic form. And like the majestic, doomed protagonists of
Greek tragedy, Dukakis was blinded in his pride by a false clar-
ity. He thought his vision, guided by his moral certainty, was
unerring. Because he was right, he felt, right-thinking people
would inevitably ratify his work. Because he was right, differences with Fran Meaney and Sumner Kaplan and Joe Grandmaison and Bill Sapers were no great loss to him, even if they
produced bitter and lasting splits. Because he was right, human
services advocates and legislators could angrily condemn him;
he was not fazed. Because he was right about the state's economy, he could predict with certainty that Massachusetts voters
would not approve a version of Proposition 13. But just when he
seemed most sure of his judgment and vision, he was most
wrong. He was blind. From his political intimates to the State
House crowd to the voters at large, he took them all for granted.
He didn't see that he needed them as much as or more than they
needed him.

Dukakis's intense single-mindedness, his drive and ambition
to do good, to get ahead, were inseparable from the arrogance
and stubbornness that permitted him to run in 1978 without
ever seeing trouble ahead.

The great difference between Dukakis and the heroes of
Greek tragedy is that Dukakis has been given a second chance.
The man resurrected from his public death and given a second
life in office has lost none of the pride and ambition evident
through his first term as governor. The question is whether his
eyes have truly been opened, whether he can avoid the blindness that pride once brought.

Nineteen seventy-eight was, of course, the turning point in his
political life. Political pragmatism dictated what changed. It was
not an alteration in character, but a shift in style, approach—a
change he had to make if he was to be successful again in
politics.

This is the key question about Dukakis. Clearly he has not

been humbled. The ambition and self-assurance that propelled his career are intact, as are his unflagging strength, endurance, and determination. He does not yield, but rather wills himself to a relentless pace—*always* forging ahead. The question is whether his vision, his own understanding of himself, are in harmony with his drive. Are his abilities now great enough to keep his ambition within their grasp? Or is he in danger of overreaching himself again? Some friends believe the changes are significant, that he is more cautious, more reliant on other people. But others see no essential change. One after another, people who knew him then say he is all but identical to the serious young man they knew forty years ago.

Notes

Chapter 7: Rematch

Page 160 Dukakis was aided: The Commission claimed: Volume 9, page 46.

Page 167 The second error: The sex tape was originally played by Dukakis's campaign manager, John Sasso, to one of the authors, Charles Kenney, who was then assigned to the *Globe*'s State House bureau. After hearing the tape played over the phone, Kenney told two other members of the *Globe* bureau, Ben Bradlee, Jr., and Chris Black, about the tape. Black mentioned it to one of King's campaign advisers, who brought it to the governor's attention.

Chapter 8: Redemption

Page 190 While ET was widely: In the spring of 1984, Theresa Amott, an economics professor at Wellesley College, released a study on ET charging that the program "gets people off welfare" but not "off poverty." Amott and Commissioner Atkins argued in the press about ET, Atkins claiming that the average wage for a full-time ET job was, at the time, $5.23 an hour, more than double, he said, the average grant under the Aid to Families with Dependent Children (AFDC) welfare program. But Amott said that even though ET graduates earned an average of $923 a month, and a mother of two on welfare got $655 a month, there were other factors to consider. She said that after taxes, and costs for child and health care payments, the ET grad was earning only about $20 a month more than someone on AFDC.

Page 191   The Massachusetts Taxpayers' Foundation: "So far, the investment in ET has paid off for Massachusetts," the report stated. "The savings to the state far outrun the cost of the program." But the report cautioned that ET's continued success depended upon the state's economy remaining robust. "A faltering labor market could cut the number of jobs available to ET graduates and its cost-effectiveness might suffer as a result," the report stated. It went on to say that much of the credit for the program's success was owed to the state's economy, "which has created a labor shortage" and "driven wages up and forced employers to consider candidates they might have ignored in a slower economy."

Chapter 10: Self

Page 235   "they recommended reasonable steps": Albert C. Ganley, *The Progressive Movement* (New York: Macmillan, 1964).

Page 235   they favored the "enforcement": Arthur M. Schlesinger, Jr., *The Age of Roosevelt: The Crisis of the Old Order* (Boston: Houghton Mifflin, 1956).

Page 236   "a far greater willingness": Richard Hofstadter, *The Age of Reform, From Bryan to FDR* (New York: Alfred A. Knopf, 1955), p. 300.

Page 236   "applauded the work of": Henry Steele Commager, *The American Mind* (New Haven: Yale University Press, 1950).

Index